Sylvia Plath

Writing About Women
Feminist Literary Studies

Esther Labovitz
General Editor

Vol. 3

PETER LANG
New York • San Francisco • Bern
Frankfurt am Main • Berlin • Wien • Paris

Toni Saldívar

Sylvia Plath

Confessing the Fictive Self

PETER LANG

New York • San Francisco • Bern

Frankfurt am Main • Berlin • Wien • Paris

Library of Congress Cataloging-in-Publication Data

Saldívar, Toni
    Sylvia Plath : confessing the fictive self / Toni
Saldívar.
        p. cm. — (Writing about women ; vol. 3)
        Includes bibliographical references. (p.   ).
        1. Plath, Sylvia—Criticism and interpretation.   2.
Self in literature.   I. Title.   II. Series.
PS3566.L27Z88   1992   811'.54—dc20   91-45858
ISBN 0-8204-1665-7   CIP
ISSN 1053-7937

Die Deutsche Bibliothek-CIP-Einheitsaufnahme

Saldívar, Toni:
Sylvia Plath : confessing the fictive self / Toni Saldívar.—
New York; Berlin; Bern; Frankfurt/M.; Paris; Wien: Lang,
1992
    (Writing about women ; Vol. 3)
    ISBN 0-8204-1665-7
NE: GT

Cover design by Jean Morley.

The paper in this book meets the guidelines for permanence and
durability of the Committee on Production Guidelines for
Book Longevity of the Council on Library Resources.

∞

© Peter Lang Publishing, Inc., New York 1992

Printed in the United States of America.

For Sam

Acknowledgements

Grateful acknowledgement for permission to quote from published and unpublished sources is made to the following:

To Olwyn Hughes and The Plath Estate for quotations from unpublished diaries, journals, letters and juvenile poems of Sylvia Plath.

To Mrs. Aurelia Schober Plath for quotations from her unpublished letters.

To Mrs. Anita Jackson for quotations from a personal letter of Dorothea Krook.

To Peter Davison for quotations from his *Half Remembered: A Personal History*. Copyright © 1973 by Peter Davison.

To Peter Owen, Ltd., and Dodd, Mead & Company for quotations from Edward Butscher, *Sylvia Plath: The Woman and the Work*, Copyright © 1977.

To Alfred A. Knopf, Inc., and Faber & Faber, Ltd., for quotations from *Sylvia Plath, The Colossus and Other Poems*, Copyright © 1962 by Sylvia Plath.

To HarperCollins Publishers and Faber & Faber, Ltd,. for quotations from *The Collected Poems of Sylvia Plath*, ed. Ted Hughes. Copyright © 1960, 1965, 1971, 1981 by the Estate of Sylvia Plath; editorial material copyright © by Ted Hughes.

To HarperCollins Publishers and Faber & Faber, Ltd., for quotations from *Sylvia Plath, Letters Home: Correspondence 1950-1963*, edited with commentary by Aurelia Plath. Copyright © 1975 by Aurelia Schober Plath.

To Doubleday, a division of Bantam, Doubleday, Dell Publishing Group, Inc., and Faber & Faber, Ltd., for quotations from *The Journals of Sylvia Plath*. Copyright © 1982 by Ted Hughes as Executor of the Estate of Sylvia Plath.

To HarperCollins Publishers and Faber & Faber, Ltd., for quotations from *Sylvia Plath, Johnny Panic and the Bible of Dreams: Short Stories, Prose and Diary Excerpts.* Copyright © 1952, 1953, 1954, 1955, 1956, 1957, 1960, 1961, 1962 by Sylvia Plath.

To Harcourt Brace Jovanovich, Inc., and Faber & Faber, Ltd., for quotations from "Gerontion" in *Collected Poems, 1909-1962,* by T. S. Eliot. Copyright © 1936 by Harcourt Brace Jovanovich, Inc.. Copyright © 1964, 1963 by T. S. Eliot; for quotations from "Little Gidding" in *Four Quartets,* by T. S. Eliot. Copyright © 1943 by T. S. Eliot and renewed in 1971 by Esme Valerie Eliot.

To Harcourt Brace Jovanovich, Inc., and to the Hogarth Press for quotations from *The Waves,* by Virginia Woolf. Copyright © 1931 by Harcourt Brace Jovanovich, Inc., and renewed 1959 by Leonard Woolf.

To *The Christian Science Monitor* for permission to reprint "White Phlox" by Sylvia Plath. Copyright © 1952 by The Christian Science Publishing Society.

To Macmillan Publishing Company and to T. & T. Clark. Ltd., for quotations from *I and Thou,* by Martin Buber and translated by Ronald Gregor Smith. Copyright © 1958 Charles Scribner's Sons.

To Alfred A. Knopf, Inc., and Faber & Faber, Ltd., for quotations from *The Collected Poems of Wallace Stevens,* by Wallace Stevens. Copyright © 1954.

To Dover Publications, Inc., for permission to quote from the Preface to *The Yellow Fairy Book* by Andrew Lang. Copyright © 1966.

Grateful acknowledgement is also made to "Father Bart" for making available the five letters of Sylvia Plath published as an appendix to this book.

Contents

Preface

No reader can doubt that Sylvia Plath wrote, as Ted Hughes put it, two "completely different kinds of poetry,"[1] though it has become commonplace to distinguish between them by calling her early work imitative and her later work original. Many readers still hear Plath speaking as a "real self" only in the later poems. And why not? She said so herself.[2] This privileging of one kind of Plath's poetry over the other, however, tends to obscure a point that my study will address: two forms of the imagination were available to Plath. One allowed her to meet the given world and to celebrate her imagination's fit with it. The other, the dominant form of Plath's talent, could find no accommodation in the given. No existing forms could satisfy its need for expression, and thus it struggled self-consciously and continually to create itself anew. This is the negating or gnostic imagination which deals with limitations by refusing them in a drive toward the sublime. Because Plath maps the destructiveness of this mode more than its creation of personal meaning, she has been faulted for an esthetics of "Resentment" by the great theorist of the gnostic imagination, Harold Bloom (*Plath* 4). Feminist critics who have appropriated Bloom's ideal of the strong poet have extended his theory to exalt the woman poet who can overcome "anxiety of authorship," that is, her doubts about her right to author herself. These readers find Plath a triumphant heroine of self-determination in her later poetry (Gilbert in Bloom, *Plath* 49–65). In contrast, the same Bloomian theory can be used to read Plath as a woman poet who, in trying to subvert the patriarchal symbolic order, subverted her will to create and her will to live (Axelrod, *Plath*). Certainly Plath's allegories can turn monstrous. In my reading, however, they attack, not the symbolic order, but the gnostic will to power that refuses any authority but itself.

For me, Plath is oddly conservative and confessional. Such a view questions studies which have rejected the label "confessional poet" as too glib for her enterprise. Is it? When M. L. Rosenthal first used that term to characterize the shocking poetic style of Robert Lowell's *Life Studies*, he aptly tied Lowell's self-display to the Romantic tradition's harrowing search for "Self" (*The Nation*, 19 September 1959: 154–155). Jean Jacques Rousseau in his *Confessions* looked for his identity in a personal style of writing (Starobinski, *Rousseau*), and he commanded the reader to take the written "I" as his literal truth. The reader knows, however, that Rousseau's "I" is a fiction, a tissue of verbal fabrications spun out of selected incident by Rousseau's desire to be his own creator and sole judge. His originality comes in his defiance of received forms, especially those in the tradition of Augustine's *Confessions*. Augustine in his book offers an "I" in writing that is also fictive, that is, also constructed out of selected incident; but he offers to the reader an "I" that is trying to become real. Augustine displays his desire in written language as a personal search for an image of reality that he does not invent. When he finds such an image in the root metaphor of Christianity, the Incarnation, he defers to that authority and in so doing structures his desire in relation to a belief in the absolute reality and priority of another Person. Different and distant as Rousseau and Augustine are from each other, both writers in their confessions were giving form to their desire for self-understanding as unique, individual men. Augustine succeeded and thrived; Rousseau failed and went mad. This says something in favor of metaphor. The Romantic poets that followed Rousseau believed in its truth value. Plath sought but did not find as a poet a single, adequate metaphoric image for her desire as a woman,[3] and this she confesses. Her later poetry of fierce self-mockery gains the moral force of satire. Like all satirists, she is energized by catastrophe, a condition which is itself a source of outrage; but like all satirists, she clears the field for those after her to structure their desire with less fear and more belief.

Plath's poetry needs the complement of the reader's own understanding of her life; it compels the reader to turn to the life. Chapter One is my interpretation of significant personal data from both published and unpublished sources. In this brief analytical biography, I trace a conflict in Plath's subjectivity: two forms of the imagination were nurtured in her education, at home and away from home. With this understanding as context, my remaining chapters offer a reading of Plath's poetry, from her early verses through her last, most distinctive and memorable poems.

I owe debts to many Plath scholars, but especially to Mary Lynn Broe (*Protean Poetic: The Poetry of Sylvia Plath*,1980) and to Lynda Bundtzen (*Plath's Incarnations: Woman and the Creative Process*, 1983), both of whose books set the tone for sympathetic and subtle interpretations of Plath's imagination in the last decade. Steven Gould Axelrod's important book (*Sylvia Plath: The Wound and the Cure of Words*, 1990), came out after my study was substantially written. The literary terrain we explore is much the same, such as Plath's tendency to allegorize, but the range and the focus of the light we throw on her work, for many reasons, are different. I am much indebted to Plath's major biographers, Edward Butscher, Linda Wagner-Martin, and Anne Stevenson, whose perspectives coincide with and extend as often as they differ from my own reading of primary and secondary materials. I am grateful for the kind assistance of Ruth Mortimer and her staff at the Neilson Library, Smith College, and of Saundra Taylor and her staff at the Lilly Library, Indiana University. I extend especially warm thanks to Aurelia Schober Plath, Olwyn Hughes, Wilbury Crockett, Anita Jackson, Thomas Bredsdorff, Edward Butscher, Diann Blakely Shoaf, and "Father Bart" for their interest in my project and their communications with me.

I want to express my deepest gratitude to the director of my dissertation (NYU 1990), Denis Donoghue. I benefited not only from his brilliance, but also from his accessibility and generosity as I developed my thesis and wrote the study which he was the first to call a book. I am grateful also to Michael Flamini and to Esther K. Labovitz for seeing its possibility for this series; to Stuart Degginger for offering encouragement as I revised for publication; to Jack Congrove for skillfully producing the final print-out; and to my husband Sam for giving, along with our sons Samuel and Matthew, affectionate and unfailing moral support as I worked on the many phases of this project.

West Point, NY   Toni Saldívar
1991

Endnotes

[1]Ted Hughes, "Sylvia Plath and her Journals" in Alexander 153.

[2]In a letter to Richard Murphy (BF 358), Plath stated that she was writing as her "real self" the fall of 1962.

[3]Arthur Oberg, "Sylvia Plath: Love, Love my Season," *Modern American Lyric* (New Brunswick: Rutgers UP, 1978) 127–173. Oberg discussed, without theorizing, Plath's doomed search for a poetic image of a "totality" (128) which would define her in "loving metaphors" (176).

Sylvia Plath

1

Learning to Read, Learning to Write: The Education of Sylvia Plath

A striking image emerges from an account of Sylvia Plath's earliest years. She is two and a half. Her mother is seated in a chair nursing the newly arrived baby brother, Warren. Sylvia sits on the floor at her mother's feet with a newspaper spread out around her, "reading" aloud all the capital letters she can find. The mother has taught the daughter to recognize the alphabet to give her an activity which would placate her jealousy of the new baby (LH 16). Sylvia has been displaced as the one child, but she has a new bond with her mother. She gives her mother pleasure as she voices the letters and in turn receives the pleasure of verbal attention and praise. The emblematic content of this scene suggests that establishing a relation by means of language in its written form was for Plath from early experience a way of connecting with the source of love. She sought confirmation of her cherished existence felt as separate from the mother, perhaps for the first time. Plath was too young to keep this experience available in her memory, but she recreated and elaborated its significance in her essay "Ocean 1212–W" (JP 20–26) written when she herself was a young mother with a two and a half year old daughter and a baby son. In her essay, Plath imagines the effects of displacement: "As from a star I saw coldly and soberly the separateness of everything. I felt the wall of my skin: I am I. That stone is a stone. My beautiful fusion with the things of this world was over" (23). She acknowledges implicitly how her life with letters—with reading and writing—had begun. Out of a sense of separateness came a heightened desire for recognition and connection: signs, letters, words became the means.

Plath wrote "Ocean 1212–W," for a BBC program on writers and their childhood landscapes. She polished this essay for publication in January, 1963, when she and her husband were separated and she was living with their two children in a London flat. Plath imagines not land but "the cold, salt, running hills of the Atlantic," a "vision which is perhaps the clearest thing I own" (20). As she begins to invoke that early image, it becomes breath, movement, a rhythm of life, a "motherly pulse" that is deep, mysterious, ambiguous: "If it could court, it could also kill" (20–21). The essay tells of going to the water's edge, jealous and brooding, when she learns that her mother is bringing home the baby brother. She looks to the sea for "a sign … of election, of specialness." The waves wash up a carved wooden monkey, a "totem" she learns later was a Sacred Baboon: "So the sea, perceiving my need, had conferred a blessing. My baby brother took his place in the house that day, but so did my marvelous and (who knew?) even priceless baboon" (24).

The sea is the mother as source. The carved totem is the power of the letter which Plath cannot read fully when first given her by her source but which, nevertheless, includes her in a family of readers and writers. This sign also excludes her from a previous privileged place, but Plath can only believe in the "blessing" of language as it comes from the mother in this new, hard and abstract form. Letters and what they demand of her have an intimate relation to life at its source and to life in its promise of a future and fuller richness—life she will reach for. In Plath's experience, mother and child participate in the circuit of feeling which writing can make possible.

The Baboon as sign is sea-born in a "caul of kelp." Plath had wanted a sign that was feminine and delicate—a "mermaid" or a "Spanish infanta" (24), but she gets a dense carved totem, "crouched on its pedestal, remote and holy, long-muzzled and oddly foreign" (24). This sign, like the brother, is masculine. Letters and the writing they constitute are for Plath a powerful male principle. Plath's essay makes clear that the mother's substitution of the alphabet for her body created distance and a sense of lack which occasioned the birth of Plath's own self-conscious desire. She yearns and she feels delight in that yearning, as when she and her brother together hear her mother, "a sea-girl herself," read Arnold's "The Forsaken Merman": "A spark flew off Arnold and shook me, like a chill. I wanted to cry; I felt very odd. I had fallen into a new way of being happy" (21). This paradoxical response is evidence of an expansion of life, not a diminishment, if she accepts desire as a gift, a *donnée*. This seems to be the case, for, as the essay continues, Plath's intimacy with the sea increases and diversifies. The sea has many moods, many "distances and miracles" (21), but it offers enduring attention. Never not there, it continues to yield an abundance of treasures and experiences in episodes that include her brother, mother, grandparents, uncle, uncle's fiancée, even a neighbor boy, but Plath does not mention her father until the last paragraph: "And this is how it stiffens, my vision of that seaside childhood. My father died, we moved inland." The result: "... those nine first years of my life sealed themselves off like a ship in a bottle—beautiful, inaccessible, obsolete, a fine white flying myth" (26).

The most significant thing about her father is that he is dead. His absence is a lack far more drastic than that occasioned by the intrusion of a rival brother and the beginning of reading, for his death removes the family from the sea, the motherly source in nature of imaginative life. The Plath children did not see their father's corpse or attend the funeral and burial. He was not anywhere for them except in the past, and so their love for him remained there also. When Sylvia Plath began writing poems not long after his death, her efforts can be understood as a means to release the "flying myth" of desire which, even when displaced in written language, could sail or soar toward fulfillment.

Plath had loved her father and had pleased him as a bright, obedient child who learned to say the powerful, polysyllabic words of his biological science (MM 9). He left her doubly bereft, for after his death her mother was absent much of the time. When at home, she was, as the father had been, often tired and ill (SP 31–35). She went to work doing what her husband had done: teaching and correcting papers. The association of written language with power over others is viewed as sinister in a 1952 short story from Plath's student days at Smith college. In "Among the Bumblebees" (JP 306–312), a feisty little girl named Alice is jealous of her younger and weaker brother who gets most of the tender attention from their mother. The story reveals much about Plath's sense of her paternal origin:

> In the beginning there was Alice Denway's father, tossing her up in the air until the breath caught in her throat, and catching her and holding her in a huge bear hug. With her ear to his chest, young Alice could hear the thunder of his

heart and the pulse of blood in his veins like the sound of
wild horses galloping (306).

Alice allies herself with her father who from her perspective seems
very great; but Plath the writer presents him to the reader as the apotheosis of the bully. He sometimes scolds the mother, "strong and proud, and
his voice would be hard, with a sharp edge to it" (308). He enjoys laughing
at his son's fears, intimidating his university students, thrilling his daughter with brave physical feats such as swimming far out to sea and catching
bumble bees in his hand. Alice watches her father correcting student papers, making "red gashes" where "the words were wrong" (308), and she
imagines him, godlike, passing judgment on a hall full of students who,
when they received their papers, made "the sound of weeping and wailing
and gnashing of teeth" (309). Her own aggression finds its authorization in
him: "Power was good because it was power" (310). Then the father sick-
ens and dies. As he languishes, Alice hears her mother's voice "... very soft
and low for a while, until Father would get cross and raise his voice like
thunder..." (311). The susurrus of the sea is the mother; the storm in the air
is the father. He blusters and vanishes, bequeathing his daughter nothing
except his pride and his arrogance and a desire for his equal. For Sylvia
Plath, written language associated with the father is a sign of elemental
and superior power that results from a Nietzschean will, while written
language associated with the mother is a sign of yearning and of mysterious connection with a reliable source, another person, who gives words as
a sign of love.
These two ways of using language suggest two modes of the imagination. The one Plath associates with the mother we can call the relational
or the symbolic imagination; the one she associates with the father we can
call the negating or gnostic imagination.[1] In the first, the writer gives voice
to her life in symbolic action through engagement with the world and its
conditions, which include other persons. Her metaphoric image of self depends on the relation of her written "I" to another who is not the same as
herself, that is, who is not merely a projection of her solitary will or desire.
It is the relation of "I" to Other—to another subjectivity, not to a mere object—that is real and realizing.
In contrast, the negating or gnostic imagination finds the world and
its conditions, including other people, intolerably foreign and hostile, full

of contradictions impossible to reconcile.[2] In this mode, the imagination rejects all existing forms as inadequate to the need for self-realization. The gnostic imagination strives to produce an original image or personal myth for the totality of its intuited essence.

If we believe that the individual imagination can live in its creations and be a revelation of the individual creator, we believe in a romantic concept: autobiography.[3] Romanticism has taught us to read lyric poetry as autobiographical expression, as a personal identity achieved in the form of a metaphoric self. We do still tend to read poetry this way unless the poet fails to persuade us of her authenticity. If that is the case, she may offer not autobiography but something else: a confession in which the poet's written "I" yearns for but does not achieve, may even despair of achieving, an adequate metaphor of self.[4] Her images bear witness to an estrangement from her goal: they stand as signs for what is not, rather than for what is, and—like magic—they can disturb and unsettle as much as they can delight us with their fictiveness. This is what happens when the alienated gnostic imagination balks in its pursuit of the sublime at the expense of relation: instead of making adequate images for intuited essence, it turns to magic and produces allegories rather than metaphors of self.[5] These are allegories of the poet's desire for a reality that her poem can mime but not satisfy. Both imaginative modes—the symbolic and the gnostic—were nurtured in the education of Sylvia Plath.

She was born into a family centered on reading and writing. When she arrived on October 27, 1932, her father, Otto, had just finished his Harvard doctoral thesis, soon to be published as *Bumble Bees and Their Ways* (Macmillan, 1933), and he was beginning a treatise on insect societies for a chapter in *A Handbook of Social Psychology* (Clark UP, 1935). Needing all the light and space he could get, Otto Plath took over the dining room for his study where his books and notes remained in strict order while he prepared the chapter. His wife, Aurelia, served as researcher, ghostwriter, editor and typist. Her collaboration in his work as a professor of entomology at Boston University characterized her obedient, loyal relation to him. Putting most of her intellectual energies into service for Otto Plath was not what she had in mind when she married him, her German professor and twenty-one years her senior, but she came to understand her husband's needs and gave up hope of a more independent life (LH 13). She would describe him years later as a practical man, a "man of science" but without imagination, a man who wrote with great difficulty but who could, with work, arrive at a lucid statement of his ideas.[6] The lively narrative style of his thesis attests to her skills in writing while the content established Otto Plath as ahead of his time in researching animal behavior (MM 5). Otto Plath's reading was of nature and natural phenomena rather than literature. When he studied and taught language, it was as a linguist, not as a man of letters. Aurelia Plath lavished her delight in the imaginary on her children. She had acquired secretarial skills in order to be financially independent as a young woman, but she had gone on to earn a master's degree in German and English literature at Boston University. Neither of her Austrian immigrant parents attained a profession in their adopted country, although they were both well educated. They had arrived in America, in fact, with more books than clothes.[7] It was the mother who read aloud:

> My highly imaginative mother, who possessed a beautiful melodic, at times, dramatic voice, was the reader, the story teller when I was a child—the oldest of three and the only one who was brought up in the European tradition. I was five years older than my sister and 13 years older than my brother. In my preschool childhood we spoke only German as the mother read to me every night at my bedtime poems, short stories, fairy tales, boarding school novels written for young girls. This memory is a treasured one and belonged to mother and me alone— she was not quite 19 years my senior.[8]

Reading aloud, then, was a family tradition descending through the mother, which Aurelia Plath continued with her own children at bedtime. Their routine was regular: supper for the children in their room, then half an hour in the living room with both parents where Sylvia and Warren would perform and recite for their father, showing what they had learned or made, then to bed and story time with their mother (LH 19).

She read to them from the classics of children's literature: works of Eugene Field, Robert Louis Stevenson, A.A. Milne and Hans Christian Andersen. She recalls that some of her children's early favorites were the anthology *Sung Under the Silver Umbrella*, the Thorton W. Burgess animal fables featuring Grandfather Frog, Reddy Fox and Johnny Chuck, and the

Dr. Seuss books, especially *Horton Hatches the Egg*. They would repeat in unison the refrain: "He meant what he said,/ And he said what he meant,/ For Horton was faithful/ One hundred percent."[9] She also read to them novels such as *The Yearling* and *Johnny Tremain*. Years later Sylvia would remember and want sent to England for her own children the Mary Poppins books, and "my beloved Red books" (LH 404). This last request is a reference to a ten volume set bought for Aurelia Plath when she was eight years old.[10] The books, now lost, were lavishly illustrated and graded in advancing difficulty volume by volume, beginning with nursery rhymes and progressing to poetry, history and myth. The Plaths also owned several of Andrew Lang's anthologies of fairy tales. Aurelia Plath recalls that these were read to her children and then later read by them, especially "Sylvia, whose delight in fairy tales exceeded that of her brother."[11] Plath's mother thinks it very likely that her daughter read Lang's prefaces as well as the stories, "for she read every printed word once she began reading for herself."[12] Lang's tone in his prefaces is one of patient, fatherly instruction directed toward children and their mothers whose enthusiasms he shared but whose ignorance he gently chastised and tried to correct.

Lang's collections offered English children at the turn of the century something different from moralistic, realistic juvenile books. His anthologies, still in print today, began with *The Blue Fairy Book* in 1889 and continued through the color spectrum until *The Lilac Fairy Book* in 1910. Lang offered tales for pleasure, nothing else, although as a scholar he developed a theory that was a fundamental contribution to cultural criticism: folklore is not, he asserted, debased myth, but the germ of sophisticated literary mythology. As he put it in his Preface to *The Crimson Fairy Book:* the tales were passed on "from savage grandmother to savage grandmother" until they at last find expression in a "Homer." Although he was a member of the British Folk Lore Society, Lang was no purist in his selections: he included the artful tales of Hans Christian Andersen. Delight was his only criterion. Sylvia probably read Lang's verse on the dedication page of *The Yellow Fairy Book*, in which he plainly told his readers what he thought the purpose of written language was:

> For every child should understand
> That letters from the first were planned
> To guide us into Fairy Land

So labour at your alphabet
For by that learning shall you get
To lands where Fairies may be met.

And going where this pathway goes,
You too, at last, may find, who knows?
The Garden of the Singing Rose.[13]

This was the experience of delight Plath wanted to give her own children when, living in England, she asked her mother to send her old books from home: "piece by piece, my favorite children's books" (LH 404). She had delighted in the power of words coming to her from the mother, but she had also delighted in her father's physical strength, imagining in "Among the Bumble Bees" the "ecstasy of terror" when carried on his back out into the dark, deep ocean and the belief he gave her that she too would one day be that strong.[14]

Otto Plath's strength began to fail when Sylvia was about four years old. From 1936 to 1940, his health deteriorated from undiagnosed diabetes. Mrs. Plath recalls that during the last four years of his life she did "all the reading for updating his lectures, handing him the condensations of the material. It was the only way he could keep going, for he was in intense pain most of the time."[15] Otto Plath was irritable, often angry, and the children were kept more and more apart from him. The story times went on, but the children were sent to bed quite early, and Sylvia began reading more to herself. Books gave comfort and company and were always available. The mother needed much time to help her weakened husband who resisted medical attention. Not until he developed gangrene in a toe which led to a leg amputation did Otto Plath know his true condition, but surgery failed to save his life. While still hospitalized, he died of an embolism in the lung. The morning of November 5, 1940, Aurelia Plath went to her children's rooms to tell them that their father had died. Eight year old Sylvia, already reading in her bed, vowed "never to speak to God again" (LH 35), but her reading increased, almost obsessively, as her childhood diaries show, and the poems started coming (MM 13).

Mrs. Plath knew she had gifted children. Warren, though more frail than Sylvia, was just as precocious. Because Otto Plath left his family without adequate support, Mrs. Plath had to provide for them. Her first recourse was to teach in a public school and to continue living in their modest Winthrop, Massachusetts, home on the bay. In 1942 she obtained a faculty position at the Boston University College of Practical Arts as an instructor on medical secretarial procedures. At this time, she moved inland to Wellesley where she bought a small house and enrolled her children in the excellent Wellesley public schools. After a long day of teaching, she would find under her dinner napkin original rhymes and sketches offered by Sylvia. These gestures are reminiscent of Sylvia's earliest association of letters and the maternal bond. According to Aurelia Plath, affection between her and her daughter was habitually expressed in writing—in such forms as notes, letters, and homemade cards (LH 32).

The letter binds but it also separates, making a space for the absence which is desire, the energy to reach toward fulfillment. This had been Sylvia's earliest experience with letters, but her relation to written language was complicating itself. She had learned that writing allows for power on the part of the writer. She could, to some extent, make her mother be what she wanted her to be by determining what responses to elicit from her. The day Sylvia learned of her father's death, she had asked her mother to sign a statement promising never to marry again (J 268; SP 29). Perhaps as a child she simply wanted to see her mother happy after the long ordeal, and in turn, to be happy herself. The notes and cards opened the space for mutual delight. Sylvia Plath was already conscious before her adolescence of that mysterious connection in which raw need becomes love in an act of the imagination that makes a circuit of desire: lover, beloved, and love.

Mixed with her experience of a loving connection with her maternal source was the legacy of her father whose will had been so self-focused that he had refused to live on any conditions other than his own. When he began losing his strength in 1936, he diagnosed himself, wrongly, as having lung cancer and he refused to submit to a doctor (SP 25). The only way to understand his wife's compliance is to take into account the almost unquestionable authority he was to her. He controlled everything in their domestic life from finances to scheduling when the children would be born (SP 19). Plath knew early on that her father was arrogant and stubborn, but he had been intelligent and powerful, and she had loved him fiercely (MM 9–10). While he lived, he had dominated the family, but he had also sustained them, as Plath had imagined the father in "Among the Bumble Bees" supporting the daughter as she swam with him in the sea. He enhanced separation from the mother; thus, he enhanced desire. His authority made the differences between them and between all of them sharp and clear. Without him, she could perhaps drown in a sea of maternal love. After his death, Plath had to be willful enough to make dry land for herself with her words. To delight and not to drown was the challenge. Desire in its energizing circuit would die if there were a collapse into identity, if she and her mother—her source—became the same.

Separation from the mother was not easy. Sylvia's home in Wellesley became a complicated matriarchy when her maternal grandmother and grandfather came to live with Aurelia and her children. The grandfather, who worked at a local country club, had given over the management of their modest financial affairs to his wife. Besides controlling the money, the grandmother drove the car. It would be years before Aurelia Plath obtained a driver's license, so she remained dependent on her mother in this way for a long time (SP 32). Aurelia Plath, however, with her professional training, commanded a steady income. The Plath household in Wellesley was that of a well-read immigrant family of three generations, each member doing what he or she could to contribute to mutual survival, with most of the energies given to finding opportunities for the youngest members. Following Andrew Lang, attention to imaginative language, cultivated and passed from grandmother to mother to daughter, would find expression in eventual genius. Sylvia felt from about the time of her father's death that she was a poet. Her mother helped her make scrap books of her writings and drawings, and helped her send verses to newspapers and magazines.

Poets write to feel the exhilaration of metaphorical thought that binds known and unknown; and they also write to exert a sharpening sense of individual power that chafes and strains at its limits of knowing. Otto Plath's legacy of imperious will devolved his daughter, but where he had disappointed his family by thundering and raging, then diminishing and disappearing (except for a book and a chapter), she became a little dynamo of achievement determined to make everybody happy at school and at home. She pleased all her teachers, almost all women, and home was a house of women. Although the household included the grandfather and Warren and at times a young uncle, the authorities were the two mothers, the older organizing the domestic life, the younger earning the main income. The matriarchy served Sylvia, freeing her from household chores and allowing her to develop her talents. She had many opportunities: art and music lessons, scouting and camping, concerts and plays. The grand-father doted on her, and the mother and the grandmother nurtured her and sacrificed for her, a little princess or a little queen bee, preparing her for a brilliant and fecund future.

In such a fairy tale, there had to be a prince. Sylvia would have a hard time with that. The reasons have to do with the intensely ambivalent feelings she had for her father. She had loved him for his strength in sus-taining her while he lived, and she hated him for his weakness in abandon-ing her when he died,[16] the ambivalence of the newly bereaved which would haunt Plath most of her life. Judging from her apparently active and normal adolescence (MM 20–42; SP 31–41), These emotions lay as deeply buried as her dead father in her unconscious. There Otto Plath would stay for a long time, a big O, an implacable absence and total indifference, an outrage to a mind structured for connections, not for contemplation of a void. Plath's mind first felt the rewards of desire from her mother, a source she re-imagines as the sea giving her out of itself masculine signs which would be a means to feel delight, not despair, in yearning. But how could her desire find its way into an actual world with no fearless yet loving father in person with whom to bond?[17] We will see Otto Plath's absence imaged as the "o-gape" of despair, a term Sylvia coined in her late verse, but as the unreachable, unknowable father, he is already a negative agent in Plath's juvenilia, growing more and more dominant as she matures. The poetry will be examined in the next chapters. What concerns us here is how Plath dealt with her emerging sense of self as a feminine person quite full of yearning, felt more and more as sexual. Effectively structuring her de-sire would be the same as finding access to the wingy myth in the bottle that had been sealed off by Otto Plath's death.

Plath's adolescent notions of romance came out of fairy tales and out of novels available to her such as *Gone with the Wind* and *Jane Eyre* (both read when she was twelve), and also out of the popular culture of the 1940's—movies, ladies' magazines, comics, the pin-up art of World War II, and the radio. In her 1945 diary, she notes that radio daytime dramas gave her a headache, but she must have listened to them. In an adult journal entry, Plath will sketch the germ of a story she plans to write: *"The Little Mining Town in Colorado*: about a young girl's plunge into the hothouse world of soap opera while she is bedded with rheumatic fever" (J 306–307). Plath's childhood diaries note many days she spent home in bed with sinus and throat infections. Her sketches in the diary of female figures are seductive in a comic book style, and she wrote at the end of the volume what appears to be a story fragment about a woman discussing her "affairs" in a voice that "skated smoothly over the dangerous ice of that topic." This voice "hammered back and forth until she at last had me nailed down." These seem very sophisticated lines for a thirteen year old, even one with an I.Q. of about 160.[18] They could be Plath's own invention, or they could be a transcription of something heard in what she called the "hothouse" of radio drama.

Such enactments would have been powerfully suggestive to a young mind like Plath's. Sylvia had seen her mother suffer in marriage. That the mother had been, in fact, miserable during much of it would put in question the reliability of sexual feelings and their object. Otto may have been roughly domineering, but he was, from all accounts, a decent man. He had, however, done something indecent when he allowed his considerable masculine strength and intelligence to be dissipated by a disease he could have lived with had he turned to others for help. "It needn't have happened!" were Aurelia's thoughts as her husband lay dying (LH 23). If Sylvia sensed that her father's death was in some way self-willed, as much of her poetry suggests, his loss humiliated her love for him and negated his love for her—as well as for the brother and the mother. There was no real or ideal father, then, even in Plath's memory, from whom she could learn emotional strength in her adolescence. Absence was better than his specter, so Otto Plath stayed submerged, but a certain luridness began to suffuse Plath's imagination, defining her sexual life. This negativity had everything to do with him. She tried to counter that force with a belief in the power of printed words to transport and transform the reader as she continued to read to furnish her mind. A verse written in her 1945 diary asserts that "A book may lead each girl and boy/ From darkest night to brilliant day."

While the 1944 and 1945 diaries record mostly school events and books read, the 1946 diary is full of rich description in different colors of ink, blue, green, pink, brown. Plath records sensuous details about weather, food, feelings, people. Her character sketch of her art teacher Mrs. Hazelton shows Plath admiring the woman's unsentimental gaze. Plath herself wants to be as direct, for she senses that the truth, whether in a drawing or in a sentence, depends on the integrity of perception. She is reading now her own experiences with great introspection and detail. The journals of 1947, 1948, 1949 are almost entirely focused on boys and dates

and examinations of her more and more powerful feelings. There is a dis-
connectedness, as if she were always alone with her own sensations, even
when she is with another. She is intensely focused on herself, and so the
journals become a private crucible for the transmutation she believed
writing could effect from dark to light, from ignorance to knowledge.

This is the start of Plath's "gnosis," her attempt, as Georges Gusdorf
would put it, to write her own "scripture," her personal myth which would
give her life its particular, unique meaning.[19] That inward turn of the
imagination is driven by its need for knowledge of a self more authentic
than the world can give. Feeling alienated from herself by the conditions in
her world, the "gnostic" will see that world as an enemy and she its victim,
entangled in contradictions. Her true self is an essence which only she can
know: the spark of the divine in her. Giving form to that essence is her
quest: "To seek myself and know who I was and who I am, in order to become once more what I was" (294). Others get in the way of the gnostic
search. Georges Gusdorf puts it this way:

> The existence of others is perceived in a mode of lack and
> dissatisfaction, of dependency in relation to this other
> whose tributary I am and who will never give me any-
> thing other than precarious and revocable satisfactions.
> It is language between men that institutes the rule of
> misunderstanding in accordance with the nature of im-
> perfect communication (284).

Thus, the poet of the gnostic imagination must assert not only the
sufficiency of her own solitary word but also its supremacy. The gnostic's
relation to the other is a power struggle. She will not be named; she will
name herself. The risks are great, however, for if she fails to create authentic forms for her unique subjectivity, she may construct merely an
idolized inner self, a beloved self-image which must be justified at the cost
of objective truth, as Jean Jacques Rousseau did.[20] Then, openness to experience is obstructed by the need to keep that "essence" the sole source of
itself, and by the defiance of all other authority. The gnostic imagination
refuses a passive stance before a world already given, an obedient stance
to powers already operative—including things already said. This form of

the imagination can turn sinister if it insists that nothing can escape its control.

Almost everything in Plath's education after her father's death would promote a gnostic turn of her imagination, but because of her earliest experiences with the mother, with language and with a rival brother as a sign of life, Plath had known imaginative pleasures which defer to others' lives. In a family, love operates within given limits and between differences which are not in opposition but in relation. Plath was normal in her jealousy of her younger brother, but her life was enriched, not diminished, by his presence. When Plath's father died, her rival became death and a gnostic duel began for her. Death as rival is nothing except one's own lack of will *to be*. Plath's father came to stand for the will to resist the limits of the world so strongly that it becomes the will *to die*. He is a lack of love: a void that is unreadable. The only way to deal with him is to out-will him, but this leads to one's own shunning of the given world. When the object of love and the rival are real, lack as desire is a force that makes the actual world readable by making it symbolic of actual relations. In the symbolic tradition, the given world includes not just self and others in present action, but also history, things already done.

For Sylvia Plath, much of what was good in her past seemed beyond reach; much of its pain, she tried to evade [21] as she sought a future of her own making. Her father had done that as a German immigrant in the American culture which celebrated as a fundamental value the courageous efforts of the autonomous self. As a young man he had renounced his Lutheran beliefs and with them ties to his parents in Germany and to other family in this country. As a second generation German-American, Plath's mother renounced her Austrian Catholic heritage for Methodism and then for Unitarianism, though she remained close to her mother and father. In high school, Plath found for a time a father surrogate in her honors English teacher, the exceptionally intelligent and dedicated Wilbury Crockett, who encouraged Plath's intellectual independence and remained her friend and mentor throughout her college years at Smith. He was perhaps the first to urge her to do graduate study in England. As early as the tenth grade, Crockett had recognized Plath's poetic talent, and he followed her published career with understandable pride. What Plath learned from Crockett was the nature of form as Aristotle defined it: a mode of action. Her high school essays show an increasing awareness of form, not only in literature but in all human activities. As a high school senior, Plath wrote in the margin of her copy of Plato's *Republic*, "All religion is man-made," and she might have been quoting Crockett.[22] Religion was not so much about God as about metaphors for God, and in the American, Emersonian tradition, the individual could make his own metaphors for his sense of the divine. Crockett taught that aesthetic forms like all forms of human action are open to criticism and change, but only as part of a moral development that constantly pursued the good and the true. Crockett provoked his students to think critically and to act responsibly. His energetic New England idealism sparked his classes and found in Sylvia an especially avid counterpart. He was all masculine lucidity for her—demanding but benevolent. For Crockett, literature and life, aesthetics and belief, were one because they were part of a great dialogue that displayed the dynamic action of moral man.[23] Plath wanted to please such an authority, and she did. She was, as Crockett put it, "singular" among the many exceptional students he taught.

By the end of high school, Plath had a firm understanding of man-made forms as means to pursue and to celebrate a higher moral order. As a Unitarian, she thought of that order as divine, but her only access to it was her own will. Individual will had become her source of value. Her stance was gnostic as she wrote in her 1949 journal:

> I want, I think to be omniscient ... I think I would like to call myself "The Girl who wanted to be God." Yet if I were not in this body where <u>would</u> I be—perhaps I am destined to be classified and qualified. But, oh, I cry out against it. I am I—I am powerful—but to what extent? I am I (LH 40).

By her sophomore year at Smith, she was a self-proclaimed "agnostic humanist" who had made her own set of beliefs. She had decided, she wrote in an essay at the beginning of a two-semester course on religion, what is "valid for myself." She went on to give what her instructor called "A remarkably clear and forceful statement for the Humanist position, especially for your first paper" (Plath MS II Lilly). Her position at the end of the year was the same: religion is a product of man's trying to come to terms with the "vast neutral, impersonal force in the universe." For Plath, the human mind had invented the dichotomy of good and evil;

therefore, the human mind had to invent ways to reconcile its duality. Plath's writing was forceful and confident, and drew praise from her instructor who differed with her radically, wanted her to read more on theism and to have further discussions with him. She seemed thoroughly convinced of the individual's power to unify her world and forge her own destiny. Perhaps for this reason, she loved Yeats more than Eliot (though she studied both at Smith with Elizabeth Drew) and would think of Yeats as her greatest poetic influence. Eliot's Christianity eluded her; only his grimness impressed her. Grimness she wanted to escape, especially that of her own family romance.

Aurelia Plath sacrificed greatly for her children, but she found reward in their successes. Plath, when away from home, faithfully reported hers in a voluminous correspondence that reveal a daughter's desire to please her mother. Plath's detailed reports seem efforts to keep their bond mutually sustaining while not engulfing. She was charting her own course as much as she could, for she had to have another kind of intimate relation: it had to be with a man, not a mirror image of herself, if she were to gain adult access to the good of the sensuous emotional life sealed off by her father's death. But this, too, would please the mother. The difficulty would be in finding the right man, the real thing.[24]

Plath's first serious romance began her freshman year at Smith. She and Dick Norton, a Yale pre-med student whose family she knew well, dated for more than two years and talked seriously of marriage. What she felt for him was probably real enough, but there were problems. His ideas of married life left no room for her artistic independence, and she knew even at age eighteen that such a life for her would be intolerable. She was reluctant to commit herself to him. He had what he called a meaningless affair which for Plath had a double effect: she was outraged that he was less the white knight that she wanted him to be, and she was guiltily aware of her own wish for more freedom (J 67; 282). When Norton fell ill with tuberculosis, he became, as her ailing father had been, self-focused. Also, he expected Plath to help nurse him. This attachment was not breaking the glassy enclosure of her inaccessible past but re-entering it as a tomb. While visiting Norton at a T.B sanatorium in upstate New York in the winter of 1952, Plath, who did not know how to ski, took a dare-devil run down the slope. She was courting death, but she suffered only a severe leg fracture and had to drag a heavy cast around campus for the remainder of the term. Literally "broken," she demonstrated her break with Norton and her openness to other possibilities.

She was not always this extreme. She behaved as most young women of her time and place did, exerting as much sexual attraction as she could in order to bring into range as many potential suitors as possible while not giving herself completely to any of them. Her quest for love was complicated by fear of choosing wrong and experiencing, as her mother had, abandonment and lovelessness. Fear, not love, dominated Plath's sexuality, leading to obsessive control and fueling her negating imagination which removed her from deeply felt connections in the world. More and more she mistrusted the world outside her own mind, as the poetry she wrote as a college junior in 1953 shows.

That year, Plath became emotionally ill during a summer internship on the magazine *Mademoiselle*. She felt degraded by what promised glamour. Though the clash between appearance and reality disturbed her, she found no way to reconcile the contradictions or to live with them. Her highly sensitive psychic state seems apparent in her response to the execution that summer of the Rosenbergs, man and wife convicted of spying for the Soviet Union. Plath imagined their deaths so intensely at the time of the actual electrocution that a rash, like stigmata, appeared on her arms (SP 100). Her agony was all within, focused on a sense of alienation and failure. Plath's mother believed that exhaustion and disappointment plunged her daughter into despair when she returned home in July (LH 123–126). Certainly Plath was worn out, but evidence of a physical cause for her emotional illness has accumulated, which better explains Plath's suicide attempt that August.

Otto Plath's family had a history of depressives which they kept secret (SP 110). Plath's underlying problem may have been an inherited bipolar affective illness which could have been helped with lithium had that drug or others like it been available in the United States.[25] The treatment that Plath did receive, electric shocks, insulin injections, and standard Freudian psychoanalysis, could not have eased a severe depression caused by the absence of an essential salt in the brain. Trauma to her body could only have increased her suffering. Attempts to explain her mental distress as "Electra complex" and "Mother obsession" could not have regulated chemical imbalances, but would have stimulated her capacity for self-focused drama and invention within given Freudian myths.

Plath's actual malady, including psychoanalytic explanations, must remain mere speculation, but one thing seems sure: attention from individuals seemed to help her, especially the weekly visits from Wilbury Crockett. He helped Plath learn to read again by moving her hands in an anagram game and saying out loud the names of the letters and the words they formed. He did what her mother had done for her years earlier: Crockett helped re-establish her relation to others by using written language in a spirit of paternal love, and he asked only that she receive it for what it was, true. At the same time, Plath's psychiatrist, Dr. Ruth Beuscher, also established a bond of warmth and trust with Plath.

Time and her own physical and mental strengths that responded to such care were the factors that probably brought Plath back to relatively stable emotional health. Her return to college for the spring term of 1954 was marked by renewed brilliance in her studies and a strong output of poetry. She won highest honors at Smith, acceptance at Newnham College, Cambridge, and a Fulbright scholarship. At Smith, however, she was not as well as she seemed. Her senior thesis, "The Magic Mirror: A Study of the Double in Two of Dostoevsky's Novels" (1955), revealed, symbolically, a problem with which she still struggled: her need to be open to the possibility of being sexually loved and the equally strong fear of being annihilated by such love. Hers was a secular problem of belief versus doubt. Plath was torn between conflicting attitudes, as Ivan in *The Brother's Karamazov* is torn between doubt and belief. Plath tried to understand psychic contradiction as symptomatic of her times, concluding her study by asserting that Dostoevsky teaches modern man to be conscious of his predicament, not to repress it:

> Dostoevsky implies that recognition of our various images and reconciliation with them will save us from disintegration. This reconciliation does not mean a simple or monolithic resolution of conflict, but rather a creative acknowledgement of the fundamental duality of man; it involves a constant courageous acceptance of the eternal paradoxes within the universe and within ourselves.[26]

To be well, then, was to be conscious and creative. In the Freudian terms of Plath's era, consciousness was creatively attained and maintained by a constant dredging up of the troublesome unconscious, a draining of the "id" or "it" by the "ego," the "I." As part of her recovery, Plath faced her fears and chose to exercise a sexual freedom which ran counter to the mores of her time and place, certainly counter to those of her mother, her father surrogate, and most of her colleagues at Smith. With her psychiatrist, Dr. Beuscher, Plath apparently theorized that heterosexual maturity would release her from dependence on her mother and from the aggression she had directed against herself. Plath had to be discreet, but by her senior year she had become a sexually active woman (SP 110). Perhaps Plath thought she could legitimize a double life by simply knowing what she was doing and why. Writing her own script would sanction her activities as she created herself.[27] The risk Plath took to gain self-direction was very great, for she did not succeed in seeing her sexual double in other than sinister images, at least not then. For evidence, we have no journals from Plath's senior year at Smith. They have disappeared or never existed, but a later Journal entry reveals something of this time:

> Promiscuity: my ingenious, evasive self-deceiving explanation: I had to give out affection in small doses so it would be accepted, not all to one person, who couldn't take it. Very queer. The fact that belies this is that I had no pleasure in anything except my relation with R [Richard Sassoon] and that was a monogamous affair for me while it lasted. So I was trying to be like a man: able to take or leave sex, with this one and that. I got even... I have hated men because I felt them physically necessary; hated them because they would degrade me, by their attitude (J 290).

If Plath took "lovers" after her return to Smith, she did so as one who prided herself on conquering shame, disgust, and fear, but whose pleasure was found in her own strength. Sex, for Plath, became an aggressive power which leads to the triumph of the will over childhood fears of powerlessness. Such a state of the mind allowed Plath in 1954 to engineer a loveless and brutal affair that may have been her sexual initiation.[28]

The one man she claimed to have loved, Richard Sassoon, a brilliant Yale senior, never was, as she knew, committed only to her. There were other men in her life, including the intelligent and gentlemanly Gordon Lameyer, but Plath remained sealed off from reciprocal human relations which were not exploitative. The poet and editor Peter Davison recalled his 1955 summer affair with Plath when she was preparing to leave for her graduate studies at Cambridge. Davison, who had studied there, recalls in his autobiography her quest for information from him, about Cambridge and "everything else" (HR 171–172). Their sexual intimacy began on the first dinner date and continued all summer, but he found her artificial and much "too exigent." Davison felt he had been in touch with her as a human being just once when, during a talk, she told him about her suicide attempt and expressed gratitude for the help certain people had given her during recovery. This seemed to Davison the only period in her life she could invest with "any real emotion in retrospect" (171). Plath's confidences can be interpreted as her way of asking to be seen as she was: spiritually dead, alive only when loved. With Davison, however, she knew that she was not. Their affair ended with the summer.

Plath's seductive behavior is not unlike that of women who have been sexually abused as children. There is not a shred of evidence that anyone molested Plath. There is, though, in almost everything she wrote the outrage of being wronged by her father's death. Never properly mourned, his loss had the effect of a gross offense, growing more troubling for her with time, not less. Justly or not, Plath felt characterized and doomed by a willful father who had not loved enough, and who had left her to fill his void by herself. As his creature, she would be as he was until some other man saw her dead soul and brought to it life. Plath's "secular scripture" had become a weird fairy tale: the engine that killed her was sexual power without love. Where was the good prince?

Plath continued her promiscuity at Cambridge. She complained to an American friend that British men were inhibited, and she extolled "our good old sensible American attitude toward sex" (Kopp 68). This might have been mere bravado, for Plath was again sliding toward disintegration. Her eroticism, inextricably part of her creativity, had to be redeemed. She went after that goal with fierce willfulness. She wrote passionate letters to Sassoon in Paris and spent her first Christmas in Europe with him traveling from Paris to southern France and back. Her Journal tells almost nothing of that trip, but her unpublished pocket diary records numerous experiences that give evidence of her highly emotional state: fights, tears, a vision of love on Epiphany at a chapel in Vence. Sassoon broke with her.

The conjunction of two powerful influences in the spring of 1956 gave Plath what she wanted: an erotic sense which confirmed her value as both a woman and a poet. The first of these two personalities was Dorothea Krook, a young and much respected Cambridge don who lectured on Henry James and the English Moralists. The second was Ted Hughes, a recent Cambridge graduate from Yorkshire who had taken a degree in anthropology, but whose knowledge of literature was even more extensive than Plath's (BF 77), and who was just becoming known for his poetry.

When Plath attended Krook's lectures on James during the 1955 Michaelmas term, Krook had been struck by her appearance, tall, rather feverish and defiant, and had wondered: Is she Jewish? ("Recollections" 49). Krook, Jewish herself, could not explain why this thought came to her. Plath was noticed, for she was attractive and gregarious, but her intensity, which lacked genuine sophistication, could be off-putting, even to a fellow American such as Lucas Meyers whom she irritated with her equal enthusiasm for Wallace Stevens and popular culture (BF 313). To the thoroughly English A.S. Byatt, Plath seemed "artificial" and "silly" with "no central reality to her at all."[29] Plath may not have known that she offended, but she did know that she might again become seriously ill. By February, 1956, she was seeing a psychiatrist and worrying over "the sterility of oppositions" that could not be reconciled when the imagination was dead. This, she wrote, "is what I fear most" (J 110). About this time Plath met Ted Hughes at a party to celebrate the publication of the new journal *St. Botolph's Review*. She had read his poems in it, liked them, and wanted to meet him. At the party, she behaved outrageously, drinking too much and deliberately provoking Hughes to make advances. He did, by kissing her and by ripping off her red hair band and silver earrings. She bit his cheek and drew blood, shocks to the nerves which Plath found thrilling, enjoying, as she put it, "my force against his" (J 113). The unpublished portion of this journal entry shows, even if imaginatively elaborated upon, Plath's indictment of herself: she leaves the party with another male student, intoxicated, and while amorously engaged with him in his room, calls herself sluttish names and begs to be scolded.[30] The Plath-Hughes courtship must be seen in the context of Plath's struggle for emotional health and strength which required that she redeem herself from a divided life that humiliated her sexual nature.

The day after the party, Plath wrote "Pursuit," a poem about lust which she dedicated to Hughes, but he did not, at this time, pursue her. She explains the poem to her mother in extravagant language that echoes both Pater and Yeats:

> ... a symbol of the terrible beauty of death and the para-
> dox that the more intensely one lives, the more one burns
> and consumes oneself, death here includes the concept of
> love and is larger and richer than mere love, which is
> part of it... (LH 222).

The poem's epigraph is from Racine, on whom Plath was writing a paper for a course on tragedy. She titled her essay "Passion as Destiny," but her instructor was not convinced that sexual passion was the "holocaust" that Plath made it out to be (Plath MSII Lilly).

Sexual passion as destiny and destiny as death were much linked in Plath's mind. She was hearing, however, about another possibility from Dorothea Krook's lectures. On March 6, Krook had discussed F. H. Bradley's *Ethical Studies*, pointing out that Bradley overlooked the re-demptive power of love. On March 8, Plath heard Krook read from D. H. Lawrence's "The Man Who Died." Krook interpreted this fable as a prophetic vision of a new value given to human sexual love. Plath felt that "an angel had hauled me by the hair in a shiver of gooseflesh ... I was the woman who died, and I came in touch through Sassoon that spring [with] ... that resolute fury of existence. All seemed shudderingly relevant ... I have lived much of this. It matters" (J 128).

Plath became attuned to the rest of Krook's discussions based on readings for the Cambridge course in The English Moralists. Krook de-signed her lectures as an argument for "religious humanism," which she later published as *Three Traditions in Moral Thought* (Cambridge, 1959). Krook's moral philosophy, her humanism as a rule of life, historically derives from the Platonic-Christian tradition, and finds, in Krook's view, its great modern artistic embodiment in Henry James and a twentieth century prophetic voice in D. H. Lawrence. Religious humanism takes from Christianity a belief in the human capacity to be transformed by love and rejects what Krook called the "utilitarian moral tradition" of Aristotle, Hobbes and Hume, which discounts love as the basis for the moral life. The humanist differs from the Christian in this way: she does not look to a divine person such as the Christian God as the origin of love's power and value; she looks to human love in various forms. The humanist resembles the Christian by recognizing a hierarchy of being, a "lower and a higher life." The moral life, for Krook, was the effort of the higher to appropriate and transform the lower. She stressed this form of humanism as a "redemptive view of human destiny" (TTMT 8), and she believed that the world would be changed by it for the better.

Plath found in Krook's moral philosophy the idealism of her early education grounded in a rich intellectual tradition which could recognize and redeem rather than ignore and humiliate her sexual feelings. Such a moral philosophy gave her the hope that her destiny was not necessarily tragic, a consolation that Freud could not offer. Krook, a brilliant, attractive, and vivacious woman in her mid-thirties, was for Plath a model of female intellectual power and independence that was neither asexual nor sinister. Krook spoke plainly: physical love between persons was always redemptive when it was true, that is, experienced as both passion and selflessness, ardor and tenderness.

Plath noted in her pocket diary for March 12 Krook's "lecture on love," apparently the closing argument which stressed the "unique contribution of Humanism to the religious knowledge of the world." This was the "affirmation of sexual love as the supremely redemptive form of love." Krook affirmed a personal belief that such understanding would resolve the modern struggle between "the terror of annihilation and hope of salvation" (TTMT 298).

Plath resolved to have Krook as her supervisor for the course on the Moralists and noted in her pocket diary for March 12: "feeling of joy and love everywhere." Hughes was at Cambridge at this time, pursuing her just a little by throwing stones at her window. She had written on March 11: "Let me some day confront him, only confront him, to make him human, and not that black panther which struts in the forest on the fringes of hearsay" (J 133). Apparently, Hughes' friends did not see him as a violent marauder, though he was very attractive to women and attracted by them (BF 76–77).

Plath confronted Hughes on March 23 in his London flat, where she spent the night before going on her spring holiday in France and Germany. She planned to look for Sassoon in a last effort to win him back, and she had arranged to meet a former lover, Gordon Lameyer, for an excursion through Germany. These attempts can be interpreted as Plath's efforts to establish with some man the connection that Krook's lectures celebrated. Much would depend on the man. She records in the pocket diary notes about spending a wild, erratic night with "Ted" whose panther-like behavior troubles her and whose callousness wounds her: he called her the wrong name the next morning. But he wrote to her, saying the thought of her went through him like brandy; and she continued to think of him. Plath's holiday in France and Germany was a disaster. Having failed with Sassoon who had fled and having fought bitterly all through Germany with Lameyer, Plath returned to London with a sense of "passion as destiny." She took a cab to Hughes' flat, and her pocket diary indicates that she took along, as Hughes had asked, a bottle of brandy. This second encounter, unlike the first one, left Plath euphoric. Plath revealed to Hughes that second night the depth of her feeling and thinking, and perhaps also the depth of her troubles. The diary records: "Bloody exhausting night of love" and "terrible dreams—multitudes seated on steps drinking vinegar in little tin cups and being sad and scornful." But then there was a steak and egg breakfast, and tapes of poems and reading aloud to each other and more "love" and sleep and finally "lovely horizontal talk—sorrow." If this was the revelation of some of Plath's personal anguish, then Hughes was neither intimidated nor put off.

She took the late train back to Cambridge. Hughes followed her there the next day which she stars in the diary and calls "the best day in the world" because of the "dawn of tenderness and miracle." Two days later, however, Plath records her doubts. After taking a long walk by herself in the cold, she writes to her mother, saying she has fallen in love with Hughes, "which can only lead to great hurt" (LH 233). Why is she so skeptical? Having found real love reciprocated, finally, by an extraordinary man, she seems terrified of the risk of losing him, as she lost her father. She musters courage in her pocket diary the next day: "incredible feeling of own faith & integrity that will come through—ted[sic] cannot ever annihilate me—I can see his flaws—egoism, bombast and lack of care for others are worst." It is likely that Hughes' brilliance and earthiness repeated her father's manliness, and thus called up the comparison and the fears as well as the intense love. Though Plath does not back away from her strong feeling for Hughes, she renounces, in an unpublished Journal entry dated April 16, any thought of permanency in their relationship. The passage, nevertheless, sounds more like acceptance of the man rather than his dismissal, and thus allows Plath to relinquish anxiety and obsessive control so that love can take its course.

The next week, as she began her tutorials under Krook's supervision, Plath was reading the *Gorgias* and the *Symposium*. The pocket diary notes: "love for ted still astounding" and "whole future gathering—accelerating." Her essay for Krook on the *Gorgias* shows her intensely engaged with Plato's argument that all men desire the good, that to do evil is to act against our deepest wish. Thus, Plath's attachment to Hughes and her close, intellectual association with Krook coincided and developed simultaneously. Each gave Plath a personal relation that answered her need to believe, as she had as a very young child, in the reality of love as a relation given, not willed, and as a potentially transforming power.

Plath's warm relation to Krook was not an infatuation but a fine example of mentoring, an "I-Thou" relation of mutual respect and affection.[31] Krook was the kind of woman Plath wanted to be, for Krook had what Plath found most academics lacked: an intelligence not cut off from feeling. In May of 1956, when Plath and Hughes had become inseparable and when Plath was beginning her weekly tutorials with Krook, Plath published a letter in the student magazine, *Isis:* "Apparently, the most difficult feat for a Cambridge male is to accept a woman not merely as feeling, not merely as thinking, but as managing a complex, vital interweaving of both" (quoted by Butscher in MM 198). On May 3, Plath wrote to her mother:

> For the first time in my life, mother, I am at peace... I feel that all my life, all my pain and work has been for this one thing. All the blood spilt, the words written, the people loved, have been a work to fit me for loving [Hughes]... I have no fear, only a faith. I am calm, joyous, and peaceful as I have never known peace. And, fantastically, I am keen mentally as I have never been. My supervisor [Krook] is a delight... I told her this week at the best supervision yet on Plato, that I was not taking this as a 'course' but as a fight to earn my humanism through the

centuries of philosophy and religion in this world (LH 248).

On May 9, Plath wrote to her mother again: "Had a wonderful supervision with dear shining Doctor Krook yesterday morning on Plato again... Already we are communicating about our own private feelings and opinions; everything relates..." (LH 251). Plath goes on to say: "Had the most moving discussion of the Trinity with her, a revelation to me of the blind, stupid ignorance I had in not even listening to such conceptions" (LH 251). What would have been the content of this discussion between Krook, a Jewish humanist, and Plath, an ex-Unitarian and a self-proclaimed agnostic? And why would the discussion have been a revelation to Plath? In response to these questions, Krook commented: "It [the discussion] would have been purely theological—what historic Christianity means by the Trinity, and how Religious Humanism re-interprets the experience of the Trinity on religious-humanist premises."[32]

The Trinity is Augustine's contribution to orthodox Christian theology. He gives it full expression in *On the Trinity*, the work of which he said: "I was young when I began it, an old man when I published it," and for which he feared there would be few understanding readers.[33] In his earlier *Confessions*, Augustine takes the reader with him through his passionate search for an image of reality which he finds in the Trinity. Augustine can apprehend "truth" only in a relation, only by knowing one thing in terms of another and thus in metaphoric images, analogies not essences. He knows himself as a man of imperfect, conflicting will when he believes that his God is something absolutely other: a perfect will, an absolute good he desires but cannot, as a human being, will himself to be. This difference between the human and the divine allows for the root metaphors of Augustine's Christianity. Metaphor enables the mind's apprehension in both thinking and feeling of what might otherwise remain an obscure intuition or raw emotion (Ricoeur 157–159). For Augustine, educated as a neo-Platonist, the most powerful metaphor is "God is Love." As a Christian, he believes that God is Love in Three Persons: Father, Son, and Holy Spirit. Thus, in relation to the mysterious unity of the Trinity of perfect love, Augustine understands himself as a singular individual who is "scattered" in his desires and acts, but whose unity of personhood is a gift of metaphoric relation. He knows himself in relation to what is not himself: the God who created him, a man, in His image. We could say, by *means* of His image, for such metaphoric understanding is an act of faith that opens perception to the truth of relation. The Trinity for Augustine is such an image, uniting his thinking, his imagining, and his feeling in relation to the world and his place in it: belief makes possible love on the part of man, but the already present love of God (which, like a father, actively seeks man) makes possible belief. This is what love is, says Augustine's orthodox Christian theology, a relation, both felt and thought, but always given before we know how to ask for it, understood because we have believed in it and acted in it.

How does the humanist re-interpret the Trinity?[34] According to Dorothea Krook, the humanist would not destroy the Christian concept of love, but would affirm it in lived relations between people. For Krook, as with Augustine, human love must be grounded in desire; love must "spring from" and be "perpetually nourished by want and wanting" (Krook OCHJ 283). The humanist would understand the human sexual bond as analogous to the Trinity as Lover, Beloved and Love: "a giving and receiving by two free spirits of a love which is good in itself and mediates good to those who share it, whether or not sanctified by a marriage rite " (TTMT 339). Krook was not advocating sexual license, but a committed union that would be based on reciprocal passion and which would endure because such a union would be sustained by mutually deep feeling, not principle or utility alone. Krook emphasized her conviction that human sexual love is intrinsically redemptive, not, as Augustine had understood it, sin, a form of corrupted will which was not subject to reason. In Krook's view, the loss of self in the sexual act is not an overwhelming of the will and the reason by carnal appetite, but an experience of another dimension which proceeds from the lovers themselves. This dimension is "the sanctifying medium of their tenderness" (TTMT 275). Tenderness is "rooted in, sustained by, and consummated in the love of the body" (TTMT 338). Such love of another person transcends reason as the mystery of the Trinity transcends reason: a person simply has to believe in order to experience its truth. Thus, in Krook's humanism, belief in the exalted love that two persons can give each other with their bodies is the supreme act of the imagination.

Plath responded to Krook's discussions with the passion of a convert: she believed that what Krook was saying was true. Two days after discussing the Trinity in humanist terms with Krook, Plath was possibly discussing marriage with Hughes. Her pocket diary notes "wedding plans," but these plans were kept secret. The sessions with Krook continued to be "sparkling" for the two women. Plath on Krook: "she is just alight and we are temperamentally most compatible" (LH 256). Krook on Plath:

> I did let myself go with Sylvia, as I have done I think with no more than five or six others in a teaching career of nearly thirty years. It was a matter of spreading one's wings to the argument, as Plato says, letting it lead whither it will. Plato was indeed the central figure in our discussions... I have racked my memory to recall what were some of the particular things I said to Sylvia or she to me about Plato and the rest... All that comes back to me is a general vision, clear and pure like the golden light of the Platonic world we had appropriated, of an extraordinarily happy freedom of communication. Love and beauty in the *Symposium*, justice in the *Republic*, the pleasant and the good in the *Gorgias*, knowledge and opinion in the *Meno*, the contemplative intelligence, the practical intelligence, the Platonic rationalism, the Platonic mysticism: these must have been some of the great topics we entered into and lost ourselves in. I remember that I pursued them with her further than I had done with any other student, drawing out implications, soaring into generalizations, reviewing my personal life's experience for illustration or proof, in a way I usually reserved only for my soul's most secret conversation with itself. The light of participation in Sylvia's eyes, shining so it seemed to me with understanding and delight, is one of the sweetest, most imperishable memories of my teaching life ("Recollections" 50–51).

Krook stresses the professional nature of their relation:

> ... full of the warmth, affection, appreciation, that its blessed communications so often breed, particularly in the Cambridge setting... Ours was indeed almost exclusively intellectual; and though the mutual impact of per-

sonalities was an inseparable part of them... I was never conscious of its intruding upon the sacred ground on which our minds met. Sylvia was extraordinarily modest, self-effacing, unassuming, unspoilt; never inviting attention to herself, seeming only to want the selfless intellectual relationship (54).

These are recollections of the first session of tutorials in the spring of 1956 when Plath and Hughes had become inseparable, and Plath's doubleness was resolving itself in a new sense of personal integration. Krook knew little of what was going on in Plath's private life at that time. She thought that Plath had earlier acquired a rather flamboyant social reputation which she seemed to have renounced in favor of serious study. Without the influence of Krook, Plath's relation with Hughes might have developed very differently. Contemplating the transforming power of human love in the intellectual company of Krook, Plath "spread her wings" not just to Plato but to a conjugal relation with Hughes—and not in desperation, but in *belief*.

They were married in June 1956 and spent the summer in Spain. No one at the university knew of the wedding, for Plath was afraid of putting her fellowship at risk. She had won a Fulbright fellowship and a place in Newnham College to achieve academic success, not domestic bliss. The two goals were thought to be highly incompatible. Thus, the couple lived apart when Plath began the fall term. Plath had written to her mother in May that she and Hughes were "capable of the most scrupulous and utter faithfulness in the world, demanding the most from each other, caring intensely for bringing each other to full capacity and production" (LH 254). Her sense of self remained, however, a fragile construct which would have to be shored up again and again by evidence of love and of productivity; but she looked to the future in which she imagined many poems and many children. Before then, however, Plath had to finish the Cambridge degree, which seemed at first an insurmountable task.

Hughes' letters to her at the beginning of the fall 1956 term are full of encouragement and advice concerning her studies and of ardent, tender concern for her well being. Still, Plath experienced a depression that prevented her from reading: words became densities she could not see through. She got better when her supervisions resumed with Krook and she became attentive to the belief which informed her life with Hughes.

Krook and Plath discussed "virginity" in October, a state Krook redefines as not the power to "renounce bodily love" but "rather the power to rediscover and relive, each time afresh, the peace, power and joy of this most intimate of unions, to experience, each time afresh its inexhaustible wonder and mystery" (TTMT 346). As Krook put it, those who can feel "a boundless gratitude for each other and for this blessed source of sweetness and strength—it is they who are the truly 'virgin,' the truly pure and chaste" (TTMT 347). A key term for Krook was "tenderness." Lawrence may have been a prophetic voice for new values in human sexuality, but, according to Krook, he failed to see the sexual relation as selfless and tender. For him sex was liberating but essentially violent and potentially destructive, "springing from the clash of incorrigibly self-centered natures" (TTMT 284). Lawrence could imagine being transformed by sexual love, but he could not imagine how its power could be sustained and its sweetness and strength perpetuated in two people who believed in it. That sustaining power, in Christian terms, said Krook, is the Holy Spirit (TTMT 285). When tenderness is gone the spirit is dead. Then, the human sexual relation is, wrote Krook, "grossly and indefensibly immoral" (TTMT 280).

Krook had been able to give Plath a way to experience the transforming and unifying power of love in the symbolic tradition, but Krook's humanism had also increased Plath's anxiety. She had to make everything right, do everything right so that the tenderness would live on. As a humanist, however, and more particularly as an American one, she had no enabling source to turn to except her own individual will. The more afraid she became, the more willful, aggressive and combative. Perhaps this is why Augustine escaped her: she could not understand his *Confessions* or *The City of God*. She wrote in her essays for Krook on these works that a dualistic world is "a more valid mirror of experience, a world in which the forces of destruction vie with the forces of creation" (Plath MS II Lilly). Her diary notes that in spite of her glowing letters home full of assertions of contentment, Plath was having nightmares about infidelity—on her part and on Hughes'. She even dreamed of Krook as an occult witch trying to levitate Hughes. On her birthday, October 27, Plath wrote in her pocket diary that the only way to survive the "nightmare of my fatherlessness" was to love, "the only way to come across."

Fatherlessness we can understand was for Plath the abyss. Otto Plath was total absence, the demonic negative that the individual will confronts and displaces with its own creative energy. Such a stance is not the stance of love in Krook's understanding or in Augustine's. For them love is making a relation that attends to rather than dissolves the boundaries of self and other. Love is three, they both say, in human experience.

By October, Plath and Hughes had decided they could not live apart any longer. Krook was the person to whom Plath went for help in how to tell the university authorities. With Krook's guidance, the situation was revealed and resolved without the dire consequences Plath feared. Plath's agitation with the rules bordered on rage, an emotion which Krook had not seen before in Plath and which surprised her. Their association continued to be warm, but Plath's anxieties were deep. Plath would characterize Krook that spring to a fellow American, Stanley Kahrl, as an Aristotelian, all intellect with no room for the spirit. Krook has written that, indeed, Plath might have thought so since that year Krook was "a passionate student of Aristotle" and Plath cared "much less about Aristotle than Plato" (MM 198). Such a comment reveals Plath's less than generous attitude toward Krook, who had lent Plath a paraffin heater to help warm her and Hughes' dreary flat in February, and who for graduation gave Plath a copy of Henry James' short stories inscribed "Sylvia, with love and gratitude, Doris Krook" (Plath Collection, Smith College). Yet on leaving Cambridge, Plath wrote: "The only person I shall miss is my dear moralist supervisor, Doris Krook, who is as close to a genius saint as I've ever met..." (LH 317). Krook loved and did not envy. Mere admiration instigates the struggle of rivals. Plath's tendency to diminish the other, even her beloved Dr. Krook, manifests an aggressive, gnostic form of the imagination that can tolerate no rival, for the rival, ultimately, is death.

Plath and Hughes left England for America after she completed her Cambridge degree in 1957. His reputation as a poet was growing, largely because of her hard work as his unofficial agent. She typed his poems and saw that they circulated widely and were read by important editors. His poetry manuscript, *Hawk in the Rain*, had just won a major prize in the United States and would be published by Harper's. Her ideal of two great talents in a beneficial, loving relation seemed to be working, but their summer at Cape Cod, a wedding gift from Plath's mother, was not as productive for Plath as she wanted it to be, and worse, her own poetry manuscript did not win the Yale Younger Poets competition. The stresses increased during the academic years when Plath was teaching full-time at Smith, and Hughes, part-time at the University of Massachusetts at Amherst. As she prepared her courses in August, she wrote: "Once I get into the blissful concreteness of this job, my life will catapult into a new phase: that I know. Experience, various students, specific problems. The blessed edges and rounds of the real, the factual..." (J 174). There is a yearning here for things resistant to her imperious imagination as will, but the "edges" at Smith were more bitter than sweet. They did not quite fit in, and as artists, they probably did not want to. Still, the situation must have been awkward for Plath, expected by her academic sponsors to be their brilliant scholarly protégée. Though she was a successful teacher, she suffered acutely from its stresses.

Early in the year, she experienced almost overwhelming self-doubt which she tried to deal with in a journal entry she called "Letter to a Demon" (J 176–179). She treated her fears as an evil double of negation. Like Dostoevsky's Ivan, she articulated her "double vision" with devastating clarity, but this tactic has its own sinister nature. It shows Plath unable to deal with imperfection or human frailty except to find a scapegoat. The victims were not only parts of herself but other people as well. More and more Hughes became a target of her fears and rage, but she proclaimed in the classroom a passionate Romantic faith, telling her students: "... man is godlike, or magnificent insofar as he creates: skyscrapers, babies, books, poems, governments. Insofar as he lives: not numb, dead, insensitive, destructive..." (Plath MS II Lilly). Inability to "create," to synthesize a wholeness or a holiness from experience, were signs of her depression and despair. Thus, she asserted that not to feel is "worse than death." In some lecture notes, she prepared to tell her students that neutrality and boredom are "worse sins than murder, worse than illicit love affairs: BE RIGHT OR WRONG, don't be indifferent, don't be NOTHING" (Plath MS II Lilly). Yet she often felt she was "nothing" when her moods plunged dangerously low. In depression, creative efforts turn into signs of failure to achieve aesthetic or ontological unity.

A journal entry from January 1958 when she was halfway through her year at Smith reveals her anxiety and fear of failure as she contemplates writing a novel based on her Cambridge experiences. She had thought of calling it "Falcon Yard" and centering it on "love, a falcon, striking once and for all: blood sacrifice ... the irrefutable meeting and experience" (J 163). This would enact being wounded by desire and healed by love, of meeting Hughes and believing in their union. She knew, however, that the story could easily become a mere pot boiler, so she conceived it as satire: "lyric cry, no ... but rich, humorous satire" (J 181). This is most significant. Plath here admits to herself that in writing, she cannot "do" love, even though she has to some extent lived it. In her writing, she can satirize, but not love.

To write anything she needs images from her past, but here she blocks memory with anxious plans: "squirrelish money-counting, paralysis sets in" (J 181). What finally comes in this journal passage of free association are images from her childhood reading which she tries to re-read meaningfully. "Re-create life lived: that is renewed life" (J 181). The images do not evoke the innocent enchantment of story hours spent with her mother. Plath's re-creations are powerful and terrible:

> A Hans Christian Andersen book cover opens its worlds: The Snow Queen, blue-white as ice. Always: sludge, offal, shit against palaces of diamond. That man could dream god and heaven: how mud labors. We burn in our own fire. To voice that. And the horror: the strange bird who knows Longfellow, perches on a wire with a back drop of English green-bushed landscapes. The white-bearded grandfather drowning in the sea-surge, the warm, slow, sticky rollers; the terror of paper crackling and expanding before the burnt-out black grate (J 181).

Plath refused to follow the horror in the "strange bird," the drowning father figure, the suffocating maternal sea-surge, and the burning paper. The charred scraps at the grate may allude to Andersen's story "The Flax," which narrates the transformations of a sensitive plant into cloth and then ragpaper on which is written an excellent story. When the story is printed, published and disseminated, the original paper is discarded and burned in the fireplace. At each painful stage, the flax tries to see only good in its situation, even as it turns to ash. This is the horror in Plath's own life, but she is held back from exploring it by her stilted question: "Whence come these images?" What might open to her is sealed, requiring on her part the aggressive tactics of forced entry: "Open Alice's door, work and sweat to pry open gates and speak out words and worlds" (J 181). An act of the imagination as love, acknowledgment of the given, cannot take its course. Plath's motive here is not love but fear. As a teacher she continued to assert that the poet as creator makes "worlds," but her own writing could only lament her separation from the real one. She called the passage under discussion "an exercise" and named what cripples it: "Hates crackle and brandish against me: unsettling the image of brilliance" (J 181–82). What does she mean by "the image of brilliance"? And what does she "hate" or what hates her?

The "brilliance" is, I think, what the "clear matter" was for Henry James. As he put it in his preface to *The Golden Bowl,* this brilliance is the essential vision of the text, the author's and the reader's sense of an "Absolute" which demands expression.[35] James called it various names— the real thing, fields of light, the shining matter.[36] All are ways to designate what brings the text into being. That motive is a great blank, "like a shining expanse of snow spread over a plain" (James 1330), but not an empty one, not an abyss. James's clear thing is a fullness that cannot be exhausted, just attended to in patterns and differentiated representations that it energizes. As a re-reader of his own work, James delighted in sensing again and again, what he called that "blessed good stuff" (James 1334) which enabled his work. He imagined his fictions speaking to him: "Actively believe in us and then you'll see" (James 1334). His fictions gave him and others access to what Dorothea Krook understood James' "real thing" to be: a vision of the transforming power of love as the human experience of selfless relation.[37]

Whatever was given, already there, is enough for James' imagination to work upon and elaborate into affirmations of that real thing. Plath's earliest sense of reading was an act that assured her of such reality. Sitting at her mother's feet, she learned to use letters to maintain her bond with the source of love, the sea-mother, the image which Plath would call near the end of her life, "the clearest thing I own." That imperative force, that "image of brilliance," was for Plath, as it was for James, love the way Dorothea Krook understood it in the symbolic tradition which evolved through Plato and Augustine: an imaginative act of meeting and believing that does not ignore the given world but is grounded in it, making the world readable, meaningful, real. Unlike James' imagination, Plath's was crippled by loss. The absconding father became the blank against which her furious imagination as gnostic will might flare, but from which she feared she would receive only indifference and, when she ceased to invent, annihilation.

Writing seemed to keep the menace off, so at Smith Plath affirmed writing as a way to stay alive. Not having enough time for that activity she understood as the cause of her anxieties and depressions. The next year, she and Hughes gave up teaching to live in Boston on grants and what they could earn from their published work. Plath's mental health, however, did not improve. In fact, as her journals show, she got worse and returned to sessions with her psychiatrist who gave her again a Freudian narrative with which to bring the past to consciousness. Plath faced her deepest fears: loss of love in the person of father, mother, husband, to a rival or to Death as rival. In her Boston Journal for 1958–59, she vented rage at her mother's limitations; she grieved for her father; and she identified her own deep insecurity. Her personal problems found explicit expression in her poetry at this time under the influence of Robert Lowell, whose poetry classes she attended at Boston University. If Lowell could write about being down and out of his mind, so could she.

Plath had a fine mind when she was well, but she had, from most evidence, an affective illness that took her at times into depressive despair, and she had that form of the imagination which envied and fought more than it loved and created. She began to deal with that negativity, finally, when she became pregnant in the summer of 1959. She and Hughes had toured the country and were spending the autumn at the artist's colony, Yaddo, in upstate New York before returning to England to settle for good. Plath had suffered from nightmares all year, but when she dreamed at Yaddo of the birth of a baby boy, her dreams got better. Hughes told her the dream meant the rebirth of her deep soul (J 323). Plath was not free, however, from fears and she still resisted the past which was "too painful … gray, laden with sorrow" (J 323). She resolved at Yaddo to be "true" to her own "weirdness" (J 323) and produced the poem which marks the beginning of her authentic style. This is "The Stones," the last of the seven poem sequence she called "Poem for a Birthday."

The poem enacts a violent parturition, the appearance of a new thing severed from the past: father, mother, the romantic poetic tradition she had been trying to serve. The poem breaks with the notion that it can give voice to an autobiographical lyric self at all. Something speaks in "The Stones," piping up, saying what it can and cannot do. It cannot create a real world, nor can it give Plath redeeming access to her origins. It can only make itself. The poem celebrates a splendid technology, the masculine technology of writing, in images whose effects are for the speaker more magical than real. "The Stones" stiffly proffers images of re-membering and re-constructing of a speaker with words, but they remain a collection of images as signs pointing toward wholeness that the linguistic structure alone cannot achieve. The poem is an allegory of its own insufficiency; it confesses its lack.

When Plath and Hughes left America for England in 1959, she had brought to consciousness a double life she could live with: first, the "trinity" of conjugal relations, based on her humanist beliefs, which kept the world readable, redeeming her erotic sense and keeping her in the world of others; and second, the pared away act of a highly self-conscious poetry that would more and more confess itself as lack of a unity of self. In Plath the poet, an allegorical form of the gnostic imagination wins over the symbolic in a negative turn which finds its level in a poetic voice painfully self-aware, self-mocking, and satiric.[38] Her strong poems, when they come as fiats say: "Let this *not* be." Plath's poetry "does" the abyss with a vengeance, but that was her talent. In less than four years, her marriage would end, a loss that would give her talent its occasion.

Endnotes

[1]Allen Tate's distinction between the symbolic imagination and the angelic imagination brings into relief these two modes: the "symbolic" is concerned with relations between persons as well as between persons and their natural world, for it keeps intellect tied to feeling and feeling tied to the body. The "angelic" scorns such relations as it drives toward some ultimate and absolute expression of itself. See Tate's "The Symbolic Imagination" and "The Angelic Imagination" collected in *Essays of Four Decades* (Chicago: The Swallow Press, 1968) 424–446; 401–423. Tate's distinctions have been eclipsed by recent theoretical debates over the nature of language itself, something which Tate more or less took for granted. He sensed, though, the dead end of Romanticism's language of protest which enacted defiance of any impingements, including those of the body. The angelic mode, once it gauged its futility, could only turn its negation as radical skepticism on its medium and subvert its own meaning.

[2]This is the turn of the imagination toward the sublime. See George Santayana, *The Sense of Beauty* (New York: Collier Books, 1961) 165. Harold Bloom celebrates only the sublime and the "gnostic" imagination. See *The Breaking of the Vessels* (Chicago: Chicago UP, 1982) Bloom's theory of "strong poetry" alone cannot account for the strangeness of Plath's poetry. See Bloom's Introduction to *Modern Critical Views: Sylvia Plath* (New York: Chelsea House, 1989) 1–4.

[3]James Olney, *Metaphors of Self: The Meaning of Autobiography* (Princeton: Princeton UP, 1972). Olney explores autobiography from the romantic perspective. Georges Gusdorf's approach is similar in "Conditions and Limits of Autobiography," *Autobiography: Essays Theoretical and Critical*, ed. James Olney. (Princeton: Princeton UP, 1980). Autobiography is "the effort of a creator to give the meaning of his own mythic tale" (48).

[4]George Gusdorf, "Conditions and Limits" in Olney gives this definition: "Confession, an attempt at remembering, is at the same time searching for a hidden treasure, for a last delivering word, redeeming in the final appeal a destiny that doubted its own value" (39).

[5]Rene Wellek and Austin Warren distinguish between mystical metaphor which is symbolic and magical metaphor which is not in *Theory of Literature*. Third Edition. (New York: Harcourt Brace Jovanovich, 1977) 205–206. The magical is causative, not expressive, an abstraction that "rigidly faces rather than follows the stream of life" (205).

[6]Aurelia Plath, letter to Ted and Carol Hughes, 2 July 1972, Plath MSII, The Lilly Library, Indiana U, Bloomington.

[7]Aurelia Plath, letter to Ted and Carol Hughes, 2 July 1972.

[8]Aurelia Plath, letter to author, 4 October 1987.

[9]Aurelia Plath, letter to author, 15 March 1987.

[10]Aurelia Plath, letter to author, 14 March 1987.

[11]Aurelia Plath, letter to author, 4 October 1987.

[12]Aurelia Plath, letter to author, 4 October 1987.

[13]"Dedication," Andrew Lang, ed. *The Yellow Fairy Book* (New York: Dover, 1966). n.p.

[14]Aurelia Plath notes that the maternal grandfather, not the father, carried Sylvia Plath as a child on his back out to sea (LH 22).

[15]Aurelia Plath, letter to Ted and Carol Hughes, 2 July 1972.

[16]In therapy, Plath traced her fear and hatred of male treachery to her father (SP 155).

[17]Jessica Benjamin, *Bonds of Love: Psychoanalysis, Feminism, and the Problem of Domination* (New York: Pantheon Books, 1988). Benjamin observes that girls may seek to bond with the father as boys do in order to value their sexual agency and autonomous will. She argues that women must structure their own desire (will) to undo classic gender polarity endorsed by Freud, who defined masculine identity in terms of repudiation of the mother and of femininity. In the Freudian family romance, the psychic strength males gain remains for girls an unattainable ideal unless they too repudiate the mother, identify with the father, and become "phallic." Benjamin proposes a different relation between genders which allows "mutual recognition" or "intersubjectivity." This dynamic requires that women find positive metaphors for their own desire (not Freud's negative ones) and that both men and women value the tension of mutual relation over the shift into domination of one by the other.

[18]Butscher quotes a teacher who evaluated Plath's intelligence quotient in the sixth grade (MM 28).

[19]Georges Gusdorf, "Scripture of the Self: 'Prologue in Heaven,'" trans. Betsy Wing, *The Southern Review* 22:2 (April 1986): 280–295.

[20]Rousseau's writing style, for example, issues from his need to believe in the purity and essential goodness of his feelings rather than his deeds. Jean Starobinski, *Jean-Jacques Rousseau: Transparency and Obstruction*, trans. Arthur Goldhammer (Chicago: U of Chicago P, 1988).

[21]At Smith, Plath wrote: "But what do I know of sorrow. No one I love has ever died or been tortured" (J 19). This is a complete blocking out of her father's long illness and death.

[22]Wilbury Crockett, personal interview, 1 August 1987. Wellesley, Mass.

[23]Wilbury Crockett, letter to author, 13 June 1987.

[24]For a discussion of Plath's ambivalent relation to her mother and to men reflected in her correspondences see Lynda Bundtzen, *Plath's Incarnations: Woman and the Creative Process* (Ann Arbor: U of Michigan P, 1983) 65–84.

[25]Catherine Thompson suggests another possibility in "'Dawn Poems in Blood': Sylvia Plath and PMS," *TriQuarterly* 80 (Winter 1990–1991) 221–249. Stevenson's biography (BF) documents Plath's fight against emotional illness without speculating on the precise nature of that illness. Any "diagnosis," physiological or psychological (including mine) must remain speculation.

[26]The Magic Mirror: A Study of the Double in Two of Dostoevsky's Novels. Unpublished Senior Thesis. Smith College Library.

[27]Plath seemed to "become her own double" after shock treatments. See Aurelia Plath, "Letter Written in Early Spring," *Ariel Ascending: Writings about Sylvia Plath*, ed. Paul Alexander (New York: Harper and Row, 1985) 126.

[28]See Nancy Hunter Steiner, *A Closer Look at Ariel: A Memory of Sylvia Plath* (New York: Harper's Magazine Press, 1973) 57–72.

[29]Mira Stout quotes Byatt in "What Possessed A. S. Byatt." *The New York Times Magazine*, 26 May 1991: 15.

[30]Unpublished Journals, Plath Collection, Smith College Library.

[31]Wagner-Martin, Stevenson and Butscher in their respective biographies of Plath refer to the Plath-Krook relation, but none gives their association the importance that I do. Butscher interpreted Plath's attachment as "a sign of a deeply buried (probably never faced) androgynous strain in her [Plath's] own make-up" (MM 199).

[32]Dorothea Krook, letter to author, 4 September 1988.

[33]John Burnaby quotes St. Augustine in his "Introduction," *Augustine: The Later Works* (Philadelphia: The Westminster Press, 1955) 15.

[34]I do not argue that there is a humanist analogy sufficient to Augustine's doctrine of the Trinity; I merely assert that the humanist beliefs which Plath took up belong to the same tradition of the metaphoric, symbolic imagination that was as much Plato's as Dante's, as much Martin Buber's as T. S. Eliot's.

[35]*Henry James: French Writers, Other European Writers, The Prefaces to the New York Edition,* ed. Leon Edel (New York: The Library of America, 1984) 1330.

[36]J. Hillis Miller, *The Ethics of Reading* (New York: Columbia UP, 1987) 113. Miller does a close reading of James' Preface to *The Golden Bowl.*

[37]See Dorothea Krook, *The Ordeal of Consciousness in Henry James.* (Cambridge: Cambridge UP, 1962).

[38]Seamus Heaney, "The Indefatigable Hoof-taps,"*The Government of the Tongue: Selected Prose 1978–1987.* (New York: Farrar, Straus, and Giroux, 1981) 148–170. Heaney finds Plath's verse from "The Stones" to "Elm" relational and everything after "Elm" fiats. The late poems "are full of exhilaration in themselves, the exhilaration of a mind that creates in some sort of mocking spirit, outstripping the person who has suffered" (151).

2

Early Belief, Growing Doubts: Plath's Juvenilia

Plath copied into her 1945 diary a verse she titled "Enchantment":

> The Soul will tread an airy trail
> To an enchanted land above the earth
> And from the highest peak will hail
> Another life ... another birth.
>
> No wall will bar this land of joy
> No sign will keep the poor away
> A book may lead each girl and boy
> From darkest night to brilliant day.[1]

This verse may or may not have been entirely Plath's own, but she liked it well enough to preserve it carefully. The commonplace affirms her early belief: books can transport and transform a reader by enabling her to experience something other than the actual and the quotidian; and the reading faculty was "the Soul." Reading was a spiritual act leading from a negative to a positive state: joyful and rich as opposed to the pain and poverty of actual experience; open to all as opposed to the injustice of the world. This romantic creed underlay Plath's earliest experiences with language and literature in the company of her mother. In "Enchantment," however, the image of the "highest peak" as access to a new, exhilarating view of existence wants to echo—not the magic gardens of Andrew Lang—but the wide, humane vision of Keats on Darien.

Plath produced a large number of adolescent poems: more than eighty written and polished during her public school years can be counted among the juvenilia collected in the Lilly Library. She pleased, perhaps more than herself, her family and her teachers with her precocity. Early on, she had a keen awareness of her audience and the effects she could have on them, though her themes emerged from deep personal struggles. Two dramatic monologues, "Persecuted" and "Bereft," written when she was fifteen, could be companion pieces.[2] The first articulates a need to separate from the mother; the second, a need to join an unreachable father. In "Persecuted" the speaker resists a "patterned" domestic life and a partner's "beseeching face." He (the speaker sounds male) wants freedom to walk alone on the shore, though he promises to return and to take up his "troubles and sorrow" again. The proclaimed weariness of the speaker is countered by the steady, sturdy ballad beat. His feet may be, as he says, "faltering," but his rhythm certainly is not, nor is his will to be elsewhere.

"Bereft" answers "Persecuted" as a feminine voice recalls her beloved's sea-side farewell. At the time, she was "glad to be rid of a part of me." Plath's father's death, after four years of suffering shown in anger and irritability, could have been felt by the young Plath as a relief. For the speaker in "Bereft," the impact of loss comes much later than the separation. Only when sea and rain have washed away all traces of the beloved is his absence felt. Then, in an "empty and bitter" autumn, the ocean roars in pain and beats "its heart out/ On sharp rocks along the shore."

Such juvenile efforts dramatize normal adolescent needs intensified by Plath's particular situation. She could not risk a drastic emotional break with the mother, but she needed to find a father, and in so doing, to identify herself as an autonomous, desiring person. In adolescence, Plath longed not to defy paternal authority, but to learn from that kind strength a way out of an undeveloped life. As this and other verses suggest, she yearned for a benevolent father. All she had was his absence. Her stance toward that absence determined the kind of poet she would become.

When the sixteen-year-old William Wordsworth, grieving for his father, wrote of "this blank of things," he found in solitude "a harmony/ Home-felt, and home-created," which came "to heal" his grief. When Plath was fifteen or sixteen, she wrote two poems about fog in which her speaker tries to evade the inner creative act of making meaning in the face of loss. In the first, a she asks for release from anxiety: "Let a haze of ocean fog/ Blur my vision/ Stop my ears/ Mute my voice/ And still my fears." In the second, titled "All I can tell you is about the fog," she reluctantly answers the demand that she use language creatively to give form to formlessness:

> Please. Don't ask me. I don't know.
> All I can tell you
> Is how the fog comes in.
> Like smoke it comes.
> It has no flavor
> Unless you count the taste
> Of grass and apples
> That mix with it.

She cannot say what the fog is, only what it does, but sensing that she has been gulled into doing what she initially said she could not do, the speaker begins the second stanza repeating:

> I don't know. Ask them.
> They talk about other things.
> They are very clever, those people.
> All I can tell you
> Is how the fog sounds.
> At night it drips like rain
> From the maple trees.
> In the morning
> It goes up in smoke,
> The color of fingernails,
> With no sound at all.

Articulating something out of almost nothing is a hard task, but the compulsion to do as bidden prevails. The figures "like rain," "in smoke," and "color of fingernails" thicken the opacity and continue the still reluctant "telling" or metaphorically counting properties of the blank:

All I can tell you
Is how the fog takes away the people
And all the houses
And the maple trees.
I think it turns them into mushrooms.
It leaves the lights, though,
Hanging up there on nothing at all.
Sometimes I think they are little lost balloons
Whizzing around in the dark and crying for their mother.

Don't ask me. I don't know.
All I can tell you
Is about the fog.

The speaker manages, in spite of her protests, to increase in each stanza her number of lines and her number of tropes "about the fog." Almost against her will, she is pulled into meaning by the power of her medium. One thing leads to another in a string of associations that only language makes possible: people, houses, and trees become mushrooms; unmoored lights become balloons; these balloons become lost souls crying for their mother. If the "soul" is the reading capacity in Plath's terms, its mother is desire for metaphoric relation that makes meaning. Written language is a means to that end, but not the end itself. The speaker has asked to be less than she might be, but two things will not allow that: language which generates both logical and tropological meaning in spite of her recalcitrance, and desire for symbolic experience which forces language into formal significance. Whose desire is it? Not the timid speaker's in the poem. It is the writer's desire and the reader's desire that put demands on language. Both maker and reader of the poem want some symbolic satisfaction; otherwise, the poet would not write and the reader would not read. Plath makes out of a dramatized resistance to imagination, an imaginative engagement.

Such attempts can, of course, fail. Some of Plath's juvenilia worry over not being able to connect in ordinary social ways. In "Wallflower" of 1949, for example, the speaker does everything right for a social evening, but is miserable: "I'll stay until the party's end/ And never try to flee it; And I'll pretend I do not know/ Failure when I see it." The self-mocking verse meshes social awkwardness with willful obtuseness. About the same time,

"The Dark River" develops the theme of social isolation and fear of losing the self in attempts to cross the space that separates people. Another verse from 1949, "Seek No More the Young," renders an even darker vision of the world after a global war in which youth's potential has been mutilated or destroyed. Plath's generation entered adolescence during World War II when many of their elders felt that civilization as they had known it was coming to an end. The pervasive influence of Freudian pessimism in *Civilization and its Discontents,* the shocking evidence of the Holocaust, and the beginning of the Cold War intensified the threat as Plath came of age. She felt the grimness of her time. Her poem "Youth's Appeal for World Peace" (March,1948) is mostly bombast and bathos, but it shows helplessness before the Four Horsemen of the Apocalypse who gallop across the plain in spite of her plea: "Oh, turn back and let this bud bloom."

A little poem from 1950, "The Invalid," might have grown out of the normal low spirits resulting from physical illness. The poem, however, enacts the mood as if it were an illness, depression, which is the incapacity, for whatever reason, to synthesize a beneficial meaning from experience.[3] Plath's influence here is early Eliot:

> Half-past four on an April morning:
> I wish the sun would never rise
> Nor the cantalope-colored light
> Stain the uninfected skies.
>
> Half past four; and after fever
> The penicillin blood now sings:
> Silver-cool through vein and fiber
> The nimble liquid sweetly springs.
>
> Strange birds twitter; and I recall
> That years ago in a Chinese sea
> A man I never knew was drowned ...
> Yet he was all the world to me.
>
> Insect like on either cheek
> My tears crawl down all hot and wet,
> And I, as Niobe, dissolve
> In green and watery regret.

Five o'clock: the orange light spills
A flood of daybreak in my eyes;
Dawn laps at the window sills;
The tall gold sun begins to rise.

Signs of depression appear in the first stanza: very early waking, not to welcome the sun as a life force, but to anticipate its menace as a staining, inflaming agent. The speaker prefers the cooled, disinfected body and the dark. Nature responds to the dawn in appropriate fashion: birds twitter. But the birds are "strange" and cannot be identified, a vague image that leads to a string of associations that do not so much express the memory of loss and the feeling of regret as they establish a code of images that say something about loss and regret.

If the reader takes as the initial clue to meaning the depressed mood of the speaker, she will not look for unity in these verses. The depressive cannot synthesize, that is, "re-member" the past as part of the whole of her experience or sense of self. The past appears as "dis-membered" parts which the reader, along with the speaker, will try to read by imposing the need for coherence and meaning. The speaker feels as guilty as Niobe—for no apparent reason—and cries abundant tears, repulsive, warm, crawling things that only add to her distress. They correspond to the ominous light coming on as relentlessly as a tide. The speaker's desire to remain cool and whole in the dark cannot hold off the dawn any more than it can hold off the undesired feelings that come from nowhere: guilt, loss, sorrow, and fear associated with the unknown drowned man. As the speaker weeps for him, the morning light takes on watery attributes: it spills, floods, laps, and rises. The speaker will perhaps drown ("dissolve") herself in the yellow light as a "Chinese sea." The lost man may be the strong (whole, healthy) will in her that would have bonded with a father as she grew into a confident adulthood. If so, she never "knew" such a well self, properly; therefore, she cannot remember it, that is, reconstruct that wholeness imaginatively. She must experience that lack as a death, perhaps at every dawn, again and again.

The best the depressed mind can do is to give form to its own disorder (Caramagno 19,22). Plath's poem composes a resistance to being dragged into life by light. With no strength to face it, she fears destruction by it as a masculine colossus. Plath here dramatizes in her writing an inability to read a unified meaning in experience, or to put it in poetic terms, an inability to project with her own imaginative strength an adequate unifying metaphor into her collection of contiguous images. But we do not need such theory to tell us that Plath is not writing poetry yet.

The reader who knows Plath's biography can bring a key to her code: a major part of Plath's struggle to grow up required that she face her father's self-destructiveness, but her tradition gave her no way to understand the problem of evil in human will, including her own will. The deep faults and gaps in her world and in herself were terrifying, yet the burden fell to her to fill them. Such deciphering turns the poem "The Invalid" into allegory, a fictional order that helped Plath live with fear of her own inadequacy and resulting melancholy. Plath's major breakdown was just three years away.

As she dealt with negative feelings and psychic pain, Plath would sometimes try for the big dramatic effect as in "Ariadne (deserted by Theseus)," dated 1949 (LH 36). She fails miserably. Throughout the poem, Ariadne has a tantrum, raging and screaming like a little girl who did not get her way and calming down only when she is exhausted. Nature cooperates by storming when she storms and by just "grumbling" when she has vented most of her fury. The verse ends with a question: "Why do you stand and listen only to/ The sobbing of the wind along the sand?" which seems less a probe into the nature of tragic loss than a rebuke for being excessive and impractical. Plath's motive here is the need to address her blank world.

"White Phlox," dated 1950 and published in the *Christian Science Monitor*, on August 27, 1952, shows Plath more able to evoke abandonment through silence than through Ariadne's howls. Here, Plath is inside the undesired and this time the effect is chilling.

> From the silver vase
> White phlox petals fall;
> Silence floods the parlour—
> And fills the narrow hall.
> The only sound's the clock
> Ticking on the wall.
>
> Is there naught to measure thought
> Save the ticking of the clock

And the fitful drift of white
Petals from the withered stalk?

Is the house asleep,
Are the tenants gone,
That the clock and I
Keep our watch alone?
Are we the only ones to mark
The petals falling in the dark?

This juvenile poem deals with the minimal: a room with no one in it but the speaker and nothing happening except the passing of time, noted by the regularity of the ticking clock and the "fitful" drying and dropping of white phlox petals from a bouquet past its prime. This is the afterward, a sense of ominous belatedness, for everything important has already occurred. The flowers were fresh for some gathering or fullness in the room. Whatever occasion the flowers honored is no longer accessible to the speaker. The loneliness here is that of a mind without memory, a reduction of imaginative capacity that makes impossible the assurance that others exist unseen in other rooms. The mind begins to question the existence of anything that cannot be empirically sensed. The ticking off of iambic trimeter and iambic tetrameter lines suggests the push of the mind against these measured limits and its defeat by them. The speaker cannot free her attention from the movement toward a dark which holds no sign of release from a reduced but insistent consciousness. There is, possibly, in the last stanza an echo of the nursery rhyme "Wee Willie Winkie," that night-gowned little fellow with his urgency: "Tapping at the window, crying through the clock/ Are the children in their beds? It's past eight o'clock." Plath's "White Phlox" is an image of a child who will neither remember nor dream and who may go mad. The speaker as such a stunted perception registers the scene but learns nothing, gets no answer in the form of poetic insight to her questions. Rather, she delineates the intense suffering of a time-trapped mind that can believe in nothing invisible. The imagination is not relied on here to ease isolation: no recollection of the past occurs; no compensating fiction emerges. Nothing can make the unseen present to this mind because it refuses the symbolic. More simply put, it refuses belief. Thus, this mind suffers loss as absolute abandonment. This is the death of the imagination, the death of the "soul" that can read symbolically.

That Plath knew another response to temporal experience was possible is obvious in a poem written the same year as "White Phlox" and published in *Seventeen* in November of 1950 (Tabor 105). This poem, "Ode to a Bitten Plum," probably done as a high school class assignment for Wilbury Crockett, strives to do justice to its object: "… resilient flesh/ translucent amber/ honey-clear,/ melting into quartz-green/ and glassed yellow ocher." We can guess the directions Plath was following: contemplate something in nature, evoke it sensuously, let the reader know how it looks, feels, tastes, smells, and then see more, its significance, and represent that as well. The poem goes beyond description of the object to imagining the invisible power of regeneration contained at its core: "inside your oval stone/ is the secret of the ages hid … gnarled boughs/ of an ancient orchard/ interlacing…." There is much posturing in this meditation on the half-eaten fruit. Nevertheless, Plath shows she had learned this: beauty in nature is transformed most acutely into art when that beauty is apprehended in the process of vanishing, for inevitable loss provokes the imagination to construct life-celebrating metaphors. This was for Plath a healthy antidote to her more usual bleakness of mind and she was trying to make those connections.

Plath was still under twenty when "White Phlox" and "Ode to a Bitten Plum" were published. The first displays the death of the symbolic imagination; the second attempts to do its work. Another poem from this same period puts the two modes together in dramatic form, and explores their differences. "Bitter Strawberries" (CP 299–300) was written sometime during the summer of 1950, after Plath had graduated from high school and she and her brother Warren were working as berry pickers, planters and weeders at a truck farm outside Wellesley. It was hard work among rough people. Plath was earning money for the fall when she would enter Smith as a scholarship student. She would begin her college career as an outsider among a privileged elite, but she could compensate by being rich in experience. That was her American birthright, almost her obligation. It would be typical of Plath, as of any strong-willed young woman of her time, to open her eyes and ears to her environment, determined not to be afraid, repelled, or demeaned by what she encountered. Rather, she would glean from it some imaginative transformation that would affirm both the rough world's value and hers.

The rousing of conflicting feeling is part of the development of "Bitter Strawberries," a poem which can be read as an anti-war statement. The Korean conflict was making the Cold War real to Americans, and Plath was, like her teacher and friend Wilbury Crockett, an outspoken pacifist.[4] The poem's narrative manages to condemn duplicity and violence by merely recognizing them. Thus, this poem is about reading right, that is, about perceiving, imagining and feeling the formal significance in the scene. There is no showing off in intricate prosody as in the verses Plath would go on to write in undergraduate courses at Smith. Here, writing for no instructor, she attends to words and acts not her own and finds her complex relation to them. The poem's narrative voice speaks as "we": small, unassertive, anonymously plural, in the scene but not of it, aware of division and distance from the opening lines: "All that morning in the strawberry field/ They talked about the Russians." A group close enough to be overheard, talk about foreigners as anonymous, faceless abstractions:

> Squatted down between the rows
> We listened.
> We heard the woman say,
> 'Bomb them off the map.'

The silent but alert "we" feels attacked and sickened: "Horseflies buzzed, paused and stung,/ And the taste of strawberries/ Turned thick and sour." Still, "we" read on with attention:

> Mary said slowly, 'I've got a fella
> Old enough to go.
> If anything should happen ...'
>
> The sky was high and blue.
> Two children laughed at tag
> In the tall grass,
> Leaping awkward and long-legged
> Across the rutted road.
> The fields were full of bronzed young men
> Hoeing lettuce, weeding celery.

Another "they," the young children have either not heard talk of the war or are not troubled by it. Their own aggression is a mere game to eliminate a competitor and establish dominance. The speaker senses the menace which the children do not. The images of the "rutted road" and a horde of "bronzed young men," unthreatening in a scene of peace, would be images of violence in the context of war. The menace intensifies:

> 'The draft is passed,' the woman said.
> 'We ought to have bombed them long ago.'
> 'Don't,' pleaded the little girl
> With blond braids.
>
> Her blue eyes swam with vague terror.
> She added pettishly, 'I can't see why
> You're always talking this way ...'
> 'Oh, stop worrying, Nelda,'
> Snapped the woman sharply.
> She stood up, a thin commanding figure
> In faded dungarees.
> Businesslike she asked us, 'How many quarts?'
> She recorded the total in her notebook,
> And we all turned back to picking.

Fear pervades the atmosphere, for "They," both conversing field workers and absent Russians, do not seem as remote as in the first stanza. Though the work goes on much the same, the harvesting has the suggestion of death, but not ennobled, tragic death. The dominant voice is that of the woman boss who abstracts Russian people into an ideology that must be destroyed. This same mentality abstracts the ripe fruit, traditionally nature's tragic emblem, into numbers in a notebook for a cash crop. Though her stance is tall and commanding, the unreflecting shallowness of her mind makes her terrifying. She cannot see the face or imagine the humanity of others. The "we" are still crouched and small and focused on their task, but the narrator perceives the potential violence within them all—the tall and shallow as well as the small and pondering.

> Kneeling over the rows,
> We reached among the leaves
> With quick practiced hands,
> Cupping the berry protectively before
> Snapping off the stem
> Between thumb and forefinger.

The "we" here refers to the pickers: all women. Their life-enhancing posture of food gathering has been read in the context of fear. Thus, although remaining outside the dialogue within the dramatic action, the narrative voice reveals in the final image her own fear and her own capacity for crudity and violence as well as for being their victim. The berry picking stands for imaginative impoverishment, the result of brutalized feeling: the act of "snapping" echoes the "snapped" speech of the woman boss. Mary Lynn Broe's response to the closing lines of "Bitter Strawberries" illuminates the depth of Plath's poetic insight: "The quietness of the final image—that simple, practiced gesture of fondling and then snapping the berries—captures all the duplicity and easy habitual violence of predatory human nature."[5] The poem, however, offers more than a mood of despair. The poem offers a remedy, a way to keep alive a soul, a reading capacity, that refuses to reduce the world to mere arbitrary signs for a fixed idea. The poem as the dramatic interpretation of words and gestures by an effaced reader offers a symbolic order to be read in the spirit of imaginative sympathy. Plath thus affirms that such acts of the reading self (or in Plath's early term, the "soul") are the only defenses human beings have against their own worst natures: their life-denying natures.

That defense came under attack at Smith College where Plath felt set apart, a brilliant but, relatively speaking, needy student. Becoming a Smith woman could eventually give her the social and economic security she had lacked. American culture had taught Plath that to be thwarted by economic or social barriers was to be weak, ignorant, and, worse, afraid; yet she was afraid most of her short life. Above all, she feared the failure of her imagination in the face of an empty and uncongenial world, and she had reason, for her belief in her own powers was assaulted again and again by the torment of self-doubt. At Smith, the world became hard to "read" with romantic conventions. Coming up against a world that she could not decipher, Plath took a harsh, ironic position, as in "Complaint" from her sophomore year. The little poem at first glance looks like an imitation of a classical *carpe diem* lyric for it begins: "Court time's favor/ With kiss and crown,/ Yet she will ever/ Gallop on." The accentual dimeter indeed gallops through the five quatrains in quick succession, flinging out images of lovers who couple, then wither, then die. The cautionary voice concludes: "So cry forever/ The raveled rose,/ No sigh will waver/ Assault of grass." No poignancy or delicacy of feeling makes of transience a life-enhancing value. Plath's off-rhymes register incongruity between culture's creatures and an utterly indifferent universe. The speaker's stare is a swaggering bully's version of the terrified child's view in "White Phlox."

"Sonnet: To Eva" (CP 304–305), also from her junior year, begins with similar tough-girl talk that develops the metaphor of a cuckoo clock for a woman's head:

> All right, let's say you could take a skull and break it
> The way you'd crack a clock; you'd crush the bone
> Between steel palms of inclination, take it,
> Observing the wreck of metal and rare stone.

This is a sonnet full of percussive sound and fury that in a brutal world signify nothing. The closing couplet shows that where a sounding, reading soul should have been is a cuckoo—a mad woman who cannot read right: "The idiot bird leaps up and drunken leans/ To chirp the hour in lunatic thirteens."

What drove her mad? An answer emerges in the poem which immediately follows "Sonnet: To Eva" in the Juvenilia appended to the *Collected Poems*. The poem "Bluebeard" echoes a sonnet by Edna St. Vincent Millay with the same title.[6] In Millay's poem, the male speaker addresses a female intruder who disobeyed him in order to seek the "truth" about him. She is self-destroyed, he says. The surprise in Millay's poem is this: there is nothing in Bluebeard's invaded chamber except his departing presence. The intruding woman is not butchered there or rescued, as in the classic tale, but left alone. Emptiness is all she can claim to know or to have, says Bluebeard as he vanishes and seeks another place. Besides Millay, Plath's poem echoes Nietzsche in "On Truth and Lies in an Extra

Moral Sense"[7] in his repeated image of Nature throwing away the key to man's self-knowledge. In Plath's "Bluebeard" (CP 305), a woman speaks:

> I am sending back the key
> that let me into bluebeard's study;
> because he would make love to me
> I am sending back the key;
> in his eye's darkroom I can see
> my X-rayed heart, dissected body:
> I am sending back the key
> that let me into bluebeard's study.

Plath's speaker, like Millay's, finds annihilation in disobedience. She explains her actions in the light of what she has just seen: her reflection in the mirror of Bluebeard's eye as a sign to be read ("my X-rayed heart") and as lifeless fragments ("dissected body"). This is Bluebeard's forbidden knowledge: at the heart of things is no other person (and thus no love), just murderous dissection in one's own mind. Bluebeard, written with the lower case "b," calls attention to the word as sign which brings the "I" to self-consciousness. Here, the sign points, not to a man, but to nothing. The "eye" of nothing stuns the woman into a new awareness. Heroic nihilism is required, but Plath's speaker is faint-hearted. She would un-do the transgression of wanting access to absolute knowledge and the power it confers; thus, she is "sending back the key." This has the ring of macabre humor, for as woman, she is asserting her "Nature" by changing her mind. She is, however, already altered by new consciousness. Having doubted and disobeyed, the speaker in the poem sees the worst about *natura rerum*: "bluebeard" is nothing, neither god nor devil. He is mere linguistic sign, but as such, powerful enough to undo her. Perhaps she knows the worst about herself: she will be haunted by her act, for having broken through to this perception of divisiveness and meaninglessness in language, she may go mad.

Plath's breakdown in 1953 was related to her increasingly bleak views of experience and her doubt that mere words could give her access to any redeeming feeling. The first poem Plath wrote after her suicidal illness, "Doom of Exiles" (CP 318), dated April, 1954, illustrates Nietzsche's definition of truth: "A mobile army of metaphors, metonyms, and anthropomorphisms" (Nietzsche 44). This is a very different poem from the dramatic freedom of the much earlier "Bitter Strawberries." As poetic language, the "exiles" take over their duties as if they could still "crack the nut/ wherein the riddle of our race is shut." The implication is that they cannot, at least not without some belief in a central animating spirit and that seems gone.

Even before the breakdown, many of Plath's poems put the efficacy of her imagination in question. "Metamorphoses of the Moon" (1953) describes the imagination deadlocked with the de-mystifying force of intelligence, that insatiable, perverse "imp" which "hangs itself on its own rope." As if to prove her corrosive power, Plath mocks and debases many elements from her literary and cultural tradition—though very cleverly. "The Dead" (1952) uses a Petrarchan sonnet to debunk a delicate elegiac mood; "Dialogue en Route" (1953) is a sadistic morality play with a "cheapened and perverted" Adam and Eve, according to Plath's own notes for this poem; "Cinderella" (1952) wears red shoes, has silver hair, looks at her prince through slanting green eyes, and goes pale with guilt and anxiety as her time for sham runs out.

Plath performs energetically in a variety of verse forms; but as Mary Lynn Broe was first to point out in her 1980 study, the core of Plath's world remains indifferent, mute, vacant (1–42). We need to remember that she felt this void as her fatherlessness. For some sensibilities, such absence offers opportunity; for Plath, it offered dread. Her anxiety was tied to an awareness that language could designate only relations, not things, and so perhaps it would designate only its own internal relations. At some point, either in 1953, just before her serious illness or in the year following, Plath retreats from attempts to be impersonal, to read what seemed to be other than herself, and follows only her own difficulties. She begins to read her own performances, such as in the 1953 poem "Circus in Three Rings," in which the speaker flaunts her sexual daring while revealing a "basic mistrust of love" (MM 80). The 1953 villanelle, "Mad Girl's Love Song," takes self-consciousness to the extreme of solipsism, but unlike the earlier poem "White Phlox," this speaker registers from beside herself her own madness. "Aerialist" suggests the same dualism, as the displayed figure is in control only when she is performing and paranoid when she is not.

The best of these self-readings is the 1955 poem "Two Lovers and a Beachcomber by the Real Sea" (CP 327) which enacts the shutting down of the imagination while imaginatively surveying the results.

> Cold and final, the imagination
>   Shuts down its fabled summer house;
> Blue views are boarded up; our sweet vacation
>   Dwindles in the hour-glass.

The elaborate conceit contemplates an afterward, as did the 1950 poem "White Phlox." Plath's only advance over that earlier poem is in technique. The speaker in this later poem is still time-trapped. The past remains inaccessible; the future seems bleak; and the present, sordid.

> A lone beachcomber squats among the wrack
>   Of kaleidoscopic shells
> Probing fractured Venus with a stick
>   Under a tent of taunting gulls.

The speaker asserts: "What we are/ Outlaws all extrapolation/ Beyond the interval of now and here." The poem's action reduces the material world and those in it to language:

> No sea change decks the sunken shank of bone
>   That chuckles in backtrack of the wave;
> Though the mind like an oyster labors on and on
>   A grain of sand is all we have.

These sounds remain sounds, not symbols of perfection that might lie beyond them. At best we have agreeable clatter; at worst, compulsion as mechanical force:

> Water will run by rule; the actual sun
>   Will scrupulously rise and set;
> No little man lives in the exacting moon
>   And that is that, is that, is that.

The conceit of reduction ends in the last line, on the the last moment, the last grain of sand in the hour glass, suggesting that this grain is like all others in a world without imagination, just as the phrase "is that" forms a bit of verbal grit that can be repeated endlessly, but neither dissolved nor transformed into significance. What is this thing I do, then, Plath seems to ask, when I write poetry? If I cannot read the world in romantic conventions, what can I do?

An answer of sorts can be found in Plath's definite shift in emphasis from impersonal reader and romantic creator, as she was in "Bitter Strawberries," to self-conscious, audacious performer in the late juvenilia. A good example is "To a Jilted Lover" (CP 309) written in 1955 and retitled in 1956 as "Apotheosis."[8] Compared to other Smith poems, this one has little cleverness or cynical playfulness. There is, rather, a strong sense of painful separation and reliance on an imaginative response to remedy the situation. This is a romantic motive and the poem does not mock or deflate a romantic reading. It does, however, unsettle such a response by offering another possibility.

Plath's opening line, "Cold in my narrow cot I lie," echoes Emily Bronte's "Cold in the Earth" with its sense of distance from a lost love. Bronte's speaker addresses a beloved, dead and buried many years, but not forgotten. Feeling in Bronte's poem depends on a continuous sense of self, available through memory. To remember is to love, but the speaker will not give in to excessive grief that would tempt her toward disengagement and death. She resists indulging in "memory's rapturous pain," concluding, "Once drinking deep of that divinest anguish,/ How could I seek the empty world again?" The force of loving increases throughout Bronte's poem in proportion to the force of resisting indulgent, self-destructive grief. The speaker has lived long, changed and experienced much, but is still the same self that loved deeply once and continues to have access to that profound feeling through recollection.

Plath's poem, like Bronte's, begins in "sorrow," but the loss results from the speaker's act and the beloved seems less a person than a power that has removed itself from her. Instead of Bronte's richly rolling, elegiac accentual tetrameter quatrains, Plath uses a version of terza rima, with four accents in the first and third lines and only two in the second. The rhyme scheme of the nine stanzas is complicated. Each group of three stanzas is bound by the rhyme of the first line. The first lines are true rhymes; the couplets are off-rhymes. The rhythm and rhyme effect a sense of control that eases and then tightens again at each beginning, yet the pattern does not vary. Rigid rule overrides desire for change in the form, but desire for radical change seems to drive the poem.

The speaker does not address her lover; she reflects on her response to his anger over an injury she did him.

> Cold on my narrow cot I lie
>   and in sorrow look
> through my window-square of black:
>
> figured in the midnight sky,
>   a mosaic of stars
> diagrams the falling years,
>
> while from the moon, my lover's eye
>   chills me to death
> with radiance of his frozen faith.

Estrangement from love results from her unintentionally inflicting pain on this dominant power. She feels guilty, not of malice, but of caprice or carelessness, as the term "jilt" in the original title suggests:

> Once I wounded him with so
>   small a thorn
> I never thought his flesh would burn
>
> or that the heat within would grow
>   until he stood
> incandescent as a god;

The pain which apotheosizes the lover seems, to her mind, out of proportion to the hurt. The focus of her attention, however, is not on his suffering but on hers, for she cannot escape his fury:

> now there is nowhere I can go
> to hide from him:
> moon and sun reflect his flame.

The beginning of the final group of three stanzas suggests a turn in the form of a facile, childish belief that the daylight will make everything all right, but as in the high school poem "The Invalid," daylight brings no comfort. What becomes clear in a romantic reading of "Apotheosis" is this: severance is absolute unless the lover will see her remorse and then pity and forgive her:

> In the morning all shall be
> the same again:
> stars pale before the angry dawn;
>
> The gilded cock will turn for me
> the rack of time
> until the peak of noon has come
>
> and by that glare, my love will see
> how I am still
> blazing in my golden hell.

Time moves, but a fixity of emotional states governs the poem. The speaker sees the lover in all the signs in the sky: moon, stars, sun. That the lover will see her is certain; that he will redeem her remains problematic. Yet the poem does not end in exhaustion: the final image attempts to keep a tension between hope and despair by means of two oxymorons: "still/blazing" and "golden hell." The speaker is "still," as in unmoving; yet she is active, continuing to burn with feeling and enriched, even if damned, by it. How we respond to this final image depends on how we understand the initial act, the wound to the flesh. If we hear the speaker reflecting on her deed and understanding it as an offense against the law of love, her closing image may acknowledge a way back to her lover through acknowledged transgression. In this reading, Plath has managed to write from within a certain kind of suffering which mars human life but which, at the same time, makes life knowable. In this first reading, Plath's speaker as "sinner" has access to the past in the way Bronte's speaker does: she sees it in the light of the present. Like Bronte's speaker, she is not innocent: she knows the price she has paid in suffering for her perspective. The nature of the speaker's offense in "Apotheosis" literally "dawns" on her as she imagines "the angry" morning light and the "glare" of noon. She places her guilty self in the inferno of the closing image, aware of what she has lost and why: the authority of love is not to be denied without damnation. But the poem's close raises an Eliotic question: "After such knowledge, what forgiveness?" In Eliot's "Gerontion," the speaker is in a similar estranged condition: "I that was near your heart was removed therefrom/ To lose beauty in terror, terror in inquisition,/ I have lost my passion." Like Eliot's "Gerontion," Plath's speaker cannot will an heroic rescue from an earthly or a divine lover. Unlike Eliot's speaker, however, she waits and hopes for one ardently.

This traditional, romantic reading can be displaced by another more analytic one if the reader understands the wound in "Apotheosis" as a mistake and the resulting gap between the speaker and the object of her desire as a space for contest. Then, the estranging "wound" allows her to face the lover and articulate her distance from him. The reader-as-analyst understands the blaze not as a humbling of the speaker but as an intensification of her desire. The original, separating act remains an error which the speaker regrets, but for which she feels no guilt or shame. The speaker is, in fact, shameless in her renewed effort to win over the alienated lover, to melt his "frozen faith" with the intensity and virtuosity of her performance. In this second reading, the speaker relies on her own invention to compensate for her loss. There is no recourse to memory to understand the past in the light of the present. The past is dismissed; only the future holds promise, and only then if the speaker can fan her desires for her object bright enough and high enough. The analytic reader will suspect that the speaker wants not the lover but the power to see not by his light but by her own.

The first reading of "Apotheosis" is in the tradition of the symbolic imagination that works within a given world that can supply what will suffice if the speaker can manage a relation with it; the second reading is in the mode of the negating imagination which arises when relations with the given world have failed, or when the given is more punishing than sustaining. Which reading was Plath's?

We can make a reasonable guess if we consider the following: the pre-Smith poem "Bitter Strawberries" and "Apotheosis," written five years later after Plath's serious mental illness, show two distinct phases of Plath's early development. In the first, Plath tried to read the world with romantic belief in the tradition of the symbolic imagination. In the second, she turned from reading the world of others to reading her own performances with an uneasy sense of the divisive forces at work in her language. In "Bluebeard," she suspected that her linguistic performances could be reduced to signs that point to nothing but more signs and that any comfort or power they might offer was specious.

"Bitter Strawberries" demonstrates Plath's ability to be open to experience, even when that experience is troubling and contaminating. She explored complicity in violence through the deadening of sensibility by habit, and also through the type of fear which can lead to the abstraction of experience for purposes of self-protection. Because language can work as a tool of ideology, the poem's voice resists linguistic display, preferring only to "read" and register the world in which she finds herself. The effaced self in "Bitter Strawberries" has the courage to sense her own potential for defensive, political violence based on fear. The only counter force to dangerous metonymic reduction of persons to signs or ideologies—mere things—is human compassion, human connection, which depends in this poem, on a belief in a shared symbolic order. Plath's poem affirms such an order by offering itself to be read with compassion and asking the reader to condemn the mindlessness of war.

"Apotheosis" also explores fear but through a performing "I" who offers two distinct interpretations of her act. Fear of loss in "Apotheosis" can be understood as a corrective, leading to understanding a past act as trespass and present suffering as atonement with the ultimate outcome openness to love. More analytically, fear can be understood as a permanent condition, a necessary spur to intensify desire. Then, the final image of the speaker's "blazing in my golden hell" becomes exhibitionistic and self-glamorizing, but also self-generating.

62

The ambiguous image in "Apotheosis" is the word "thorn" and the nature of the injury it gives. In the first reading, the wound suggests a denial of divine love, a black transgression that, when understood in the light of the beloved, is a means to forgiveness and reconciliation with the source of love. In a secularized, romantic reading, this wound is an erotic punctilio symbolizing the hazards—both ways—in wooing the rose and the necessary suffering of lovers that can lead to bliss. In the second, analytic reading, the barb is a disruption that splits the original union into opposing elements. The thorn is both a means for inscribing and, quite literally, the inscribed letter itself. Read this way, the thorn stands for the power of signification. Such power is a great negative, a "NO!," which puts the desired object forever out of reach and leaves desire to operate in a compensatory play of language. If the thorn in "Apotheosis" is read not as a symbol but as a sign for the ever elusive object of desire, the poem becomes a metonymic arrangement, an allegory of the unbridgeable distance between lover and beloved. In this reading of "Apotheosis," the female speaker as writer discovers her ability to "wound" and its effects. The "thorn" is a linguistic power she does not renounce but intensifies as she writes on toward the strong final image that does not resolve the issue of separation at all. This second reading decodes an allegory of desire for identification with the power of the estranged lover, an erotic fable which does not close the distance between its images as signs and the meaning they might point to. This second reading differs radically from the first, in which erotic desire is a symptom of love, a radiant symbol of the possibility of a redeeming mutual relation in human experience.

John Bayley detected Plath's direct playing to her audience as a "display the patient makes up for an analyst," but which remain "verbal games of attention and observation, beautifully controlled and not—as the Lowell's and Berryman's [confessional poems] are—the history and projection of a self."[9] Bayley sees the fictive images Plath creates out of her neurosis both concealing and revealing her "desperation of nothingness, the sense of not being anyone" (20). In my view, the oddness, the distinctiveness of Plath is just that: though her projections do add up, finally, to an incontestable voice, that voice often does not seem to belong to an "I" that is person. This is precisely what she will find herself confessing as a poet.

Traditionally, the lyric voice is as singular, unified and authentic as the living person who produces the poem. Plath's personal history and cultural legacy, as well as her affective illness, which worked against her symbolic imagination and stimulated her negating one, tended to put her personhood in question. "Apotheosis" makes plain the conflict of modes of imagination. In the symbolic reading, the speaker must acknowledge her transgression of love's authority in order to renew connection. In the analytic, allegorical reading, the speaker must acknowledge a necessary break caused by the act of writing. This disruption leads her to self-consciousness and her power to read and write herself as text. Turning herself into language can go on as long as she can endure the necessary isolation. This strategy requires some domination to struggle against and that, in the second reading, is what the lover, as starry influence, has become. The love affair has turned to war. The erotic impulse to meet the other in a mutual relation has become an impulse to displace the other with the self-quickened textual "I." The speaker makes present her "golden hell" of awareness in which she can assert her agonistic role as writer of her own "scripture." The price for this power is lover-turned-rival. The stronger he grows, the brighter she will flare, not repenting the wound, but enabled by adversity to discover and use her demonic creative power.

Plath wrote "Bitter Strawberries" when she was seventeen and in good emotional health. She wrote "Apotheosis" when she was twenty-two, recovering from suicidal depression and institutionalization, and attempting to live at odds with the mores of her time and place as she sought more autonomy in both her life and her art. By 1955, she had shifted away from shared human concerns toward self-scrutiny and her own particular problem of staying alive. "Apotheosis" might be read as address to a lover by a speaker who can still believe in the transforming power of the symbolic imagination. The final image, however, strikes a pose with a hint of hysteria. The speaker may be ardently waiting for her alienated lover to act, but she has no assurance that he will. The poem offers a form of action that remains indefinite. Its force seems aimed at unsettling relations, at promoting, not easing, anxiety over the lost connection imaged and felt as "frozen faith." If the speaker is left with nothing other than her own desires, the burden of her redemption falls to her solitary will to power confronting the opposition. In a senior essay at Smith, Plath had praised Nietzsche's hero "who evolves by a dynamic dialectic of struggle and surmounting."[10] Can she powerfully reinvent her reality in adequate metaphors of self or is she doomed to allegories that point to nothing except her lack of them? These are the major concerns in her first volume,

The Colossus and Other Poems (1960). There, Plath comes to terms with her frustration over her inability to make a viable personal myth or to affirm a universal one, and with her own peculiar, aggressive power when facing the "blank of things."

Endnotes

[1]Diary. Plath MS II. Lilly Library. Indiana University.

[2]The largest collection of early poems is in the Plath Collection, Plath MS II, Lilly Library, Indiana University. All references are to typescripts from that collection unless otherwise indicated.

[3]Thomas Caramagno, "Manic-Depressive Psychosis and Critical Approaches to Virginia Woolf's Life and Work," *PMLA* 103 (January 1988): 16.

[4]Titled "Swords into Plowshares," in early draft, 7/10/50.

[5]For a thorough reading of the Smith College poems, see Mary Lynn Broe, "Early Fiction and Poetry," *Protean Poetic: The Poetry of Sylvia Plath* (Columbia: U of Missouri P, 1980) 1–42. Broe's thematic reading concludes that the overriding concern in Plath's early work is a conflict between a harsh, intractable reality and a powerful, transforming imagination whose symbolic order cannot alter blunt fact, and that Plath's entire poetic career is a working out of this conflict.

[6]Sonnet vi, "Bluebeard," *Collected Poems. Edna St. Vincent Millay.* ed. Norma Millay (New York: Harper, 1956) 566.

[7]"On Truth and Lies in an Extra Moral Sense," *The Portable Nietzsche.* trans. Walter Kaufmann (New York: Viking, 1954) 44

[8]Under the title "To a Jilted Lover," this poem was included in Plath's senior poetry collection, *Circus in Three Rings*, and was published in *The Lyric* (Winter 1956) as "Apotheosis." With this second title, the poem appears in Plath's Cambridge MS which she submitted to her examiners as partial fulfillment for her Cambridge degree, June 1957.

[9]John Bayley, "Death and Co.," rev. art., *New Statesman* 2 October 1981: 19–20.

[10]"The Age of Anxiety and Escape from Freedom." History 38b essay. Plath MS II. Lilly Library.

3

Becoming Improbable:
The Plot of *The Colossus and Other Poems*

The dualism of eye to "I" in Plath's early poem "Apotheosis" subverts the theme of contrite love and raises questions of power. Other poems written by Plath around 1955, extend these questions as they follow the implications of the poem "Bluebeard," the fearful consequences of the insistence on knowing by solitary seeing. There is nothing to see in that poem but the speaker's image reduced to signs and fragments. No unified self dwells in this chamber, not even Bluebeard. He is a mere structure of words working as a vacant yet potent mirror that leaves the speaker with the challenge such an absence poses. In another 1955 piece, "On Looking Into the Eyes of a Demon Lover," Plath's speaker does not back off from such demonic power, but exerts her own force to gather herself into a coherent image. The poem concludes:

> I sought my image
>   in the scorching glass,
> for what fire could damage
>   a witch's face?
>
> So I stared in that furnace
>   where beauties char
> but found radiant Venus
>   reflected there.

The aggressiveness Plath discovers in "Apotheosis" and severely questions in "Bluebeard" is celebrated in this poem. What annihilates lesser wills exalts her own because she has not been afraid to exert her strength and triumph with it. The speaker's swift transformation from witch to love goddess is, however, too facile to be anything other than magical. It comes like a rabbit out of a hat, done with a bit of reckless swaggering of crude rhyme, rather than grace. A genuine transformation is wanted but not poetically achieved.

Plath admits this want and gives it expression in a poem written in the spring of 1956, "Strumpet Song," which she would include in her first published volume, *The Colossus and Other Poems* (1960):

> Walks there not some such one man
> As can spare breath
> To patch with brand of love this rank grimace
> Which out from black tarn, ditch and cup
> Into my most chaste own eyes
> Looks up.

Here, the same kind of surprise ending occurs as in "On Looking into the Eyes of a Demon Lover." This time, however, the transformation is not asserted but longed for. The speaker's own eyes, though she claims them "chaste," can see only sinister reflections in nature. The poem acknowledges a desire for some force other than herself that would redeem her with his "breath" or "brand of love." Such an encounter was indeed what Plath was hoping for in the spring of 1956 when she wrote this poem. Under the influence of Dorothea Krook, Plath came to understand her passionate relation to Ted Hughes as just such a redemptive blaze.

The love poems Plath wrote that spring are full of images of fire. For example, "Firesong" ends: "dream/ not of staunching such strict flame, but come,/ lean to my wound; burn on, burn on." In "Song for a Summer Day," a noon sun which is not angry or offended "Took my heart as if/ It were a green-tipped leaf/ Kindled by my love's pleasing/ Into an ardent blazing." In "Wreath for a Bridal," "two burn in one fever." The extravagant "Epitaph for Fire and Flower" elaborates the conceit of two ardent lovers perishing blissfully in their own conflagration. Though not very original, these poems show Plath stressing desire for another who is a real person, not a phantom or a fiction, not a "demon lover." Plath's 1956 poem "Ode for Ted" conveys the density of his physical bulk, his sounds, his earthiness. He is not a mirror. Plath celebrates him as an independent existence. In this new mood, Plath asserts that mirroring is damning. In "Vanity Fair" a witch seduces foolish young girls by their own reflections so that they do not believe there is any "fire" beyond their own hearts' "flare" or that any force from without can hoist "soul up after lids fall shut." These girls, in love with their own images go to hell: "Some burn short, some long,/ Staked in pride's coven."

This new note in Plath's love poems which modulates her poetry into a different key is the note of belief. It sounds most clearly in "Black Rook in Rainy Weather," written in the autumn of 1956 after Plath and Hughes had been married a few months. Quietly, without hysteria, the poem accepts the ordinary life of routine, bad weather, and fatigue, because this life is lit by "A certain minor light" which can hallow "an interval/ otherwise inconsequent/ By bestowing largess, honor/ One might say love." The poem affirms relation:

> I only know that a rook
> Ordering its black feathers can so shine
> As to seize my senses, haul
> My eyelids up, and grant
>
> A brief respite from fear
> Of total neutrality.

Such moments of "radiance" come unwilled to the speaker who is grateful for them and who finds them sufficient to "Patch together a content/ Of sorts." This speaker is expectant, but able to wait for the "angel," probably an allusion to Stevens' ordinary one and, in Plath's line, for its "rare, random descent." Plath's tone is a bit too nonchalant to make the speaker fully convincing; however, the acknowledgement of the given, unwilled nature of what is beautiful, which is a relation, not a thing, and of the need to be responsive to such gifts whenever, however, they come, sets a new direction in Plath's maturing poetry.

The important images in "Black Rook" are of feathers and eyes and how they relate. In the poem's action, it is the feathers that open the eyes, not the eyes that invent the feathers. The speaker hesitates to call such experiences "love," as if to blunt the event by that much used and abused word, but this *is* the experience of receptivity to what comes unwilled: desire which focuses attention and allows relation. The triad of rook, the speaker, the radiance that binds them results not from a dissolving of the material world, but from the patient, obedient working within it. The speaker is as committed to duties as the poem is committed to its five-line stanza form and its subtle but binding rhyme scheme, a pattern that repeats only the final consonant sound. Somehow, within this given, the hallowing happens. It comes and it goes, begins and ends, but the "interval" could not have been felt without a gracious deference to those unwilled edges between self and not self.

Willfulness in Plath's seeing takes her into the gnostic mode, that rejection of what is other than the self in favor of a strong sense of a solitary subjectivity. In Plath, such practice is haunted by fear, for when she fails to dissolve the given world, that world turns to stone. Thus, for Plath, the inward eye can be evil, a witch's, a snake's, or a Medusa's who is a combination of both.

Sister Bernetta Quinn has discussed the Medusa in her many forms (from the literal jellyfish to the staring lunar Lucinda) as the presiding muse in Plath's poetry (97–115). Quinn's understanding of the fundamental importance this image for Plath coincides with that of other readers who find Plath resolving poetic tension with deadly control (Phillips, 186–205); with the "lithic impulse" (Howard 349–357) or with a sorceress's "animistic projection" (Perloff 179–184). The magical impulse is especially telling in Plath's early poems to which few critics, including Quinn, pay attention. These poems show Plath's resistance to her Medusan power, her poetic "death wish."[1] In "Prologue to Spring" (1955) the sky is a "gorgon's eye" that freezes the winter landscape "within a stone tableau." The view is the speaker's perception, for her own eye fixes the scene in words. This is an undesired condition, and the speaker relies on nature's "countermagic" to undo her spell: "Green-singing birds explode from all the rocks." Plath tells a parable in "Crystal Gazer" (1956) of the curse of too much vision and too little belief. Lovers who believe in each other and are content with what nature gave them will have a fecund future, according to Gerb, the fortune teller. She herself had doubted her lover's faith and had practiced black magic to learn their future. Thus, she saw in the crystal ball only "gorgon-prospects" for herself: "each love blazing blind to its gutted end," the whole earth for her an "ever-green death's head." In "Winter Landscape with Rooks," (1956) the speaker is another cursed Medusa-witch whose eye turns the lover's image to "ice" and "rock" from which she can expect no solace. "Black Rook in Rainy Weather" is strong evidence of another potential in Plath which is neither monstrous nor deadly. That poem allows for the "miracle" of love within the given world. The feathers, the wings, have it over the eyes which are human and which are acted upon rather than act to freeze or petrify an object.

Besides missing Plath's own critique of the Medusan stare in the early poems, Quinn does not extend the Medusan myth to her offspring, the winged horse Pegasus. When Perseus killed the cursed woman-turned-gorgon, Pegasus sprang from her blood. In Ovid's *Metamorphoses,* Pegasus' hooves struck the earth and released the spring or fountain sacred to the Muses. The Medusa motif in Plath's poetry elucidates Plath's struggle to affirm a redeemed erotic sense, but only if we remember that the Medusa as protean sorceress in Plath must suffer severance from her body and as a result, bleed. As Plath will declare in her late verse: "The blood jet is poetry." Pegasus as poetry is not death. He is a flying horse that affirms rather than denies desire for an ennobled erotic life. His hoof-taps wound the earth, but only so that the creative imagination can be fed by a conjunction of thinking and feeling.

Medusa can also symbolize the perversion of spirituality, that is, spiritual pride: seeing the Medusa is seeing one's "self" as vanity and guilt laid bare, a sight so terrible that no one can survive it (Diel 71–73). The gnostic poet eludes and dissolves fatal Medusan vacuity by believing in the rightness, the goodness, of the artist's will to power. The poet who fears the negating turn of the imagination, however, is like Perseus. He penetrates the horror and transforms it with the aid of the mirroring shield of Athena in an act that requires memory, understanding and will. Perseus must remember the horror, understand it via symbols or emblems, and will to overcome it in a spirit obedient to a divine force greater than his own. Three things occur, not one: the death of Medusa, the birth of Pegasus, winged desire, and the flow of the Muses' fountain, results that Perseus did not will for himself. Pegasus' hooves wound nature but in a form that emphasizes how the mind can triumph over its own perversity. In 1957 while teaching at Smith, Plath wrote "Perseus: or the Triumph of Wit Over Suffering" in which the earth is Medusa:

> ... the whole globe
> Expressive of grief turns gods, like kings, to rocks.
> Those rocks, cleft and worn, themselves then grow
> Ponderous and extend despair on earth's
> Dark face.

What can break the despair of petrified gods and kings in deadly eye-lock with a cursed earth? Plath's solution comes in rather forced wit, "feathers to tickle as well as fly," and heavy-handed satire, a "fun-house mirror that turns the tragic muse/ To the beheaded head of a sullen doll." Though facile, Plath's "Cosmic/Laugh" affirms a belief in something beyond a tragic plot. If she can mock the vanity in her life, perhaps she has found a mirror in which to safely view both its destruction and her survival.

No one found Plath's first volume of poems a "fun house mirror." Plath shows cleverness in *The Colossus and Other Poems*, but there is too much gravity in the poetry she wrote from 1955 to 1959 to suggest parodic amusement. Her selections may be, in fact, about "gravity," the downward pull of a density with which the poet must establish a relation. What is the density that draws Plath? Is it the given world of living, breathing persons with whom she can form a relation, or is it the world gone blank in Medusan stone which she must overcome? In other words, what is Plath's poetic stance in *The Colossus*: symbolic or gnostic? relational or negating? metaphoric or allegoric? autobiographical or confessional? These questions, which are all forms of the same question, are the driving force of this first collection in which Plath tests out what her poetry does. What follows here is a reading of that volume as Plath's own arrangement of her poems which lead to that discovery.

The Colossus begins and ends with poems about birth, both written in 1959 at Yaddo when Plath and Hughes were expecting their first child. This placing of work written over a period of four years between two poems both written in November 1959, invites a reading for plot.[2] Plath opens with "The Manor Garden," written "for Nicholas," the masculine name she gave to the baby she was carrying. The month is November, a time for decay and death; but the hour is dawn, a beginning. The entire movement of the poem is a struggle to overcome the falling rhythms of the first line: "The fountains are dry and the roses over."

The speaker in this inaugural poem reads the signs in her garden and what they portend for the gestating life within her. There are good signs: "The pears fatten like little buddhas"; and there are fearful signs: the dead roses emit "incense of death," while a "blue mist is dragging the lake." The term "dragging" suggests a continuing search for a drowned person. This figure in Plath usually evokes the dead father, appearing early in such juvenile poems such as "Bereft," and "The Invalid." Otto Plath did drown, in a sense, from an embolism in a lung following surgery. He drowned, in another sense, because he refused or did not know how to accommodate himself to what could have sustained his life. The speaker tries to evade the menace of the lake by turning it into an emblem for the womb which is safe for the living, growing fetus:

> You move through the era of fishes,
> The smug centuries of the pig—
> Head, toe and finger
> Come clear of the shadow. History
>
> Nourishes these broken flutings,
> These crowns of acanthus,
> And the crow settles her garments.
> You inherit white heather, a bee's wing.

The child repeats an evolutionary process, but he is heir to a particular family history and orientation, which include violence and predaciousness. The starkness of the crow perched on a ruined classical column is softened by images of small delicate things which a lover of nature would prize. The grimness, however, remains. Besides a father at home on heathered moors and a grandfather fascinated with bees, the child's legacy includes a history of psychic illness:

Two suicides, the family wolves
Hours of blankness. Some hard stars
Already yellow the heavens.
The spider on its own string

Crosses the lake....

The stresses in this stanza work vigorously against a downward pull.
Trochees and dactyls are countered by the spondees "hard stars" and "own
string," as the plucky little spider crosses the blank space between the
penultimate and the ultimate stanza and ends on an upbeat iamb. The lake
has appeared again as a blank into which the perverse father sank, but
over which another life can travel and, like the spider, spin out of inner resources what is needed to stay alive. The spell works:

... The worms
Quit their usual habitations.
The small birds converge, converge
With their gifts to a difficult borning.

An image of decay is vacated and then followed with the most up-beat, energetic line in the entire poem, consisting of the spondee "small birds" and
the repeated iambs of "converge, converge." Until now, the images have
been predominantly visual, but here, at the poem's close, is the promise of
sound as well as sight in the coming together of winged creatures and their
"gifts," blessings that will accompany the breaking into life of the child.
The child must utter his own cry in order to breathe and to live beyond the
mother's womb. The necessity for breaking and crying invites the comic
mode, for the cries of the birds which accompany the breaking of the dawn
traditionally mean appetites for life, for sustenance and for mating and
procreation. The rising energies of "converge, converge" counter the
falling rhythms set in motion in the first line. Still, the poem ends with the
drag of a dactyl and a trochee in "difficult borning." The pull down in this
poem is toward death in various images: death of the imagination as a dry
fountain; death of love as ashes of roses; and death of a family, cursed
with willfulness, for whom an essential element is a killer not a source of

life. The speaker holds within her that which nourishes the fragile flesh of a new being. Belief in that life's potential defies the death signs which, nevertheless, do not go away. Thus, the "difficult" birth raises a question. Beyond the protection of the mother's body, what will preserve the flesh and a feeling for the flesh? What can work toward a breaking into life, not a sinking into death?

The poem which follows, "Two Views of a Cadaver Room," explores this problem. In the first nine-line stanza, flesh is analyzed and studied in a medical dissecting room where bodies, though useful, are not loved. They rivet the gaze, "black as burnt turkey," but they arouse no feeling. A cut-out heart is merely "a cracked heirloom" one must receive dutifully. In the second stanza of equal length, the scene observed is not from life but art, Pieter Brueghel's sixteenth-century panorama of carnage, *The Triumph of Death*. Plath must have read Brueghel's title ironically. Two lovers, occupying the corner of the canvas where the eye might come to rest, have turned their backs on death. They look only at each other and at the sheet music she holds for him and from which he sings to her. Plath's second stanza talks only about this pair, "Blind" and "deaf" to the rest of the scene in which death reaps his harvest in every violent way. The lovers' presence speaks of the artist's desire that death should not triumph over love. Plath's two line coda interprets Brueghel's intent. For her, his "desolation stalled in paint, spares the little country/ Foolish, delicate, in the lower right hand corner." Plath both echoes and reverses Auden's "Musee des Beaux Arts" that responds to Brueghel's *The Fall of Icarus*. Auden's poem contemplates tragic suffering which occurs unnoticed by the world in the corner of the scene of an ordinary day. Plath's poem contemplates comic affirmation, the motion of desire toward the beloved and thus toward renewed life, as a power to be attended to even in the midst of an apocalypse.

That feeling, the desire called love, cannot survive a brutal world if the rhythms of the heart are lost in the din and the allure of impersonal force. The next poem "Night Shift" follows a pounding rhythm, "It was not a heart, beating...," to its source in a silver factory. The speaker, stunned to the "marrow" watches factory workers "Tending, without stop, the blunt/ Indefatigable fact." The speaker, looking hard at a world that exists independently of her desires, feels the attraction of mindless power, though next to it her human flesh seems fragile and powerless. The following poem, "Sow," comically exalts female flesh in the image of a huge pig as fertility goddess. Her powers, however, are also mindless and, in excess, destructive:

> A monument
> Prodigious in gluttonies as that hog whose want
>
> Made lean Lent
> Of kitchen slops and, stomaching no constraint,
> Proceeded to swill
> The seven troughed seas and every earthquaking continent.

Plath's distortion is a way to see what otherwise might strike her dead: the fatal Medusa as mirror reflecting her human vanity in the endlessness of desire, the unappeasable wants that consume all that they can. Plath's fictive pig is the imagination's own excesses, attempting to dissolve the world into one glorious sow's need.

Next, "The Eye Mote" bemoans too much self-knowledge. When an injury distorts the sight of the speaker, she loses her innocent vision and knows the dark side of desire: "I dream that I am Oedipus." Feeling the limitations of the Freudian myth, she yearns for freedom from "this parenthesis," but in an earlier, less conscious state, "a place, a time gone out of mind," not one which she must create for herself. In "Hardcastle Crags," the speaker does muster energy to strike her creative spark against a flinty, frozen world in order to make a more congenial place for herself in relation to its density. She walks on a winter night through a village landscape, making a great deal of noise, "a racket of echoes from the steely street," but not changing a thing, not even "The blank mood she walked in." Beyond the echoing, sheltering walls of the town, the wind pares "her person down to a pinch of flame."

> All the night gave her, in return
> For the paltry gift of her bulk and the beat
>
> Of her heart was the humped indifferent iron
> Of its hills, and its pastures bordered by black stone set
> On black stone.

The world has turned more not less forbidding. This is the world "in its earliest sway ... unaltered by eyes." To go on would be to have the "quick of her small heat" snuffed out and to become one with this dense world's absence of human desire. Before that can happen, "she turned back," an act that acknowledges her incapacity to overcome a hostile environment by means of her solitary will to power, though she can face and acknowledge a density unredeemed by any spirit congenial to human kind.

Plath warms the natural landscape in the next poem, "Faun." The scene is still cold and dark, but a man is in it, blending into the sights and the sounds of animals, at home among them as a presiding spirit, no doubt inspired by Hughes. Plath's own relation to the natural world remains, as the next poems shows, one of "penury." In "Departure," a speaker leaves a seaside where "the sun shines on unripe corn." Her "retrospect" does not "soften" the unresponsiveness of nature, but merely exposes it again and again:

> The scraggy rock spit shielding the town's blue bay
> Against which the brunt of outer sea
> Beats, is brutal endlessly.

The title poem of this collection, "The Colossus," explores the speaker's now characteristic isolation and tries to come to terms with it. As a castaway on an island, she ponders the littered ruins of a stone effigy. Whatever the giant statue once meant is lost to her. In a quiet mood, she vows to live among the fragments, not attempting a reconstruction of the past for her understanding or anticipating a rescue from her state of incomplete knowledge. Fatherless, but beyond anguish for lack of a knowable origin, her piety turns toward a conjugal relation. A lover is, however, for this speaker, a fantasy effect of the father's absence: "My hours are married to shadow." This solitude takes her to apparent acceptance of her condition: "No longer do I listen for the scrape of a keel/ On the blank stones of the landing." Such resignation to estrangement has its own danger which the next poem elaborates.

In "Lorelei," the promise of absolute knowledge beckons a spirit cut loose from emotional connections in the natural world. Plath's use of terza rima connected by off rhyme and slant rhyme frustrates expectations for the pleasures of exact rhyme while at the same time leads the eye and ear on, like a siren promising an eventual satisfaction in matching words and desire. This is what sirens promise: absolute knowledge, a total revelation. What they deliver is death. The poem is the siren, enhancing the disaffection for the world of others with its powerful pull into itself, opening with Plath's now familiar effect of a mirroring surface that shows her sinister doubles and her attraction to them.

> This is no night to drown in:
> A full moon, river lapsing
> Black beneath bland mirror-sheen,
>
> The blue water-mists dropping
> Scrim after scrim like fishnets
> Though fishermen are sleeping,
>
> The massive castle turrets
> Doubling themselves in a glass
> All stillness. Yet these shapes float
>
> Up toward me, troubling the face
> Of quiet.

The poem holds as long as it can a calm balance between the material world and its reflection, but out of the "black ... bland mirror-sheen" come the terrible "sisters" of the speaker, sirens in a most seductive form promising tranquility:

> ...From the nadir
> They rise, their limbs ponderous
>
> With richness, hair heavier
> Than sculptured marble. They sing
> Of a world more full and clear
>
> Than can be.

The speaker knows these are forms of madness:

> You lodge
> On the pitched reefs of nightmare,
>
> Promising sure harborage;
> By day, descant from borders
> of hebetude, from the ledge
>
> Also of high windows.

Although evoked in images of derangement, the callers have irresistible allure as "great goddesses of peace." The poem ends with a plea: "Stone, stone, ferry me down there." The distinct echo here is Theodore Roethke's "The Lost Son," but where Roethke wants renewal in aboriginal life, Plath wants her experience even more reduced. Her stones seem to be the lorelei themselves, forms of the Medusa in their effect. The speaker gives in to the falling rhythms which sounded in the collection's opening poem "The Manor Garden." In "Lorelei," all resistance to a quietus melts away as the speaker falls completely in love with easeful death.

In Plath, to drown means to die as her father had done, refusing an accommodation with life, exercising the will to such an extent that the uncongenial world loses its dominance. Such exaltation of the will spurs the imagination to do only what it wants, rejecting all other conditions as barriers and limitations. In the next poem, "Point Shirley," done after the *Life Studies* style of Robert Lowell, such a will haunts a scene, trying to break the world's unresponsiveness but failing, as the speaker in "Hardcastle Crags" had failed, to get from the landscape any sign of recognition or love. Here, the speaker returns to her dead grandmother's house by the sea and tries to feel the life that once animated the place. Though the speaker can remember the woman, her activities, her care, her "wheat loaves and apple cakes" cooling on the sill, the woman does not live again in the poem because she does not live again in the speaker's memory. What is evoked is her absence: "A labor of love, and that labor lost." The will cannot retrieve her, but only because it does not really want to. The bleak scene is more engaging that the dead person, and such lines as these reveal how the speaker knows she is lavishing her imagination on something other than the memory of a loving grandmother:

> I would get from these dry-papped stones
> The milk your love instilled in them.
> The black ducks dive.
> And though your graciousness might stream
> And I contrive,
> Grandmother, stones are nothing of home
> To that spumiest dove.
> Against both bar and tower the black sea runs.

The poem cannot "do" love any more than the speaker can get milk from a stone. As the speaker contemplates the vacant scene, she sees not the grandmother but her own reflection: she is "nothing of home" to the memory of what was. She knows she should be, but the facts are otherwise. What familial connections might have been made at the poem's close are negated in the image of the black ducks, going their own appetitive way, at one with the sea's power. In the line, "The black ducks dive," the focus of the poem begins to become clear, finally stated boldly in the last line: "Against both bar and tower the black sea runs." The force that corresponds to the speaker in this scene is the charging black sea that would destroy whatever barriers thrown against it—including memories of the past. The poem which follows "Point Shirley" allegorizes that sea as "The Bull of Bendylaw." The bull, image of male power, evokes the awesomeness of the imagination as will: nothing intimidates it, no laws of thou shalt or thou shalt not:

> The bull surged up, the bull surged down,
> Not to be stayed by a daisy chain
> Nor by any learned man.
>
> O the king's tidy acre is under the sea
> And the royal rose in the bull's belly,
> And the bull on the king's highway.

With this force given its due, Plath can go on to give an unsentimental rendition of her relation to her antecedents in the next poem. Plath's epigraph for "All the Dead Dears" informs the reader of her inspiration: the stone coffin of the fourth century A. D. which contains the remains of a woman, along with those of a mouse and a shrew, one of which had "slightly gnawn" the woman's ankle-bone. The dead in this poem witness to "the gross eating game," clinging to consciousness like barnacles, intrusively haunting communal events:

> ... be it by wakes, weddings
> Childbirths or a family barbecue:
> Any touch, taste, tang's
> Fit for those outlaws to ride home on,
>
> And to sanctuary: usurping the armchair
> Between tick
> And tack of the clock, until we go
> Each skulled and crossboned Gulliver
> Riddled with ghosts, to lie
> Deadlocked with them, taking root as
>   cradles rock.

The dead's claims are petrifying, and the Medusa motif shows itself in the lines:

> ... As I think of her head,
> From the mercury backed glass
> Mother, grandmother, greatgrandmother
> Reach hag hands to haul me in.

The quickly shifting imagery proceeds from the speaker's view of the glass-cased skeletal remains to the sight of her own mirrored head in the place of the skull, to her ancestors extending the reflection so that they threaten to overwhelm her. Giving in to their claims on her would be fatally constricting. Like Swift's Gulliver who is taken home by pirates but who does not want to stay there, Plath's speaker is riveted by outlaw ghosts again and again to a past in which she finds no comfort, only paralysis and death.

Plath's imagination works hard with its penury. It can find no delight in remembrance of things past and it can be oppressed by its own visualizing capacity, as the next two poems "Aftermath" and "The Thin People" show. The first briefly explores the human need to see grandeur in catastrophe and the human tendency, not admirable but perhaps salutary, to turn away from other people's misery when it seems merely banal. The second explores what happens when a mind cannot turn away from human suffering. In "The Thin People," the speaker is threatened by the images which have lodged in her mind but which she can neither transform nor erase:

> They are always with us, the thin people
> Meager of dimension as the grey people
> On a movie-screen.

In both the printed press and in newsreels, Plath had seen, like everyone else of her generation, deeply disturbing photographic images: casualties of war that included victims of German and Japanese concentration camps, as well as of the United States' bombing of Hiroshima and Nagasaki. The horror of that time, which closely followed her father's death, never left her imagination. The world's anguish, at first momentary stimulations on the optic nerves, takes up permanent residence in the mind:

> They found their talent to persevere
> In thinness, to come, later,
>
> Into our bad dreams, their menace
> Not guns, not abuses,
>
> But a thin silence.
> Wrapped in flea-ridden donkey skins,

Empty of complaint, forever
Drinking vinegar from tin cups: they
   wore

The insufferable nimbus of the lot-drawn
   Scapegoat....

Plath had recorded in her Cambridge pocket diary a dream of multitudes drinking vinegar from tin cups. In her life, she awakened to a promising relation with Ted Hughes. In the poem, the thin people do not disappear with dreams when the dawn breaks, but "persist in the sunlit room." As they multiply, their presence dulls and drains the natural world of glory. No escape to any pristine frontier is possible. As psychic realities, these images will print themselves on every experience, like evil—willful, arbitrary, haunting:

We own no wilderness rich and deep
   enough
For stronghold against their still

Battalions. See, how the tree boles flatten
And lose their good browns

If the thin people simply stand in the
   forest
Making the world go thin as a wasp's
   nest

And grayer; not even moving their bones.

In this poem the material world gives way to the visual imagination that is morbidly obsessed, not visionary. Images stubbornly refuse a symbolic reading and turn instead into signs that reduce nature to a paper-thin text which both demands and defies a reader.

"Suicide Off Egg Rock" evokes a state of blank depression immune even to obsession, but as if in response, a redemptive attempt goes on in the next poem, "Mushrooms," as thin grey images plump into animated, proliferating fungi who are "nudgers and shovers/ In spite of ourselves." Such small energies exert their own desires: "We shall by morning/ Inherit the earth./ Our foot's in the door." The meek shall inherit the earth, but the meek do not put their feet in doors. Here is the same old menace in disguise. As the sow's world became sow, here the world will become mushroom. Big or small, strong or weak, aggressive or merely busy with themselves, most things seem to want to take over the world and make it into their own images. Plath gives this theme another treatment in the following poem, "I Want, I Want," in which the "bald, immense" baby god cries, not for the mother as person, but for his mother as his need satisfied. When frustrated, he cries for the father's blood and from those exorbitant desires comes all the suffering in the world: "Barbs on the crown of gilded wire/ Thorns on the bloody rose stem."

Plath's imagination will find in almost every scene evidence of this appetitive motive for life and the sinister nature of transforming the world into oneself. In "Watercolor of Grantchester Meadows," she skillfully evokes an idyll of the Cambridge rural scene, "a country on a nursery plate" but only to stall in paint a double desolation. A gentle water rat out of *Wind in the Willows* is in danger, while the students in the scene, "hands laced, in a moony indolence of love" are:

> Black-gowned, but unaware
> How in such mild air
> The owl shall stoop from his turret, the rat cry out.

The next piece, "The Ghost's Leave-Taking," tries to make Plath's vision seem less bleak. She evokes the spirit of a *visio*, a dream that is true. To such a capacity for belief, things "Speak" as Plath's poem puts it, "in sign language of a lost otherworld." This would be the world of the symbolic imagination as Dante knew it, perhaps lost to modern man except when the mind hovers at certain moments between the chaos of dream and the order of awakened consciousness. In that liminal state, the mind seems receptive to orders, in the sense of directives as well as of arrangements, other than its own. In Plath's poem, a mound of bunched sheets becomes signs of "our origin and our end" before they "thin to nothing." The poem fails to be more than clever, mainly because the otherworld is signed too coyly with images out of nursery rhymes, but the poem is important in the overall scheme of *The Colossus* as one more attempt to re-see and thus usurp and re-image the death's head, the Medusa's revelation of vain will. Here, the head as "dreaming skull" is a "profane grail" that holds, however briefly, the promise of some region of psychic life that is "pristine" and "new," a place for beginnings. Plath tried to give form to that elation, but her talent lay elsewhere.

Her real gifts are these: she makes the reader feel the density of the actual world; she shows how the awesome human will rails against the limitations this world imposes; and she makes the reader yearn for a less destructive relation with that real, objective density. All this is abundantly clear in the next poem, "A Winter Ship."

The first line alerts the reader to the speaker's attempt to be just, to relate the scene as it is: "At this wharf there are no grand landings to speak of." This will be no fable of bulls or colossi or otherworldly sirens, only a cleanly observed cold harbor, and yet, that negative sounds another alert. If there are no "grand landings" then the poem may make its own; for, after all, that is what the speaker is looking for in order to speak of something. The reader suspects that she will indeed have one and thus reads to find out how the poem leads to a great event, an heroic act in the midst of a drab and uneventful scene.

First, Plath makes the dense, ordinary world really there, its intransigence felt in the many internal rhymes like the first one, "grand landings," and in lines like these: "Red and orange barges list and blister" and "A gull holds his pose on a shanty ridgepole." These repetitions of internal vowel sounds in quick succession work like a spondee to slow the flow of sound and add weight and density to the line. Like the barges that tilt and decay, these lines are "shackled" and not going anywhere. The gull in his "jacket of ashes" gains substance in that repeated "a" as his image would gain substance in a second grey-paint-laden stroke of the brush. The next stanza ends:

> The whole flat harbor anchored in
> The round of his yellow eye button.

The very neat end rhymes, though slant, seem to have the scene securely fixed, but another eye is looking, that of the speaker who continues to enhance the scene with her rhymes. The repeated interior vowels become insistent, more like a volley of sounds to attack what has been made substantial, only to be felt as insufficient:

> A blimp swims up like a day-moon or tin
> Cigar over his rink of fishes.
> The prospect is as dull as an old etching.

The view has turned boring as all those short "i's," even a bit maddening. The next line, "They are unloading three barrels of little crabs," attempts to stay, as promised, with the dull facts, but the desire brought to bear on this ordinary scene won't be satisfied with mere scrupulousness. It wants, in fact, to destroy what it sees and does so by imagining the pier pilings collapsing:

> And with them that rickety edifice
> Of warehouses, derricks, smokestacks and bridges
> In the distance.

As soon as the desiring speaker has gotten rid of the inadequate actual, she denigrates the sounds of a language tied to it:

> All around us the water slips
>
> And gossips in its loose vernacular,
> Ferrying the smells of dead cod and tar.

Now with all that dreary reality evoked and dismissed, the speaker can get on to the big event worthy to "speak of." She imagines, "Farther out, the waves will be mouthing icecakes…." This is what happens when the world is not enough in Plath's imaginings: it becomes uninhabitable, "A poor month for park-sleepers and lovers." And she becomes visionary. But suddenly, as in a Wordsworth poem, the speaker makes the reader aware that she is not alone: "Even our shadows are blue with cold." The poem comes to a close in a shared vision:

> We wanted to see the sun come up
> And are met, instead, by this iceribbed ship,
>
> Bearded and blown, an albatross of frost,
> Relic of tough weather, every winch and stay
> Encased in a glassy pellicle.
> The sun will diminish it soon enough:
> Each wave-tip glitters like a knife.

The speaker and the person with her do not see the sun come up, but they believe they know what he will do when he does. The poem has broken free of the harbor-mirror eye of the gull. The ship in its skin of ice is, in the speaker's vision, a magnificent alternative bird: an "albatross of frost." In this rhyme-dense, literary image, the speaker's desire for event, for the "grand landing," is being satisfied. The frozen, immobile ship as ancient, bearded, dead "albatross" echoes Coleridge's image of insufficient feeling for the world and its creatures. Plath makes the ship-bird an image of frozen Eros which is another version of the Medusa. She looms, eery and otherworldly, a monster the sun as hero approaches with his blades of light. What will the sun as hero do in this fable that got underway in a poem that at first promised no such tricks, a fable which, having begun, has nothing to do with the actual harbor and its business? The speaker says that "The sun will diminish it soon enough." The ship is beautiful but it is also terrible and must be made ordinary, part of the rest of the real world in which the sun does come up and ice does melt. It is the ordinary scene that the speaker can inhabit with another person. They want to see together, not the frozen ship, but the sun. The presence of their mutual desire, their affirmation of the stronger, melting power of that reliable energy finally suffuses this poem, as the sun will suffuse and free the ice-bound vessel. Such a shared event has become grand, because it redeems for the speaker the ordinary scene and, within it, her relation to another person.

What happens when this real world loses out, when the speaker goes with the fabulous and the magical as far as she can? The next poem takes that turn. "Full Fathom Five" is addressed to the drowned "old man" that is for Plath the intransigence of the will, not the world. He surfaces "seldom," but when he does he is more mesmerizing than the lorelei, perhaps because more inscrutable. The lorelei promise "peace"; he promises nothing as he draws the speaker's will toward his, looming in image after image as an icy absolute: "You defy other godhood." The speaker is, to borrow from the previous poem, "mouthing icecakes," turning perception into an artifact that is sublimely satisfying. This cold, sea-man-god is the articulator of desire that will not be satisfied by anything other than itself. The speaker is his offspring:

> I walk dry on your kingdom's border
> Exiled to no good.
>
> Your shelled bed I remember.
> Father, this thick air is murderous.
> I would breathe water.

The poem flows in terza rima, one stanza linking with the next, usually in slant rhyme, but with enough true rhyme to create an undulation that moves irresistibly toward the source of its power, the drowned man in the sea who personifies defiance of the limits of the given. Most of the end words are in falling rhythms, like those in the last stanza, where the downward pull is felt most strongly and the force is called "Father." The speaker has been fathered by a power that refuses accommodation with the world, which is what Freud understood as the death drive. Plath's personification may be not so much a desire for death and stasis, as the desire to have everything on his own terms, including death. Harold Bloom restates the death drive this way: "An organism wishes to die only in its own fashion."[3] The poem enacts what happens when Plath's gnostic imagination is allowed to range. Death is the direction it takes as we hear the speaker exercising her own defiance of limits in the last line: "I would breathe water."

The following two-part poem, "Blue Moles," literally "grounds" that desire for "the heaven of final surfeit" in an attempt to accommodate it to a natural and a social world. The speaker observes two dead moles, which, while tunneling and searching for food, were unearthed and killed by "some large creature." Their little bodies are the focus of interest for the two stanzas that form part one of this poem. At first the moles seem victims, "Blind twins bitten by bad nature," but the shock of their discovery diminishes for the speaker as they become part of the larger scheme:

> The sky's dome is sane and clear.
> Leaves, undoing their yellow caves
> Between the road and the lake water,
> Bare no sinister spaces. Already
> The moles look neutral as the stones.
> Their corkscrew noses, their white hands
> Uplifted, stiffen in a family pose.

Initial surprise recedes as events in history recede, and the results of violence begin to be felt less, to take on, in fact, an order of calm, familiar arrangement. The event is beginning to fade like an old photograph. Having evoked the dense world, Plath's imagination is now about to dissolve its insufficiency and to replace it, but the poem resists that particular menace: the will that cannot be satisfied with the inscrutable given. Part two begins with a shift away from such obsessive control. The speaker stops "seeing" and ordering the scene like a general, and becomes one of the "old veterans," blind to any grand design, simply obeying commands to stay alive. She slips into a dreamworld where her own appetitive nature works, mute and solitary and unseen as moles deep in their tunnels, and just as untroubled by necessary repetitions. The search for what sustains life is endless:

> ... beetles, sweetbreads, shards—to be eaten
> Over and over. And still the heaven
> Of final surfeit is just as far
> From the door as ever....

All willfulness and anxiety melt away as the poem ends:

> ... Whatever happens between us
> Happens in darkness, vanishes
> Easy and often as each breath.

Just as in "A Winter Ship," the speaker suddenly makes the reader aware that she is not alone. "I" becomes "we" and the final image is a tender one: two sleepers, each deep in his or her own dreamwork, not threatened by their separate needs but trusting the rightness of them and feeling safe in that trust. Like "A Winter Ship," "Blue Moles" keeps the speaker in a living world by means of a shared experience. The other person is essential.

This theme is repeated in the two following pieces, "Strumpet Song" and "Man in Black." The first, discussed earlier in this chapter, is a plea for a redemptive, erotic relation, and the second is a celebration of it. The world will not dissolve for Plath if her vision includes a beloved who is a real person and who functions in the poem as an opaque situating device: "... there you stood/ Fixed vortex on the far/ Tip, riveting stones, air,/ All of it, together." With such a secure base, Plath moves out in the next three poems into those regions where she is alone. "Snakecharmer" reads like a Wallace Stevens meditation on the supreme fiction:

> As the gods began one world, and man another,
> So the snakecharmer begins a snaky sphere
> With moon-eye, mouth-pipe. He pipes. Pipes green.
>   Pipes water.

The poet's sounds take control and makes a "place to stand on," a metaphoric world "of snakes,/ of sways and coilings, form the snake-rooted bottom/ of his mind." This is what happens, the poem says, when one imagination blanks out the world and in that void makes its own: "And nothing now but snakes/ Is visible." Plath's earlier poems have been uneasy with this gnostic poetic practice. She fears the gorgon effect of exorbitant takeovers, and mocks this tendency in such poems as "Sow" and

"Mushrooms," but in "Snakecharmer" she allows her defiant power out for a brilliant exhibition of the world as snake in a multitude of variations, and then puts it away, as neatly as a cobra in a basket.

Pipes the cloth of snakes

To a melting of green waters, till no snake
Shows its head, and those green waters back to
Water, to green, to nothing like a snake.
Puts up his pipe, and lids his moony eye.

The reader is invited to be charmed by the artist's skill, to be pulled into its peculiar realm where the eye sees what is not, not what is. Plath's fictive music is piped, enjoyed, but not at all succumbed to. She is just showing off her magic. "The Hermit at Outermost House" hearkens back to a more threatened position for the artist who must not allow "Tablets of bank blue" in nature "flatten" him out. The hermit survives a hostile material world by flooding it with "a certain meaning green."

The snakecharmer and the hermit are tentative poetic stances for Plath. Can she pipe just what she wants and control it? Can she make the harsh world less brutal with a form of imaginative resistance? In the following poem, "The Disquieting Muses," Plath faces, perhaps for the first time, the nature of her particular poetic gift. Here, Plath identifies her strange muse: three Medusae minus their snake-hair, lunar divinities in the shape of grief (Quinn 110–111). The speaker begins with the words, "Mother, mother," both lament and reproach. As the poem develops, the reader sees that the mother is at fault for a number of reasons: she slighted some important power at her child's beginning; she did not say the right charms to ward off its evil intent; she did not admit that evil that had taken up residence in their world and in her daughter; and she floats away in false gaiety, leaving her daughter to travel alone with her awful muses as vain will and thus death to look upon.

Day now, night now, at head, side, feet,
They stand their vigil in gowns of stone,
Faces blank as the day I was born,

Their shadows long in the setting sun
That never brightens or goes down.
And this is the kingdom you bore me to,
Mother, mother. But no frown of mine
Will betray the company I keep.

The kingdom is that of the ultimate abstraction, death. The three stone-gowned figures out of the de Chirico painting with the same title are signs for nothing: negatives, zeros, voids, dense and dead as stone. They are letters as signs, O's, that can point only to vacancy and whatever they spell will turn to nothing. There is no sun as hero with blades of light to come to the speaker's rescue, because in this kingdom, the sun never moves. For Plath, this is a linguistic place where there are no beginnings, no endings, and thus no space for the natural rhythms and distinctions of erotic life. Eros has been frozen by the Gorgon muses. The speaker's imagination inhabits the kingdom where the only power is will—no memory, no understanding. This is the mother's kingdom, too, though she does not know it. All her willful, cheerful efforts were for nothing: the big O. The last line redeems the speaker's reproaches from cruelty: the daughter will not insist that the mother see the same horror that she sees. The poem takes on its full measure of anguish in that last line, for the last lament, "Mother, Mother," is to a person whose perceptions are as vacant as the visages of the muses. Only the speaker is conscious of both kinds of vanity—of the mother's unacknowledged limited vision and of the speaker's own unblinkered one. The last line is a hero's boast. The speaker, now masculine in her stance, will protect the mother and will deal with the blank which is her inheritance. The speaker is the only sun/son in this scene, an imagination acceding to an agonistic, solitary poetic destiny. It is the phallic language of the father that the mother has, unwittingly, given her daughter who now, doomed to dominance, must somehow wield its power.

The next poem, "Medallion," works like a coda or formal stamp on this discovery: a dead snake becomes her signet. The poem opens as if describing an emblem or an escutcheon with precious inlay:

By the gate with star and moon
Worked into the peeled orange wood
The bronze snake lay in the sun

The next stanza undoes the illusion of adornment:

> Inert as a shoelace; dead
> But pliable still, his jaw
> Unhinged and his grin crooked
>
> Tongue a rose-colored arrow.

"Medallion" follows the tradition of poems of Dickinson and Lawrence who use the snake to make clear an attitude or a moral position toward its symbolization of good and evil, innocence and experience, and, of course, sexual power (Oberg 138). Dickinson does not love the snake, but her respect is felt as "Zero at the Bone." Lawrence grieves that he kills the snake and feels diminished by denying the snake its place in his experience. Arthur Oberg's reading places Plath's poem on a "purer plane of lyric" than either Dickinson's or Lawrence's pieces, for her "image has become so internalized and exacting that it is more autonomous than anything we encounter in either of the other poems" (137). The reader is left to ponder this emblem with Plath, wondering with her how her image can, as poetic images traditionally do, share in "creation and health" (138). The final stanza gives much to ponder:

> Knifelike, he was chaste enough,
> Pure death's-metal. The yardman's
> Flung brick perfected his laugh.

Plath's relation to her snake is less baffling when tied to the destiny announced in "The Disquieting Muses." The snake's power lay in its striking potential: his "tongue a rose-colored arrow" and his clean, "knifelike" darting. Dead, he burns with decay; only his "laugh" is perfected by death, which is the clue to this emblem. The dead snake reminds Plath that, as a fecund woman, her deepest allegiances are to the comic mode, and that her "disquieting muses" are the accidents of her time and place and particular history. Her fate is this: as poet, she must exercise her negating, gnostic imagination, which means heroic efforts to face an empty, father-less, godless world of natural appetite and mechanical force. Plath figures the blank most often in Medusan figures, emblems of vain will. If she can make the Medusan blanks bleed, there is hope for a flying horse of enno-bled eroticism, that is, for sexual and creative power in some relation other than a struggle of wills for dominance.

The two following poems return Plath to the world of the human body. First, "The Companionable Ills" praises the body's limitations that keep the spirit from pretensions to perfection. Then, "Moonrise" meditates on whiteness inimical to life: the unripe or the dead. Colorlessness is a form of blankness and, as Jon Rosenblatt has noted, "'Blankness' in Plath's lexicon, is the perceptual state that occurs when the world is seen as hard stone" (62). The firm repulsiveness of white is announced in the first line of "Moonrise":

> Grub-white mulberries redden among leaves.
> I'll go out and sit in white like they do,
> Doing nothing. July's juice round their nubs.

The speaker makes the point that she is no Emily Dickinson by alluding to that white-gowned solitary in her own voice of petulance. Plath's speaker wants something to happen to her that she cannot do for herself alone. So like the tight, white berries, she trusts to the sun to work the change from stone to life, but as she sits "in white" her mind cannot stop working on blankness:

> This park is fleshed with idiot petals.
> White catalpa flowers tower, topple,
> Cast a round white shadow in their dying.

The speaker's tone disdains this nineteenth-century organic form, seeing it as self-immolation. She finds a truer analogy for her efforts in the next stanza:

A pigeon rudders down. Its fan-tail's white.
Vocation enough: opening, shutting
White petals, white fantails, ten white fingers.

The reader becomes aware of the decasyllabic count of these lines—each one from the beginning a perfect count of ten. The count is done, as the image tells, as the fingers press the speaker's nails into her hands, bringing blood to the surface:

Enough for fingernails to make half-moons
Redden in white palms no labor reddens.
White bruises toward color, else collapses.

The phrase "doing nothing" deepens in intensity when placed in contrast to "labor" that would redden hands with the pain and effort of actual child-birth. The labor of the poem is to make only itself, mere sounds, a structure of syllables and images that the speaker wants to "bruise toward color." The images become more shocking: a dead body "Rots, and smells of rot under its headstone/ Though the body walk out in clean linen." The speaker is becoming obsessed, seeing the oppressiveness of white everywhere she looks:

Death whitens in the egg and out of it.
I can see no color for this whiteness.
White: it is a complexion of the mind.

Though tired of this variously repeated blank, the speaker cannot stop making anything else. In spite of wanting to be ripened naturally into life by the sun and the season, the speaker cannot address the desired solar energy. She has access only to a muse who is another form of rejection of color and who enables only more violent images of the same:

Lucinda, bony mother, laboring
Among socketed white stars, your face
Of candor pares white flesh to the white bone,

Who drag our ancient father at the heel,
White-bearded, weary.

The calcified moon muse labors, not to bring to life, but to drag the drowned male figure tied to her. He is the now familiar sign for the will which refuses accommodation with the world as it is. Pared to bone, the dead father signs nothing, for he is the inverted image of the moon as O: he is the abyss. This use of language fills the speaker not with Nietzschean delight for a flexing of her own power, but with weariness and dread. Against this particular "complexion of the mind," Plath places a concluding image: "... The berries purple/ And bleed. The white stomach may ripen yet." Because an unseen sun ripens berries, the speaker hopes for some shining element besides her own whiteness of mind. With only that, all she can do, or in a Jamesian phrase, all she can "put" as image-maker is "nothing," the dead blank, deadlocked in its many forms. She cannot will the sun, but she can hope for it and what it enables: the ripening of her skills toward the eventual evocation of life, a stained conception which will be a sign for something other than herself.

"Spinster" and "Frog Autumn" follow, each a grey evocation of life sealed off from energizing forces: a woman, in her disdain of disorder and imperfection, from love; and nature, as the days grow shorter and colder, from the sun. Something very different happens in the poem Plath placed next. In "Mussel Hunter at Rock Harbor," the speaker manages an encounter with the sun via an image which elicits enough imaginative sympathy from the speaker to establish a new relation to this life force. The poem begins:

I came before the water-
Colorists came to get the
Good of the Cape light that scours
Sand grit to sided crystal
And buffs and sleeks the blunt hulls

> Of the three fishing smacks beached
> On the bank of the river's
>
> Backtracking tail.

The speaker comes early to "get the/ Good" of a light not yet strong enough for the painters and their palettes, but still a working light. The morning sun illumines the beachscape so that it seems clean and polished. The sun's activity, however, is not the focus of her attention. As the sun goes mildly about its business of dawning and scouring, the speaker goes musingly about hers:

> ... I'd come for
> Free fish bait: the blue mussels
> Clumping like bulbs at the grass-root
> Margin of the tidal pools...

Plath's skill makes the dense world palpable for the reader in strong, sensory detail:

> Dawn tide stood dead low. I smelt
> Mud stench, shell guts, gulls' leavings;
> Heard a queer crusty scrabble
>
> Cease, and I neared the silenced
> Edge of a cratered pool-bed...

Plath sounds this world into density for the reader, in the thud of "d's" and the grate and tack of "g's" and "t's", the crackle of "qu" and "cr", but in tones hushed, not harsh, that bring the senses to alertness so that the faintest diminishment is noticed. It is at an edge of sound that the speaker's attention is focused—an interval between the end of one sound, the "crusty scrabble," and the beginning of another. That space or lack is felt delicately, but intensely as an absence of both sound and movement:

> The mussels hung dull blue and
> Conspicuous, yet it seemed
> A sly world's hinges had swung
> Shut against me. All held still.

The speaker sees the mussels, but senses what is not there, what excludes her. The hendiadys, "blue and conspicuous," is the pleasurable jarring and loosening of equivalence: these two adjectives joined by a co-ordinate conjunction are not quite parallel. The disjunction engages the speaker's attention, heightening her sense of dissimilar spheres. The closed world of the sea-side creatures unhinges, but after a lapse of time that is relative to a completely alien perception:

> Though I counted scant seconds,
>
> Enough ages lapsed to win
> Confidence of safe-conduct
> In the wary otherworld
> Eyeing me.

The speaker describes the emerging fiddler crabs as miniature armored warriors, displacing their domes of mud, in Seamus Heaney's reading, "as tiny knights might doff their casques." Heaney finds in the use of "casques" Plath's invitation to the reader to indulge her,

> ... ever so slightly, to allow her to raise her eye a fraction from the level of crabs to the level of casques. Casque, a word chivalric, plump and metallic, takes our eye off the object for a millimoment ... the reader's pleasure comes from just this sense of being on a linguistic tour where the point of the outing is as much to relish the guide's vocabulary as to see what is being talked about (156).

Heaney notes that the elevated diction of "casques," as helmet, leads into the speaker's fanciful perusal of the crab community: "sibilant/ Massmotivated hordes," but he does not note another sense of casque, the same as cask, relating to *casco*, pot or skull, an encasing that can be broken. Casque is etymologically rooted in mud and bone. The mud is "displaced" by the pushing of the crabs, as the unglamorous, literal material scene is displaced by the fanciful pushing of the speaker's metaphoricity of thought. We do enjoy the tour, but keep expecting a more powerful breakthrough, an engagement that this heightened language seems to desire, even though the speaker admits that linguistic invention does nothing to reveal the crabs' motives or sensations, which remain unknowable to her:

>   ...I
> Stood shut out, for once, for all,
> Puzzling the passage of their
> Absolutely alien
> Order as I might puzzle
> At the clear tail of Halley's
>
> Comet coolly giving my
> Orbit the go-by, made known
> By a family name it
> Knew nothing of.

The nature of this alien sphere, first felt in the hendiadys and then responded to by the elevated diction of "casques," has opened a space between the speaker and the unknowable, and has intensified the desire for relation. This opportunity eventually occurs when the speaker finds a real *casco*, an empty crab shell:

> High on the airy thatching
> Of the dense grasses I found
> The husk of a fiddler-crab,
> Intact, strangely strayed above
>
> His world of mud.

The separate wanderer could parallel the speaker herself, but the poem resists the metaphoric urge to find similarity in dissimilarity and instead continues to evoke the distance between the speaker and what she observes:

> ... green color
> And innards bleached and blown off
> Somewhere by much sun and wind;
> There was no telling if he'd
> Died recluse or suicide
> Or headstrong Columbus crab.
> The crab-face, etched and set there,
>
> Grimaced as skulls grimace: it
> Had an Oriental look,
> A samurai death mask done
> On a tiger tooth, less for
> Art's sake than God's.

Rather than immediately reaching for the obvious metaphoric connection between herself and what was once another created being, the speaker continues to refuse similarity. Her careful scrutiny of the lone wanderer's remains leads her to observe yet another difference in the alien crab scene, that between dry land and sea. Plath manages to hold apart all the differences in her poem until the very last line:

> Far from sea—
> Where red-freckled crab-back, claws
> And whole crabs, dead, their soggy
>
> Bellies pallid and upturned,
> Perform their shambling waltzes
> On the waves' dissolving turn
> And return, losing themselves
> Bit by bit to their friendly
> Element—this relic saved
> Face, to face the bald faced sun.

One crucial find in this poem, as Heaney's reading notes, is the vital contrast of the dry land and a "truly malignant" sea (159). He understands this as Plath's personal drama of identity and survival, "the attainment of a dry, hard-won ledge beyond the welter and slippage of Lethean temptations" (159). My reading differs from his somewhat, for I want to emphasize Plath's understanding of how her use of language and survival are related. Plath's words as signs are those abstract substitutes for the mother's body, we might as well say, as Ransom did, the "world's body," but her signs, used in the right spirit, could nevertheless link her to a source of love. That right spirit is another and greater accidental find in the poem which results from searching, not for herself, not even for crabs, but for mussels for bait. The speaker never does get on with actual fishing, but through a series of acute distinctions among differences, she herself is finally caught by surprise in the closing line which is a powerful unwilled metaphoric image for will. Plath has abandoned the blank-obsessed stance of "Moonrise" and is using in "Mussel Hunter" a masculine sign for will (desire) to understand the world, not to replace it or to completely succumb to it. The white stomach of "Moonrise" becomes the "bellies pallid and upturned" in this poem, an undesired, mindless giving in to life cycles that, no matter how biologically fitting or "friendly," leads to decomposition in the sea. Plath wants a more passionate, vigorous, self-conscious relation to the world, and that requires those keenly felt edges of things—of differences between sound and silence, of sand and sea, crab and human, self and not self. The crab becomes an emblem of a sensibility that refuses to collapse into identity, preferring a relation, even a lonely and agonistic one, to a merging of all things into the dissolving single element.

This is a way of talking about the illuminating, energizing impulse of desire. This is the "good" of the sun that Plath's speaker came to get from the first line, but she did not know this good until it struck her—first as a sense of lack of connection, signaled in the unsettling "blue and conspicuous," then as a need to know what is not known, in the imaginative tour of the crab world, and finally as that imaginative leap toward an object that offers to make a metaphoric connection possible.

This poem ends with a triangulation: the speaker, the crab face, and the sun. The linguistic tour has become a linguistic place, a means for relation, not dissolution. The little crab's out-facing, or defying the sun, is understood tenderly but not sentimentally. Who can explain such impulses to break away from the mindless herd and to exert an individual force unless as a passionate need to be conscious, to see and reflect an awareness of differences between one thing and another? The crab is for the speaker a reflector, a little shield perhaps, in which she can see the power of the good light which floods the final line, dissolving nothing, but rather burnishing keenly felt distinctions to brilliance.

In spirit, this poem resembles the earlier "Black Rook in Rainy Weather," in which a moment of radiance ("you might say love") comes unwilled to a speaker going about her tasks. Plath's later poem reaches farther, though, for a relation and attains a clearer, drier, less glamorized state of awareness. There is no mention of "love" in "Mussel Hunter," but there is a use of patterned language that Frost would call loving meters. Plath's seven syllable lines move steadily and carefully until they can achieve the clarification in the very last line when the crab becomes more than a dead, foreign object: he becomes an emblem of deep and vital connection. Yet there is no lover in this poem, unless it is the source of life itself, the sun. And there is no beloved, unless it is the willful, defiant crab who left his herd to approach the source. And there is no love, unless it is the language of the poem itself, a scoured and resonant vessel open to the mysterious workings it registers. The mystery is that of human feeling and thinking in some unequivalent relation to the world. The poem works like the coordinating "and" in the hendiadys which first alerted the speaker to things beyond her. The poem is the binding, loving spirit of conjunction that brings into relation unmatched things: what is and what is not. As such an act, the poem affirms both the value of individual human imagination as will and the value of a given world that survives it.

The new poetic strength in "Mussel Hunter" comes in that double affirmation of boundless possibility and of the givenness of things. The crab as an emblem says: I may willfully make my history, but I also suffer it. Where the dead snake defied death with a "perfected" laugh in "Medallion," the dead crab faces his fate with a "grimace" of dissatisfaction and pain. There is nobility here, not anxiety, in relations held with a justness tempered by tenderness.

The image of the crab who chose a lonely, higher ground allows Plath a penetrating look at the nature of willfulness in the form of "recluse or suicide or headstrong Columbus crab." Plath's father had been all these: a solitary focused on his chosen work, stubborn and self-willed to the point of recklessness with his own health and his family's welfare, yet a pioneer in his field of entomology, especially in reading the signs of animal behavior. In this poem, Plath is doing as a poet what her father did as a scientist, but her vital find is not a sense of identity or security, so much as a mood in which she can meet the influence of her dead father without fear or rage. The reader senses a blessing for the speaker, and for Plath herself, in what her poem symbolically achieves. However, when the father is perceived as an unknowable absence which she must out-face, he triggers Plath's gnostic imagination, as the earlier poems in *The Colossus* have shown. Plath's writing then becomes the place where the drama of unfulfilled desire for a relation of love enacts itself. In the next poem, "The Beekeeper's Daughter," Plath develops a new approach to the negative father as a generator of her writing.

The poem opens with "A garden of mouthings," not a child's garden of verse, though the phrase recalls Stevenson's collection as well as Lang's nursery rhyme image for the mysterious delights to which written language may lead. Plath's garden resembles more a Roethkean hot house which she makes seductively, even oppressively, feminine:

> The great corollas dilate, peeling back their silks.
> Their musk encroaches, circle after circle,
> A well of scents almost too dense to breath in.

In this space moves a powerful male force:

> Hieratical in your frock coat, maestro of the bees,
> You move among the many breasted hives,
>
> My heart under your foot, sister to a stone.

The "maestro" has an aspect of writing older and simpler, less pictorial than the hieroglyph, more remote and more holy. As an archaic power, he commands—orchestrates—nature's energies into some particular arrangement for maximum effect. The opening lines of the poem lead the reader to expect development of the theme of sexual desire. Plath's poem is an uncanny anticipation of Jacques Lacan's extension of Freudian theory to language.[4] Freud's understanding of humanness rests on his Oedipal theory of repressed desire. For Lacan, the power that makes difference knowable and signification possible is the law of the father that prohibits Oedipal impulses and simultaneously creates language as the symbolic order of that repressed desire. Lacan calls the sign for the father's authority "phallic," not so much to designate gender as to name that which, through opposition to desire, enforces distinctions and generates a meaningful order of relations out of difference. The lowly, inert speaker, contemplates erotic images within the garden:

> Trumpet-throats open to the beaks of birds.
> The Golden Rain Tree drips its powders down.
> In these little boudoirs streaked with orange and red
> The antlers nod their heads, potent as kings
> To father dynasties. The air is rich.
> Here is a queenship no mother can contest.

Among the flowers, the speaker finds little prohibition of generative energies, but without a phallic marker of limit, she cannot proliferate herself linguistically into a structure of desire. The dash arrests and turns the speaker toward the father as orchestrator. His "NO" renders ultimate knowledge, not as fulfillment of desire in him, but as the knowledge of difference: good and evil, life and death, "A fruit that's death to taste: dark flesh, dark parings." In Freudian-Lacanian terms, the primary prohibition against incest is the phallic sign which generates everything: consciousness and unconsciousness, writing and the civilization that writing makes possible. In such a concept of writing, desire is repressed, dispersed, diversified, and sublimated in metonymic forms, endlessly. The bees in Plath's poem are signifying energies, ordered by the Law of the Maestro, which brought the higher form of creative life (higher than the flowers) into being. The pun is unavoidable. To gain access to the phallic father, the origin of moral and aesthetic consciousness, within his signifying system is impossible, because he is simply not there except as a negative command. The desire to know this unknown, however, is very great. The only way is the way of the gnostic imagination: visionary seeing, but what the speaker sees and knows is, finally, not the "father" but her own desire engaging its inventions:

In burrows narrow as a finger, solitary bees
Keep house among the grasses. Kneeling down
I set my eye to a hole-mouth and meet an eye
Round, green, disconsolate as a tear.

The hole-mouth is the space of the speaker's poetic language, and in it she reads the sign of the unaccommodated will, "disconsolate as a tear." Plath's diction rises in "disconsolate" to emphasize the dark, deprived, even underworldly condition of separation from community for a solitary creative endeavor. The single bee becomes the sign for the imagination that defies the given order. This defiance, for Plath, finds expression in language associated with her actual father: language as a power that makes itself its own origin and end. Otto Plath made himself in this country and he made his own death. The speaker in "The Beekeeper's Daughter" accepts his Nietzschean will as her own. She will be a queen bee and marry the bee-father, defying the incest taboo. The conjugal meeting, however, will be immediately displaced by a funeral, for after the male bee has engendered a new order, he dies. Plath's familiar abyss as bald blank is here a candy Easter egg. Sugar was death to Plath's diabetic father who craved sweets. Her desire to be her own sweet will is death to her experience of her father, because defiance means her autonomy at the price of his usurpation. She is brought to life, no longer "with her heart under your foot, sister of a stone." She, too, now defies the given. As a queen bee, defying gravity like a flying stone, she is self-generated by writing, full of desire to signify on her own terms, to "be" original. She is now willful, dominant, and fecund, having taken from the father what she needs, his power: "The queen bee marries the winter of your year." She is proud, yet sorrowful, for the disconsolate "eye" is the reflection of her own imperious and solitary spirit.

Language understood as a system of differences enabled by an absence, an unknowable source, is the language of the Plath's gnostic imagination. Such language is not understood as a link to a source of love as authority. Plath kept trying to make her poetry "relational," to borrow Heaney's term, in the Platonic-Christian symbolic tradition and she succeeded in such pieces as "Blue Moles," "A Winter Ship," and "Mussel Hunter." But by late 1959, she realized that she could not "do" love in her writing as well as she could do other things. She had been terrified of the nature of her poetic gift, and she had been reluctant to assert it. She had tried to hide that orientation, as in "The Disquieting Muses," and when exploring it, she had found it dangerously seductive as a death wish in "Full Fathom Five " and "Lorelei." When she accepted her way of poetic knowing, as she seemed to in "The Bee Keeper's Daughter," she began to trust it without fearing annihilation by it. She was able to do this because her own life had taken on not just the solidity of a passionate relation in marriage but also the embodied miracle of child-bearing. The last five poems in *The Colossus* seem attempts to put her particular form of imagination in its place. "The Times Are Tidy" signals the departure. Her poetry no longer has the heroic, romantic, social role she once thought it had: "But the children are better for it,/ The cow milk's cream an inch thick." She does not want the terrible, death-wishing, self-focused power of her poetic imagination loosed on a world into which she is bringing children. She must relate this energy to something other than its own capacity for making fictions. She tries by setting it in a space marginal to the vital concerns of her quotidian life. Thus, she can live as a woman striving for a soundness of existence as both a wife and a mother and as a responsible human being in a complex, social world, and she can pursue an artistic endeavor at some distance from her actual life. She does not write, then, her personal myth or her "secular scripture" in order to give her life coherence and meaning. Her life already has plenty of coherence and meaning. She writes to affirm something else: what her gnostic imagination can do when set free to know only itself in language. Such desire cannot live in the real world of other people; this kind of sublimity is dangerous and must live only in poems.

Plath marginalizes her gnostic will in "The Burnt Out Spa" which begins: "An old beast ended in this place." The stanzas that follow elaborate the ruin of a house once a place for finding health. The spa, figured as a decaying organic carcass, can offer none of that now:

> I pick and pry like a doctor or
> Archaeologist among
> Iron entrails, enamel bowls,
> The coils and pipes that made him
>   run.

The speaker's attention in the next stanza shifts from the ruin of the old spa, which seems an emblem for notions of art of a bygone romantic, even modernist, era, to what remains unchanged by time and fashion:

> The small dell eats what ate it once.
> And yet the ichor of the spring
> Proceeds clear as it ever did
> From the broken throat, the marshy lip.

Plath uses her familiar tactic of the suddenly but subtly elevated diction in a single word to alert the reader to the poem's concern. The term "ichor," the life fluid of the deathless gods, makes the reader wonder along with Plath: If the fountain of the muses continues to exist, what is it? What is poetry if it is no longer part of the enterprise for social and individual coherence and health? From a sagging bridge the speaker sees an answer:

> Leaning over, I encounter one
> Blue and improbable person
>
> Framed in a basketwork of cat-tails.
> O she is gracious and austere,
> Seated beneath the toneless water!
> It is not I, it is not I.

The speaker sees either her own reflection or a sunken stone statue—or both. Whatever she sees beneath the water of a stream has the aura of a medusa not a saint: the image has a wreath of "tails" not a halo. This gorgon does not threaten, however, for the speaker is not drawn into her particular peace of frozen desire as she was drawn by the lorelei or the old man of the sea in earlier poems. The difference emerges from Plath's new sense of separation and difference between her art and her life. She can say of what she sees in her poetic constructs: "It is not I." She says this with strong emotion, signaled by the apostrophe, a rare utterance in *The Colossus* poems. We have seen it only two other times and will not see again in this collection. In "The Bull of Bendylaw," the "O" helped mainly to fill out the ballad line, but in "Lorelei" it carries the awe that it does here in "The Burnt Out Spa." The sign O, semantically both apostrophe and lament, is now the negative sign of phallic power for Plath: the emptiness that divides and creates an order of proliferating desire. She knows that her muse is this negative O, but she also knows the order it creates is removed from her life:

> No animal spoils on her green doorstep.
> And we shall never enter there
> Where the durable ones keep house.
> The stream that hustles us
>
> Neither nourishes nor heals.

The phallic sign will bring into being a linguistic order that enacts its own drama, sufficient unto itself, but not sufficient for fragile, perishable actual life that does need both nourishment and healing among many other things.

Exploring this as well as other possible connections of art to life is the function of art, as it both confirms and unsettles our sense of ourselves as makers of that relation. Asserting this value is Plath's motive in the next poem "Sculptor" in which she praises Leonard Baskin for giving the "bodiless" a "solider repose than death's." The marginal space that art makes out of desire has its own special density, not life but not death either. In that region, some of the anxieties that plagued Plath's early poetry simply disappear or become so small as to seem to disappear. The penultimate poem, "Flute Notes from a Reedy Pond," diminishes and then empties one imaginative construct in favor of another. As the natural scene in this poem deadens into winter, Plath's poetic scene cools into something she can contemplate without horror:

> Puppets, loosed from the strings of the puppet-master,
> Wear masks of horn to bed.
> This is not death, it is something safer.
> The wingy myths won't tug at us anymore:

Desires loosed in poetic language may give us dreams that are true, but they will still be dreams. The life of the real woman who lives in her body, both rooted in the actual and enmeshed in the wingy myth of eros will go her own responsible way, while her divine spark of gnostic will goes another. In the last stanza, this creative will slips out of all empirical restraints, but on such a quiet, miniature scale that it will scarcely be noticed and will certainly not cause alarm:

> The molts are tongueless that sang from above the water
> Of golgotha at the tip of a reed,
> And how a god flimsy as a baby's finger
> Shall unhusk himself and steer into the air.

Too easily read as a myth of death and rebirth in nature, "Flute Notes" gains power when understood as a conscious shedding of an old symbolic style for a new allegorical one. An image of emptiness dominates this final stanza: mouths without tongues, perhaps the mother tongue, that no longer sing of the old plenitude of death and resurrection. All that remains are the "molts." Plath wrenches this verb into an odd substantive. The violence of the turn leaves behind in another discourse mythic associations of life and death cycles. The metonymy of "molts" for tongueless birds is an image of shedding as a casting off of one form after another, not necessarily related to any given pattern. It is difficult, in fact, to shift back to a traditional image, to think, for example, "nightingale" and all of its classic and romantic associations. If the reader thinks of them, it is only to dismiss them, and rightly, for this poem dismisses such restraints. No symbol, no metaphoric relation based on mythic belief, can hold in a linguistic space that insists it is a process of groundless difference and absence. In such a conception of language, symbols flatten and harden into allegorical signs that point to what is not, or into magical metaphors that make illusory gestures toward what is desired but not achieved. That, quite specifically, is the poet's desire to come to life, truly, in an adequate metaphor of self.

The last poem in *The Colossus*, "The Stones," can be read as Plath's dramatized entrance into an order in which the "I" confesses its fictiveness in an allegory of unappeased desire. The poem, not a person, speaks, articulating Plath's most distinctive poetic voice. For Plath, this is the voice of "Not-I." Her first line, "This is the city where men are mended," comes from the title of an African folktale that Plath found in Paul Radin's collection.[5] In that story, a daughter is killed by a hyena who lures her to destruction by a false voice. The dead girl's bones are found and re-membered by the efforts of her good mother who refuses all seductions on her way to the "city" and is thus judged worthy to have her daughter back, more beautiful than she ever was. Noting the change, an evil mother de-liberately kills her ugly daughter in hopes of a similar reconstitutive effect. The bad mother not only willfully destroys her offspring, she also stops at every invitation to satisfy her appetite along the way to the "city." The bad mother's re-membered daughter returns uglier than before. Obviously, the outcome of the mending depends on the spirit which desires it. The appeti-tive, evil mother was dissatisfied with the given and was punished. Plath submits herself in "The Stones" to her creative spirit, sensing it is more like the folk tale's evil mother than the good one. Making and then dissolving the made thing is the act Plath tried to resist in earlier poems such as "A Winter Ship" and "Blue Moles." This poem, "The Stones," tells of its gen-esis, not in mythic ritual of death and rebirth, but as a pattern of unmaking and making that figures the irreducible doubleness and undecidability of language when divorced from the metaphoric, symbolic tradition. Understood this way, "The Stones" witnesses to a fragile, fictional "I" in construction. It will not last, for it will only be "good as new," that is, good while new. If value rests on newness, this fabrication is destined for more of the same treatment by the "mother of pestles," i. e. the unaccommo-dated spirit which is both passionate, dissatisfied, and violent.

This is not life and it is not death: it is theory, an imaginative con-struct which in "Sculptor," Plath called "something safer" than both and in "Flute Notes," something not subject to the "wingy myths" of the body's erotic desire and its symbolic transformations into spiritual desire for an absolute, something universally good and true and beautiful. Thus, this "city" is not the desiring mind in a trinity of functions obedient to the given. Plath's is the city of the creative spirit as sheer will which must reduce the given to nothing and then re-make it in its own image. The poem recounts this process. Whatever previous form this poetic voice had was blanked out when taken into the "city where men are mended." In Plath's city of will, prior expression is reduced to fragments and silence:

I entered the wordless cupboard.
The mother of pestles diminished me.
I became a still pebble.

Its new voice is in the making: "The head-stone quiet, jostled by nothing."
This is still language, very "still," for it is desire in repressed form be-
coming writing, making a sign. The sign is O, the hole-mouth, which is for
Plath consistently both the deadly Medusan muse and the absent father.
Plath gives the O as sign a negatively generative function:

Only the hole-mouth piped out,
Importunate cricket

In a quarry of silences.
The people of the city heard it
They hunted the stones, taciturn and separate,

The mouth-hole crying their locations.

The word "people" suggests that for Plath the creative spirit was
many, not one, or its manifestations were multiple. As the poem begins to
occupy the space of its own mouthing, it becomes "Drunk as a foetus/ I
suck at the paps of darkness." This is the primal desire, and the rest of the
poem works to diversify its energies into an esthetic form. The attention
lavished on devices, from food tubes, chisels, electric volts, and catgut
stitches suggests the delight in craft that the "people" of this city take.
What is done is done well, even though violently. If there is love in this city,
it is love of technique:

On Fridays the little children come

To trade their hooks for hands.
Dead men leave eyes for others.
Love is the uniform of my bald nurse.

Love is the bone and sinew of my curse.
The vase reconstructed, houses
The elusive rose.

Ten fingers shape a bowl for shadows.
My mendings itch. There is nothing to do.
I shall be good as new.

In a reconstructed state, the "I" of this poem speaks as the mysterious delight of language, a thing made out of words. The pleasure in this poem comes in sophisticated self-consciousness, in being unlike anything that has come before in the collection. "The Stones" carries awareness of itself as linguistic artifact into a new dimension. When the speaker concludes, "There is nothing to do," the reader of Plath's first published collection of poetry has come to read her "nothing" as the grief which generates her writing. The word "love" is both the covering for blankness which she makes out of her own need, and the curse of desire that will drive her spirit from one theoretical "self" to another, endlessly. Plath is "doing" the abyss, for it is her *writing*, her articulated emptiness that speaks in this poem, not her autobiographical "I." Plath's speaker in "The Stones" confesses a lack of an adequate metaphor that would present her to the reader as a living soul: the speaker is a self-conscious fiction.

This chapter, dealing with Plath's poems from 1955 to 1959, especially those which she chose and arranged for her first published volume, *The Colossus*, has traced a dialectic in Plath's poetry. At times, Plath writes as if her language could connect her with a loving presence and her personal reality. In that belief, she deals with lack as a space for affirming relations that keep her in the given world. This is the Platonic-Christian-Humanist tradition of the symbolic imagination which allows for poetic autobiography. At other times, Plath writes as if to ward off threats to her existence. This use of language, associated with the willful, absent father, deals fearfully and anxiously with limit as a challenge to her autonomy. This is the American tradition of the highly individualistic gnostic imagination that tries to see through the given world in order to see itself in some reassuring self-generated formal identity. The gnostic imagination can achieve poetic autobiography if it believes strongly enough in its own powers. The reader experiences then, in Harold Bloom's terms, a clarification in "the overwhelming self-revelation of a profoundly subjective consciousness."[6] In Plath, however, gnostic belief is qualified. The result is the confessional mode which yields the opacity of the fictive self with no claims to symbolize her as an autonomous, actual woman.

Plath anxiously resists "gnosis" when she conveys the overwhelming density of the world in such poems as "Hardcastle Crags," "Departure," and "Suicide Off Egg Rock." She could sometimes do poems of relation, in such pieces as "Black Rook in Rainy Weather," "Blue Moles," "A Winter Ship," and "Mussel Hunter at Rock Harbor." The balance she achieved in these affirms the tradition in which desire locates a speaker in the world of others by means of the gift of love for that world and its creatures. Because Plath understood this tradition well, she felt the power of her particular gift as dangerous. She tried to mock it in "Sow," "Mushrooms," and "I Want, I Want," but she had to acknowledge the attractions of otherworldly and unrestrained regions beyond the given that draw her in "Lorelei," "Full Fathom Five," and "Point Shirley." She faces the nature of her orientation to language in "The Colossus" and understands its divisive and tragic aspect in "The Disquieting Muses." The way Plath deals with the blank of things in *The Colossus* collection shows her gradual acceptance of her powerful gnostic imagination. The last poems in this volume show also her growing sense that her poetic acts are not mimetic in relation to the acts of Plath as wife, mother, daughter, complex person occupying a specific time and place. What she does as a poet is other than what she does as that empirical self. This seems clear because the birth Plath contemplates in the opening poem, "The Manor Garden," is not at all the birth of the closing poem, "The Stones." In the first, the speaker, about to bring a new human life into a world of death, looks within herself for the courage to affirm her capacity to be herself a good mother, i.e., a living source of love. In the last poem, the speaker acts as an allegorical poem, which is neither life nor death, telling of its linguistic generation in the space which is nothing.

The poems that Plath placed between these two "births" show her coming to terms with two things: her father's death and her own form of poetic talent. Plath makes peace with her actual father's memory in "Mussel Hunter at Rock Harbor." The exquisite precision of her inquiry leads to surprising sympathy for the solitary willfulness of a fellow creature and allows for an illumination at the poem's end. There, the searcher finds not so much the thing she sought as the place in which to look. This place is where love as charity occurs and with that experience an expansion of consciousness and of human potential. Plath looks not at an empty crab shell, but at the imaginatively perceived soul of another and she felt the capacity to love it.

Her orientation to her father changes radically in "The Bee Keeper's Daughter," and so also does her orientation to language. In this poem, Plath takes on her father's spirit of defiance, filling his absence with her own powerful imagination as will. The last poems in her collection act out acceptance of her negative turn of imagination which frees in her poetry that strange yet compelling voice that would be her definitive one: the voice of unaccommodated desire. She has taken over "bluebeard's" chamber and will make it her own. She is the divisive, passionate, violent spirit of that empty place, but as a "mother of pestles," she hopes to house somehow in her fabrications the "elusive rose" which is still what she wants and why she writes.

Endnotes

[1]Paula Bennett finds the Medusa a muse for women poets who are caught between conflicting needs for relationships and for separation and individuation that lead to an autonomous, creative self. "The Muse as Medusa," *My Life a Loaded Gun: Female Creativity and Feminist Poetics* (Boston: Beacon, 1986) 241–267. Thus constrained, argues Bennett, they subvert "the very power they seek to claim" (264). Steven Gould Axelrod explores Plath's subversive poetic in *Sylvia Plath: The Wound and the Cure of Words* (Baltimore: Johns Hopkins UP, 1990). My study was largely written before Axelrod's book appeared. Though we see many of the same things occurring in her poetry, I deal with Plath's conservatism: her use of the Medusa-muse to articulate allegory that confesses an unachieved metaphorical self.

[2]My reading is of the American edition of *The Colossus and Other Poems* (New York: Alfred A. Knopf, 1962) which is shorter than the English edition (London: William Heinemann, 1960) by ten poems. Stanley Kunitz recommended Plath's book for publication but without the poems too obviously influenced by Roethke (Tabor 10). Plath chose the ten for deletion: "Metaphors," "Black Rook in Rainy Weather," "Maudlin," "Ouija," "Two Sisters of Persephone," "Who," "Dark House," "Maenad," "The Beast,"

and "Witch Burning." Plath kept the remaining poems in the same order as in the English edition (Tabor 5–10).

[3]Harold Bloom, *A Map of Misreading* (New York: Oxford UP,1975) 91.

[4]Jacques Lacan, "The Insistence of the Letter in the Unconscious," in *Modern Criticism and Theory: A Reader,* ed. David Lodge (New York: Longman, 1988) 79–106. See also Terry Eagleton, *Literary Theory* (Minneapolis: Minnesota UP, 1983) 151–193; and Malcom Bowie, *Freud, Proust and Lacan* (New York: Cambridge UP, 1987).

[5]Paul Radin, "City Where Men are Mended," *African Folktales and Sculpture.* Bollingen Series XXXII (New York: Pantheon Books, 1952) 250–253.

[6]Harold Bloom, "Introduction," *Modern Critical Views: Elizabeth Bishop* (New York: Chelsea House, 1985) 1.

4

Looking Out on Nothing:
Poems of 1960–1961

In the year 1960, Plath completed twelve poems.[1] The first of these, "You're," addresses her unborn child in a series of fancifully exuberant metaphors:

> ... vague as fog and looked for like mail.
> Farther off than Australia
> Bent-backed Atlas, our traveled prawn.
> Snug as a bud and at home
> Like a sprat in a pickle jug....

The progression of images has no argument, no sense of beginning, middle or end, and could be scrambled in any fashion without doing harm to logic, for felicitous as these descriptions are they do not add up to what the baby is. He remains what is yet to be, still an unknown, addressed in the final line as "A clean slate, with your own face on." The poem does not want to write on that blank. Its assertions do nothing more than fill the space where the baby is not, which is the space of the poet's anticipation or desire. The real baby stays safe in another realm. This is a good example of how Plath's metaphoric urge to relate balks in her poetry and breaks into a series of displacements, magical metaphors like little philosophers stones doing their work in a void.

Again, we are aware of Plath's fear of her imaginative power as a solvent that might be more destructive than transforming. "The Hanging

Man" (June, 1960) reads like a highly condensed version of "The Disquieting Muses."

> By the roots of my hair some god got hold of me.
> I sizzled in his blue volts like a desert prophet.
>
> The nights snapped out of sight like a lizard's eyelid:
> A world of bald white days in a shadeless socket.
>
> A vulturous boredom pinned me in this tree.
> If he were I, he would do what I did.

The speaker tells of events that led to a significant, though unnamed act. The reader knows only its cause: the speaker's election by a god who charges her with knowing by visionary seeing. Such a poetic dissolves the ordinary world of differences into an intolerably undifferentiated state. The speaker cannot endure being prey to a demonic force that is itself "nothing." Her defiance is empowering. Why should she remain obediently "pinned" in the tree like Christ on the cross if her god is not a loving, present father? If her god is unknowable, she has only the energy of the imperative to affirm a satisfying order of her own. Plath's speaker refused to suffer passivity and acted to overcome the blankness of her conditions. The last stanza suggests this: If Christ had had no loving father, he, too, would have exercised his own will. The rhyme scheme enacts the willed reversal of the given pattern. What began as a b c, ends as b a c. The caesura in the last line slows the conclusion and allows the reader to sense the unidentical natures of "he" and "I." The speaker refuses identity with any god and she also refuses to be his victim. The speaker confesses in "The Hanging Man" that she acts, that is, *writes* poems, to fill a void which is the agent of her act.

Two poems of 1960, "Love Letter" and "A Life," suggest different ways Plath dealt with the hanging man's gift. "Love Letter" was written close to Plath's twenty-eighth birthday in October, the same month that *The Colossus* was published by William Heinemann in England. Plath's first baby, Frieda, was six months old. Linda Wagner-Martin calls this poem a tribute to Hughes, the husband who drew Plath "away from a life of apathy to one of complete emotional fulfillment," for loving him leads her to "a nearly transcendent state" which "Ted shares" (SP 79). Wagner-Martin's reading holds but does not account for the poem's strangeness. Certainly the poem was for Hughes, for he would have understood it better than anyone, knowing well the nature of Plath's talent. She had, as he put it, an "instant special pass to the center, and no choice but to use it" (JP 5). The center was, however, empty. By 1959, Plath had learned not to fear so much as to resist and utilize that void by being, as she wrote in her Journal, "true to my own weirdness" (J 323). If the reader understands the "you" in "Love Letter" merely as a beloved man, the poem enacts a woman's transformation from an unfeeling, unselfconscious material object into the expanded consciousness of a purified soul; however, if the reader understands the "you" which the poem addresses not as person but Plath's own peculiar creative spirit or spark, then the poem enacts something else.

My reading understands that "you" as Plath's capacity to turn the blank into her writing's own forms and fictions. Thus, the reader listens to Plath's will to power speak in that distinctive sound first heard in "The Stones" where a nullity is transformed into a space for desire to image itself. As in "The Hanging Man," Plath would at times refer to her poetic power as "the god." In 1959, she wrote in her Journal: "Every day is a renewed prayer that the god exists, that he will visit with renewed force and clarity" (J 328). The poems in *The Colossus* show Plath often personifying the force of the absent and indifferent father-origin and associating him with the cold depths of the ocean, an empty sky, blank world, or barren moon. The poem "Love Letter," then, can address "the god" as Plath's own creative resistance to the abyss, a resistance which the abyss makes possible. The "nothing" brings her "everything" into play.

The poem should be read as literally as possible, beginning with the title which provokes this question: which letter is love? The poem answers the riddle: the letter O, the sign for nothing when it becomes a sign for perfection. This happens for Plath when her will resists blankness and articulates desire for complete fulfillment on her own terms. What this form of the imagination wants more than anything is transparency: its own seeing as all there is to see. For this to happen, consciousness has to awaken to desire: a sense of lack. Plath's speaker traces her shape-shifting from blank O, "bald eye," to black O, a coiled snake indistinguishable from black rocks on a white sheet of snow. As one of many such signs, unable to perceive difference, she recalls that she was unable to write or read herself. When she tropes to a "bent finger," she has gained that potential, without knowing "what to make" of her new sense of difference and distance. Compelled to act, she does what desire does: she flares and moves toward an object:

> I shone, mica-scaled, and unfolded
> To pour myself out like a fluid
> Among bird feet and the stems of plants.

The coiled, inert O became intent, a power in the form of a running line of released desire, a streak of articulated energy. The term "mica-scaled" adds sparkle and extends the image of unfolding, for mica is a crystal that readily separates into very thin leaves. The density of stone has become a segmented silver shimmer of moving particles which flows into nature, flooding its ground. The sign as inert zero has been diversified by desire and thus enabled to seek and to find what it wants to signify: "I wasn't fooled. I knew you at once." The sign O wants to point not to emptiness but to fullness. In the void of "sheer air," the speaker opens to her own desire and "knows" it, as the gnostic intuits her essence and wills to make her own expressive form for it. Thus empowered, the sign O moves toward the faultless, pure will or desire it wants to become:

> Tree and stone glittered, without shadows.
> My finger length grew lucent as glass.
> I started to bud like a March twig:
> An arm and a leg, an arm, a leg.
>
> From stone to cloud, so I ascended.
> Now I resemble a sort of god
> Floating through air in my soul-shift
> Pure as a pane of ice. It's a gift.

The speaker has come to see her object of desire as identical with herself: O as desire satisfied. In a landscape out of nature, she moves toward her object in a series of turns, from silver scale to lucent glass to budding arms and legs. The prehensile appendages multiply the finger image; her will or desire apprehends or grasps her intent to ascend from "stone to cloud," to become transparent and to mean something, not nothing. Transparency has been achieved when desire and its object become one. Can the reader assent to this? Only if the reader is as desirous a space as the speaker and that is the "gift." The poem ends on a Rousseauesque note that leaves, not the poem, but the reader culpable if he cannot see the change that the first line warned was not going to be easy: O the nullity becomes O the perfect. Read this way, the poem can still sound on a personal level. Hughes had not only redeemed Plath's erotic sense, he had also believed in her poetic gifts and had encouraged her to take more and more imaginative risks. The poem enacts a "soul shift," a visionary power in the making, learning to read itself right. For the reader, principally Hughes himself, who can "see" poetically as strongly as she does, O as fulfilled desire, or in Harold Bloom's terms, as poetic victory, is for Plath the "love letter." The relation Plath celebrates in "Love Letter" is not in her domestic life, but in her life as a poet for whom identity as such is achieved through the gnostic, romantic quest for a perfect matching of words and will.

A month later Plath wrote another poem, "A Life," in which she looks at the conditions for such a quest in a voice of cool detachment, like an indifferent god peering into an alien scene under glass. The creatures are, however, human, and pathetically unaware of how exposed they are to scrutiny. Within this miniature seaside village, sealed off from the turbulence outside, a family of inhabitants seems perfectly content, their lives moderated and pleasant: "They ring true, like good china." But, "Elsewhere the landscape is more frank/ The light falls without letup, blindingly." This is the familiar terrain of Plath's imagination in the oppressive shadeless blank, and sure enough, there she is in it:

> A woman is dragging her shadow in a circle
> About a bald, hospital saucer.
> It resembles a moon, or a sheet of white paper
> And appears to have suffered a sort of private blitzkrieg.
> She lives quietly

> With no attachments, like a foetus in a bottle,
> The obsolete house, the sea, flattened to a picture
> She has one too many dimensions to enter.
> Grief and anger, exorcised,
> Leave her alone now.

Apparently, the worst has happened: the figure has been cut off from the sea and from community by private suffering. Although no longer agonizing over a past obliterated by the violence of a lightning war, she is afraid of the future: "Age and terrors, like nurses, attend her." Her endurance of the barren present effects a surprising and eerie advent: "a drowned man, complaining of the great cold,/ Crawls up out of the sea."

The man in an autobiographical context is Otto Plath. The father's absence, however, became for Plath as poet the sign that could not be read, but which, as a negative, articulated her desire into language. The woman could be Plath's mother, but is not, simply because this figure is about to write a poem, a powerful willed reversal to the empty conditions of her life. The drowned man who also refuses his conditions is an image for Plath's own unaccommodated spirit.

Such writing is for Plath the language of the unloving, inscrutable, yet empowering father, the enactment of desire as will, brought into play by his absence. In much of the American poetic tradition, absence is opportunity. For Plath, absence remained an outrage, in spite of her various efforts to turn it to benign effect, as in "Love Letter." Like an awful crack in the world, her native tradition pulls her into that realm of absolute freedom of desire, a beautiful but a terrible place, for there her language must aspire to achieve a total victory over the given, dissolving it and making it over into forms that satisfy the autonomous and solitary will. As much as Plath wanted to separate from any identity with her own mother, she nevertheless remained nostalgic for the language of the mother in her earliest experience: language spoken by bodies accommodating themselves to each other in a temporal world; sounds and signs assuring her that such connections sustained a fabric of life that was sufficient and would survive her will.

The first poem of 1961, "Parliament Hill Fields," affirms Plath's old belief that language could connect her as a writer (and a reader) to a world that her imagination could not negate. Plath wrote this shortly after she had miscarried in February, 1961. The speaker, a woman who has experienced this loss, begins:

> On this bald hill the new year hones its edge.
> Faceless and pale as china
> The round sky goes on minding its business.
> Your absence is inconspicuous;
> Nobody can tell what I lack.

Here are the now familiar Plath images of emptiness: things bald, featureless, colorless, hard and round. The landscape, however, does not correspond to the speaker's loss. Hers is an absolute, a life never seen and never to be seen, not even in this poem. Yet she addresses this vacancy, filling it with what she can see.

The second stanza begins: "Gulls have threaded the river's mud bed back/ To this crest of grass." A rhyme has been achieved, a matching of sounds in the last line of the first stanza and the first line of the second: lack/back. This linking will continue, a delicate thread spun out of the speaker's language to bind together the ten stanzas. The technique recalls Plath's image in "The Manor Garden," of the spider who "crosses the lake on its own string." Getting across the dark water of the abyss is the drama in this poem. Plath had affirmed in her Cambridge diary her ability to do it: "Love is the only way to come across...." For Plath, loving required not things, present or absent, but real people, actual lives, potencies that impinged on her own. The poem is a search for such solidity. Gulls argue among themselves, alien and thus powerless in the poem's context: "Settling and stirring like blown paper/ Or the hands of an invalid." The sun is also weak; it cannot warm her; it can only make her cry and dissolve the world:

> The wan
> Sun manages to strike such tin glints
> From the linked ponds that my eyes wince
> And brim; the city melts like sugar.

These are not real tears of grief as the next lines make clear:

> A crocodile of small girls
> Knotting and stopping, ill-assorted, in blue uniforms,
> Opens to swallow me. I'm a stone a stick
>
> One child drops a barrette of pink plastic;
> None of them seem to notice.

There is no potency here: eyes may water, but not from grief. A group of children may engulf her, but will not connect. In the "silence after silence" that follows, the speaker addresses the lost infant: "I suppose it's pointless to think of you at all./ Already your doll grip lets go." What does engage the speaker is the excessive impersonality of this scene and her mood. When she taps that mood, she confesses the ease for her of what Keats thought impossible for the poet: the forgetfulness of nature which he called in "In Drear-Nighted December" the "The feel of not to feel it." Keats had envied the "Too happy, happy tree" that, though blown bare of leaves does not remember its "green felicity." Plath reverses Keats:

> You know me less constant,
> Ghost of a leaf, ghost of a bird.
> I circle the writhen trees. I am too happy.
> These faithful dark-boughed cypresses
>
> Brood, rooted in their heaped losses.
> Your cry fades like the cry of a gnat.

Just as in the earlier poem "Point Shirley," the speaker is drawn less to grief over lost happiness than to the power of absence that grief has led her to:

I lose sight of you on your blind journey,
While the heath grass glitters and the spindling rivulets
Unspool and spend themselves. My mind runs with them,

Pooling in heel-prints, fumbling pebble and stem.

The speaker is being funneled off through the aperture into that space where her desire for fullness might be satisfied in her own solitary imaginings, emptying out everything else as

The day empties its images
Like a cup or a room. The moon's crook whitens
Thin as the skin seaming a scar.

But something breaks into this movement of her desire to do the world on her own terms. The present breaks in, with "Now ..." and just in time, in the last line of this stanza, to link this desire for fullness to life already there:

Now, on the nursery wall,

The blue night plants, the little pale blue hill
In your sister's birthday picture start to glow.

This is an act of memory for the speaker, not a flight into fantasy or an escape from pain. She remembers how her living child's glow-in-the-dark picture in the child's room lights up as daylight diminishes. This rendering of an actual, recalled, not invented object, works like a lodestone or a lodestar to guide the speaker home. It is suddenly more vivid to her than the sights before her eyes:

The orange pompons, the Egyptian papyrus
Light up. Each rabbit-eared

> Blue shrub behind the glass
> Exhales an indigo nimbus,
> A sort of cellophane balloon.
>
> The old dregs, the old difficulties take me to wife.
> Gulls stiffen to their chill vigil in the drafty half-light;
> I enter the lit house.

The empty speaker is drawn by memory back into her actual life, full of things that will not dissolve, "dregs" and "difficulties," but, nevertheless, full. She is part of that fullness in both its history and its future, felt acutely in the word that relates the two: "Now." This poem is a re-emergence of Plath's poetry of relation. Like the new year referred to in the opening line, she has honed her "edge" throughout her reach of desire, the "lack" that set the poem going. Each stanza is an attempt to make accurate distinctions, to multiply them into a satisfying texture out of the blank of the opening lines. The refusal to stay solely within the generating lack is the most crucial choice in the poem. This occurs when the speaker connects with a memory and acts upon it in such a way that she accepts the given world. Only then is she able both to love and let go, to release and accept the reality of loss and of life. Only then is she able to be Keatsian. Through such obedient desire, the poem turns, not toward the dark, but toward the light. As in the poem's beginning, the outside and the inside do not match, but they connect, relate, illuminate, and energize the speaker for contact with the sources of her life, dregs and all. There is no identity, no transparency, but there is a clarification.

Besides the miscarriage in 1961, Plath underwent an appendectomy and moved with her husband and small daughter from London to a house in Devon. She completed twenty-two poems during the months of February through October. Of these, only "Morning Song," also written in early February, repeats the strategies of "Parliament Hill Fields" as the vacancy demanded by the negating imagination becomes the fullness of interacting lives. The speaker addresses her infant and thus gathers herself from her various imaginative dispersals: "Your arrival shadows our safety." She solidifies into one, heavy and tired, nursing mother, who responds with bodily love to the body that depends on hers for its life. The poem ends with a metaphoric clarification of her relation to the child. The infant's cry and need are clarions that lead her into a light and a lightness without negating or lamenting physical limits: "Your clear vowels rise like balloons."

Most of Plath's other poems of 1961 give shape to forms of discontent with the given world. This impulse, however, is questioned in these poems as it displays itself in a variety of dramatic situations and personae. In "Whitsun," the speaker experiences the nausea of existential angst when she finds the town and its seaside, "not what I meant." In "The Zoo Keeper's Wife," the anxiety of the sleepless depressive is given a humorous performance as the speaker vents her disgust with the earthiness of a husband who previously had charmed her. Such former delights as "wolf-headed fruit bats" are among the many particulars of their life that she has found imaginatively "indigestible." The speaker's rejection of the gritty clutter of married life generates a plethora of repulsive images that compete for abusive power. The mood of this poem resembles a flyting, but it is a contest of only one beset imagination trying to outdo itself and in the process trying to do away with intolerable conditions. This is the gnostic impulse used for satiric attack.

Another poem of sleeplessness, "Insomniac," delivers a less original set of images that harken back to Plath's juvenile poem, "The Invalid." In that early poem, the ill speaker lives through the night only to face the threat of drowning in daylight. In the later poem, "daylight" is a "white disease." "Insomniac" tries, like its earlier version, for pathos rather than satire, but the speaker is herself too detached to achieve that force. Two other poems of 1961, "In Plaster" and "Tulips," can be read as a pair of theme poems, the first rises to satire, the second, to pathos. In each, the voice of Plath's frustrated gnostic imagination speaks, chafing against the limits set against it.

First, "In Plaster": the speaker is showing off. She opens by claiming, "I shall never get out of this," and then like a Houdini, she not only assures the reader and herself of her control of her escape, but also begins to experience a premature nostalgia for the form she claims to be in the process of destroying.[2] This is Plath's version of the old dialogue between body and spirit, though the spirit here is that which has always been but which has not always been acknowledged by its own imperious forms. There is fine irony in the last stanza:

I used to think we might make a go of it together—
After all, it was a kind of marriage, being so close.
Now I see it must be one or the other of us.
She may be a saint, and I may be ugly and hairy,
But she'll find out that that doesn't matter a bit.
I'm collecting my strength; one day I shall manage without her,
And she'll perish with emptiness then, and begin to miss me.

See what I can do once I get going, says the voice in "In Plaster." There is no end to her inventions as she seeks a way to have everything on her own terms. She calls herself unattractive, the "old yellow one." Her seductiveness, however, is in how she voices what she sees. The reader misses her when she stops talking, for she ends on just the right note of petulance, reminding the reader that the entire poem is an attack on restrictions by the spirit that lives by rejecting all received forms. The poem ends before the radical undoing begins, but the loss of meaningful relations, unstable as they are, is already being parodically lamented.

In the second poem of this pair of laments, the mood is serious, the pathos moving. The voice in "Tulips" wants to give shape to a tranquility so complete that it will be not an enunciation but a renunciation of the world and its complications. The voice begins in protest: "The tulips are too excitable, it is winter here." The flowers pun on "two lips," organs of both enunciation and desire. The voice of this poem wants neither to be spoken or written. It wants to be a "nobody" without history, a white pebble underwater, free from human want that insists on action. The desire for no articulation is, however, a desire itself articulated by the rejection of the given—the gift of red tulips. The first five stanzas develop the desired blankness, reaching a concluding image in

The peacefulness is so big it dazes you,
And it asks nothing, a name tag, a few trinkets.
It is what the dead close on finally; I imagine them
Shutting their mouths on it, like a Communion tablet.

The speaker desires completion, not death, a critical difference which keeps the poem attentive to many fine distinctions. The next stanza begins with a second critique of the tulips, the "something" which her desire to be pure must resist: "The tulips are too red in the first place, they hurt me." They hurt like life: an "awful baby," her corresponding "wound," upsetting tongues, and the "red lead sinkers" that ground her when she would prefer to float away. But when the speaker has given the tulips their due in the fifth stanza, she loses her dominance. They take over the rest of the poem, watching her, hauling her into a relation:

> Nobody watched me before, now I am watched.
> The tulips turn to me, and the window behind me
> Where once a day the light slowly widens and slowly thins,
> And I see myself, flat, ridiculous, a cut-paper shadow
> Between the eye of the sun and the eyes of the tulips,
> And I have no face, I have wanted to efface myself.
> The vivid tulips eat my oxygen.

The tulips, which will not be dismissed, have insisted on a triangulation of eyes: the sun's, the flowers' and her own. Although she still protests this as a violation of her desire for autonomy, the speaker can no longer pretend to see everything on only her own terms with her own blank eye, the "stupid pupil" that has to "take everything in." The tulips demand attention. As she gives it, reluctantly, she sees the real danger to her negating imagination: another force, a life both outside and inside her, opposing her will. It warms the walls, animates the tulips, and makes her acknowledge her own grounding in an organic world: "And I am aware of my heart: it opens and closes/ Its bowl of red blooms out of sheer love of me." This pulsating world will not let her go. What resists her will is itself the heart of a great mystery that holds her to itself: "The water I taste is warm and salt, like the sea,/ And comes from a country as far away as health." Thus, the poem ends with nostalgia for the body. The tears are signs of wanting a relation with a living source of love which is the complex dynamic of "health," principally of emotional health. The speaker has been, in spite of her desires for emancipation from materiality, a nuncio for the symbolic imagination that believes in a redeemed eroticism and refuses desperate escapes from the given world.

Emptiness and Plath's relation to it are her unabashed obsessions in the poems of 1961. About two months after "Tulips," Plath wrote "Widow" with the provocative first line: "Widow: The word consumes itself...." Emptiness consumes itself, for "widow," derived form *videre*, means one who is bereft, robbed, voided, destitute, empty, because separated from the source of her fullness. This word for lack of relation sits alone at the beginning of the first stanza which goes on to develop loss as immolation of the "widow's" body, valueless as yesterday's news: "Body, a sheet of newsprint on the fire..../... That will put her heart out like an only eye." The second stanza repeats the theme: "Widow. The dead syllable, with its shadow/ Of an echo...." The searing pain of separation is over, as in Dickinson's poem, #341, which Plath echoes in this exploration of the "formal feeling" resulting loss of relation. As emptied vessel, the word "widow " becomes the metaphor for language that

> ... exposes the panel in the wall
> Behind which the secret panel lies—stale air,
> Fusty remembrances, the coiled-spring stair
> That opens at the top into nothing at all....

The blankness of the present and the rigid, insufficient forms of the past move the desire (which is the poem) out of an old, intricate, yet deadened structure into an undefined space. The self-consuming emptiness then takes up that space:

> Widow. The bitter spider sits
> And sits in the center of her loveless spokes.
> Death is the dress she wears, her hat and collar.

This black widow is not the plucky little spider of "The Manor Garden," or the wounded spirit of "Parliament Hill Fields." This is the "stiff Heart" of Dickinson's poem, after the initial "great pain" when, though impaired by shock, it can still question and function. Plath's poem keeps her desire in this stage, not taking it to Dickinson's "Hour of Lead" and "letting go."

Plath's desire, too insistent to give up, may have to "sit ceremonious," but it will not grow "regardless." She sees and sees in the void, looking for what will suffice, but all the while afraid that her seeing which turns everything into her own vision is a form of death:

> The moth-face of her husband, moonwhite and ill,
> Circles her like a prey she'd love to kill
>
> A second time, to have him near again—
> A paper image to lay against her heart
> The way she laid his letters, till they grew warm
> And seemed to give her warmth, like a live skin.
> But it is she who is paper now, warmed by no one.

Getting a memory into a form for love is what this poem wants to do but cannot. The poem is a "widow," a desire in written language that cannot consummate itself, only consume, that is, destroy or deconstruct itself and everything that comes into its deadly orbit:

> Widow: that great, vacant estate!
> The voice of God is full of draftiness,
> Promising simply the hard stars, the space
> Of immortal blankness between stars
> And no bodies, singing like arrows up to heaven.

This "voice" is the poem's own venting of discontent with vacuity. Plath's unease with her poetic practice sharpens when we hear her as a contrasting echo of Stevens' "Stars at Tallapoosa." In that poem, Stevens celebrates the mind contemplating dark and empty spaces: "there is no body to be seen/ But is an eye that studies its black lid." The unfathomable darkness of the sky is matched in this inward dark: "But in yourself is like:/ A sheaf of brilliant arrows flying straight...." For Stevens, no dark is too dark for his mind to drown in, while Plath is afraid of her dark mind's power. When her poem "Widow" turns toward landscape, trees are vaporized to shadows or "black holes cut out of it," and there is no delight in this dissolution.

Nothing impinges here and that is troubling: "A bodiless soul could pass another soul/ In this clear air and never notice it...." The final stanza boldly states the problem:

> That is the fear she has—the fear
> His soul may beat and be beating at her dull sense
> Like blue Mary's angel, dovelike against a pane
> Blinded to all but the gray, spiritless room
> It looks in on, and must go on looking in on.

Plath is haunted by the doubt that her visionary seeing may be faulty as a one-way view. The one who sits at the center and sees must be powerfully full or she will see only her own pained blankness in the space which her tradition leaves her as its widow.

Plath's poetic worries result from her sense that her gnostic stance is dangerously self-focused. Autonomy as artistic obsession could threaten ordinary life by refusing to acknowledge limits. When Plath accepted that mode of imagination as her inheritance in *The Colossus and Other Poems*, she tried to do so with restraint and care, on a very small scale, as she did in the poems that conclude collection, "Flute Notes from a Reedy Pond" and "The Stones." Plath echoes Stevens "Stars at Tallapoosa" again in just such a restrained effort in one of her finest 1961 poems, "Stars Over the Dordogne." Interestingly, she wrote at the same time "The Rival," a satirical attack on the impulse that makes such an American poem possible. Both poems come from July after Plath and Hughes had spent two weeks vacationing in France, an episode touched on by all three of her biographers. Linda Wagner-Martin says that their time there was "disappointing," but does not say why (SP 191). Anne Stevenson's biography gives a detailed account of the strained social relations between Plath and her hosts, Dido and W. S. Merwin, who found Plath disturbingly possessive of Hughes (BF 215–218). Edward Butscher notes that Plath was upset by her and Hughes' visit on the way to the Merwin's farm to Berck-Plage, a seaside home for ill and crippled Algerian War veterans. Butscher quotes Ted Hughes: "It was one of her nightmares stepped into the real world" (MM 302). The poem "Stars Over the Dordogne" is a welcoming of an empty, clean cold space that the imagination can respond to with its own health—if it is healthy.

In the Stevens poem, the speaker looks at an American night sky and sees not the stars but the lines "straight and swift between the stars." The lines are not singing of the night: "The lines are much too dark and much too sharp." They are singing of the mind's own "simplicity," as the body disappears and poetic insight takes up all the space. This is Stevens' delight, a "pleasure that is all bright edged and cold." In Plath's poem, the speaker looks at a European sky in all its abundance, heaviness, depth and appetite. She is scrupulously attentive in the first stanza, like a tourist making notes:

> Stars are dropping thick as stones into the twiggy
> Picket of trees whose silhouette is darker
> Than the dark of the sky because it is quite starless.
> The woods are a well. The stars drop silently.
> They seem large, yet they drop, and no gap is visible.
> Nor do they send up fires where they fall
> Or any signal of distress or anxiousness.
> They are eaten immediately by the pines.

Fullness, not emptiness, drives the speaker to stop her transcription. She cannot read anything in an abundance that leaves no gaps for her to fill with her own "lines," so in the second stanza, she looks inward and imagines an American sky. She thinks of the sparse, tired stars of home, that arrive, "dulled by much travelling" and humbled by the great spaces. The "smaller and more timid never arrive at all." Thinking of those she cannot see makes the necessary difference so that the speaker can read a little more in those she can. The stars that have not had the hardships of crossing the Atlantic appear above this French river as "self-assured as the great planets." Yet the speaker can make out few patterns and no messages in all their placid splendor. Thus, she returns again to her own imaginings, the remembered stars that are "plain and durable," not wanting "this dressy backcloth/ Or much company, or the mildness of the south." Plath manages to face absence and to create within herself that home-felt, home-created comfort so rare for her:

They are too puritan and solitary for that—
When one of them falls it leaves a space,

A sense of absence in its old shining place.
And where I lie now, back to my own dark star,
I see those constellations in my head,
Unwarmed by the sweet air of this peach orchard.
There is too much ease here; these stars treat me too well.
On this hill, with its view of lit castles, each swung bell
Is accounting for its cow. I shut my eyes
And drink the small night chill like news of home.

Plath clears her seeing by looking inward, as Stevens did, but she wants not the solitary pleasures of her mind, so much as a connection with the world that her sharpening poetic insight affirms. Her American stars are singular and missed; their absence makes their remembered shining an object of desire. As the poem reaches for that clear thing, it refreshes and comforts like a message from a place of sustaining relations—home. Certain stars, their absence, her desire for them set up the old triangulation of love that she had accomplished in earlier poems. Plath clears the air in order to realize what Stevens called in "Evening without Angels," "...our unfashioned spirits realized/ More sharply in more furious selves." The fury is for meaning, for Plath as well as for Stevens, in sufficient poetic form. Plath's speaker does not so much reject the given in "Stars Over the Dordogne," as search for a set of relations that will generate a space for an order of "selves" in her poetry she can read with understanding and delight.

She achieves order in "Stars Over the Dordogne" by keeping her rage for it small and well-behaved, as if obeying Stevens' command in "Puella Parvula": "Keep quiet in the heart, O wild bitch" and let the imagination tell "the human tale." But Plath's poem, "The Rival," shows what energy she was holding in check. This poem is addressed to Plath's muse: the empty O that looks like the moon and leaves "the same impression/ Of something beautiful but annihilating." This is Plath's furious self who makes "stone out of everything," only to destroy it and then remake it to say "something unanswerable." Plath shows no fondness for this force: "Spiteful as a woman, but not so nervous," and not to be ignored. "No day is safe from news of you/ Walking about in Africa, maybe, but thinking of me." Ted Hughes says that this poem was "... leftover from a series specifically about that woman in the moon, the disquieting muse."[3] Plath lets this muse's "O-mouth" which *is* the "rival" speak out in "Wuthering Heights" where the flesh as "grass" is "too delicate/ For life in such company; Darkness terrifies it." Of the frightened, threatened body, this muse as vacancy can only say, as it says of people: "Black stone, black stone." In this vision, communal, bodily life becomes "small change."

The best poem in this vein is "Blackberrying," for it goes as far as it can in accordance with the strict will of Plath's muse: beautiful, annihilating, and unanswerable. Plath begins with that intent focus on things which has become characteristic, a quick look around, a sizing up of the situation in detail, but in the voice of detachment: "Nobody in the lane, and nothing, nothing but blackberries,/ Blackberries on either side, though on the right mainly...." There is not much poetry yet, just notes, some repetitions that move into metaphor in the third line and, finally, into interior rhyme in the fourth: "A blackberry alley, going down in hooks, and a sea/ Somewhere at the end of it, heaving...." There is nothing attractive here, unless it is the absence of people and the suspicion of the indefinite, unseen power of a sea which for Plath, as for almost all her American precursors, is the source of imaginative life. The voice is reportorial, not at all keen on the abundance of berries that seem to beg to be picked. The berries are big and "dumb," silent but also stupid to "squander" their "blue-red juices" on the speaker. Her speculation, "They must love me," carries a note of disdain for bleeding nature, "a blood sisterhood" the speaker does not especially want. Nevertheless, she takes them, but on her own terms: "They accommodate themselves to my milkbottle, flattening their sides." The engagement with nature flags in the second stanza, where the speaker looks at the sky full of "choughs in black, cacophonous flocks...." The berries were too eager to please; the birds, too eager to frustrate: "Theirs is the only voice, protesting, protesting./ I do not think the sea will appear at all." But what else is there? The lushness of the berry bushes becomes an almost unbearable riot of juice-drunk flies:

> Hanging their bluegreen bellies and their wing panes in a
>   Chinese screen.
> The honey feast of the berries has stunned them; they
>   believe in heaven.
> One more hook and the berries and bushes end.

Disdain drips from the speaker's view of the sated flies, stunned into be-lief. The "hook" of the lane, or the hook of the line which the poet writes, brings this blind, dumb, and too-satisfied scene to an end. The speaker wants the open, even corrosive, sea and must struggle against a "sudden wind" that "funnels" at her: "Snapping its phantom laundry in my face." The place of force is still out of sight: "These hills are too green and sweet to have tasted salt." The voice is not at home in sweetness and must move on:

> ...A last hook brings me
> To the hills' northern face, and the face is orange rock
> That looks out on nothing, nothing but a great space
> Of white and pewter lights, and a din like silversmiths
> Beating and beating at an intractable metal.

There is relief in reaching this freedom from relation. Until now, every-thing the speaker imagined had accommodated itself to her or had ad-dressed her: the berries loved her, the birds warned her, the flies showed how nature might satisfy, the wind bullied her to keep her in the green, sweet place. But the lane of hooks has its own insistence, like Eliot's lane in the beginning of "East Coker," that takes his speaker to a place of heat and light, a place to imagine. Plath wants that, too, and so she keeps hooking letter to letter, word to word, image to image, in the belief that there must be a place to get to where the mind can know something unrestrained and limitless. Plath's mind wants freedom, but most especially, freedom from itself. Like Eliot, Plath wants her poetry to attest to something beyond her own fabrications, something true and unanswerable. Thus, her poetry must be more than enactment of a mood.

In Eliot, the unanswerable is the "nexus of terror and desire;"[4] in Plath, the image that astounds or wounds or both, in the name of the muse. In "Blackberrying," Plath is writing what Robert Graves called "muse po-etry" which comes from "the back of the mind" and delivers a frisson that only "fearful or supernatural" experiences can.[5] Sufficiently stunned, Plath, too, might believe in something beyond herself. There, in that great blank of space and light, nature falls away, leaving the speaker to con-template in awe the power that drives her beyond limits. Does she achieve the sublimity she seems to seek? The dauntless "din" of the sea heard amidst those "white and pewter lights" has all the wildness and unsponsored force the negating imagination could ask for. This could be Plath's grand echo of Stevens' lines from "Man on the Dump": "One beats and beats for that which one believes/ That's what one wants to get near." For Stevens, that is himself as "invisible priest." Plath's poem, however, does not end with a matching of her words and will, but instead avoids that transparency at the very last moment. The sea as the forging imagination beats unseen at the base of the cliff's blank face without dissolving that edge of the given world. The closing metallic image shines, but not as a clear light. "Blackberrying" ends in an opacity, for the final effect is an obstinate, impenetrable luster. Light and sound do not clarify: they stun. Does such seeing satisfy Plath?

A dark and troubling answer comes in "The Moon and the Yew Tree," written in October of 1961. Plath wrote the poem on assignment given by Hughes. She "insisted that it was an exercise on a theme," but Hughes felt depressed by it, reading it as "a statement from the powers in control of [Plath's] life."[6] Plath, too, must have been distressed by the darkness in her art, but also exhilarated by its original power. There is no necessity for calling Plath's poetry an image of her desire as her "true self," as opposed to a "false self," especially when there is much evidence that she tried to keep her time with her muse and her time with her family separate. Plath's personal life was very full, and at times very difficult, but from most accounts, she had a talent for domesticity.[7] As a poet, however, Plath's interior paramour was a terribly weird sister that Judith Kroll has well documented as Robert Graves' sinister moon goddess. Kroll has read Plath's poetry as a personal myth, a secular scripture, that Plath wrote to give her life coherence and meaning. My study argues that Plath's poetry contains a critique of that gnostic practice, not a subversion of that mode but a way to see its energies in relation to life structured by mutual relations in the actual, social and familial world. Plath needed that harbor in which to anchor. Her social self was not false but fragile and flawed by emotional illness, and at risk when sustaining relations gave way or when she feared they might. For a poet like Plath, actual survival would depend on trust in an unwilled, daily life responsive to the life-in-the-flesh-needs of people who loved her and whom she loved: husband, children, extended family, friends. Such activity requires enormous physical and emotional stamina, neither of which she had ever had in large measure. The year

1961 had been one of great physical and emotional strain. Her poem "Last Words" finished the day before "The Moon and the Yew Tree" extols the comfort of material objects by a speaker who sounds very tired and who would like to sleep a long time. Put to rest in a royal Egyptian sarcophagus, the speaker seeks from things other than herself a comfort that her own spirit never gives her:

> I do not trust the spirit. It escapes like steam
> In dreams, through mouth hole or eye-hole. I can't stop it.
> One day it won't come back. Things aren't like that
> They stay in their little particular lusters
> Warmed by much handling....
>
> ... the shine of these small things sweeter than the face of
> Ishtar.

Ishtar in the ancient myth goes into the underworld to rescue her brother-lover, Tammuz. Sweeter than resurrection or rebirth are the hand-warmed things loved during a singular life, says the speaker in this poem, who chooses them over all other desirous forms her spirit might make.

In "The Moon and the Yew Tree" the reader listens to Plath's spirit trying to delineate the nature of its making. This had been Plath's concern since her Smith College days. The poems of The Colossus brought her gnostic imagination to the fore. The poems of 1960–61 extend that awareness, but in a continuing dialectic with Plath's human need for a tradition that validates or creates the self in relation to the given world that resists and refines the solitary will. We see that need defeated in "The Moon and the Yew Tree," although it is a search for clarity via the poet's own light. The speaker begins with all the gravity of a dead star.

> This is the light of the mind, cold and planetary.
> The trees of the mind are black. The light is blue.
> The grasses unload their griefs on my feet as if I were God,
> Prickling my ankles and murmuring of their humility.
> Fumy, spiritous mists inhabit this place

> Separated from my house by a row of headstones.
> I simply cannot see where there is to get to.

The second line which introduces "trees" jars the reader's expectation by opening a gap between the first trope for the mind of starry wandering and the second one of the fixity of its contents. Each gap marks a new turn in the pattern of tropes that make the poem. What is being imagined about the poet's acts of the mind in these spaces? Plath's blue light, like the blue volts in "The Hanging Man," descends from Shelley and Stevens and many other poets who took blue or azure as the color word for the imagination. In "The Moon and the Yew Tree," there is something metallic in Plath's "blue." Each poetic line crackles like another jolt of electricity delivering another disjunction. After the fixed and inanimate trees, the reader is asked to look at personified grasses, a pathetic fallacy that disrupts a movement toward a unifying image. Like the berries in "Blackberrying," organic nature leans to the speaker as if there were a loving hierarchical relation between them. The speaker disclaims such mutuality; she is irritated by the suffering and obsequious grass, a term Plath has used before in "Wuthering Heights" for delicate, perishable flesh. The speaker also disclaims any resemblance to "God." She is, rather, an agitated spirit of a region cut off from "my house." Another troubled speaker had entered "the lit house" at the end of "Parliament Hill Fields" in a movement toward sustaining relations in the given world. In this later poem, such a maneuver is blocked by "headstones," irrefutable evidence of death. If fixity could be broken, as it was in "The Stones," the poem could perhaps at least hope to "house" the rose of incarnate love, but the speaker in "The Moon and the Yew Tree" does not have the strength to pulverize the barriers set up against her: "I simply cannot see where there is to get to." In this frank admission of weakness the speaker finds her theme and thus continues her erratic scrutiny of her conditions:

> The moon is no door. It is a face in its own right,
> White as a knuckle and terribly upset.
> It drags the sea after it like a dark crime; it is quiet
> With the O-gape of complete despair. I live here.
> Twice in Sunday, the bells startle the sky—

Eight great tongues affirming the Resurrection.
At the end, they soberly bong out their names.

The moon limits the speaker's poetic power, for she cannot make the moon be what she wants, a redeemer who says knock and it shall open, ask and you shall receive. The moon's mass is no way to a more abundant life, for it coldly resists her needs, as she resisted those of the grasses. Thus, she can only look at its face, not beyond it. Though "face" suggests an autonomous presence, it also suggests artifice, an exposed surface that is prepared or fashioned in some way. "Face" is also a surface that receives ink and transfers it to paper. The moon is a face that prints out, that is, makes visible and readable a particular anguish. The speaker's blue imagination is informed by the moon's hopeless emptiness. Worse, this vacancy is the place in which the speaker resides, not in the "house" beyond the gravestones which could be a place for love as *agape*, but in the imagination governed by despair in the familiar shape of grief: "the O-gape." Lack of love, which is lack of relation, prevents the speaker from hearing any message in the bells. The shift from visual to aural imagery is another disjunction that, like the bells, startles rather than comforts. The speaker tells what the bells tell but with no flicker of finding a paternal relation in their sounds which are endured, not understood. Plath used this perception in her 1962 short story, "The Mothers," written a few months after this poem. When the carillons pounded the countryside, there was for the narrator "no escape from the probing notes" (JP 13), yet they make her feel "left out, as if from some fine local feast" (13). The speaker in "The Moon and the Yew Tree" is similarly on the outside of shared belief. In silence, the speaker finds her true familial tie:

The yew tree points up. It has a Gothic shape.
The eyes lift after it and find the moon.
The moon is my mother.

This seems a moment of clarification toward which the poem has been erratically, coldly moving. In the American tradition of Whitman and Stevens, the moon-mother, night and death formed a complex of romantic images for tender feelings. Plath distinctly echoes the first line of Stevens' "Lunar Paraphrase," "The moon is the mother of pathos and pity." Plath, however, reverses this possibility:

> ... She is not sweet like Mary
> Her blue garments unloose small bats and owls.
> How I would like to believe in tenderness—
> The face of the effigy, gentled by candles,
> Bending, on me in particular, its mild eyes.

Death, the night, the mother, the moon-muse and her control of the speaker—all are terrifying presences for Plath. They are, however, empowering, and the speaker, in her weakness, needs power of some kind, even if dark. The "face" of Plath's form of the imagination becomes more sinister in the term "effigy," which can name a crude, finger-formed image of a hated thing. Although surrounded by three words for tenderness, "gentled," "Bending," and "Mild," the effigy or face of the speaker's muse is not softened by the mere proximity of warm images. The candles' warm energy does not penetrate the realm of this poem. Here, the only power is negative: the poet's cold, blue "light of the mind." The only thing it illuminates in the scene is the vacant mother whose "blue garments" yield creatures designed for the dark. The poem is the face of despair printed out. Its eyes are the speaker's eyes, and they are not mild.

The poem's final stanza reaches an ironic clarification. Instead of enlightenment, the speaker accepts her sphere of limitation, which is a place for making her own forms:

> I have fallen a long way. Clouds are flowering
> Blue and mystical over the face of the stars.
> Inside the church, the saints will be all blue,
> Floating on their delicate feet over the cold pews,
> Their hands and faces stiff with holiness.
> The moon sees nothing of this. She is bald and wild.
> And the message of the yew tree is blackness—
>   blackness and silence.

The speaker's poetic vision cannot achieve the beatitude of transparency or identity in either the meaningful sound of the bells or the warm light of candles. Nevertheless, the speaker resists for as long as she can being pulled into a total lack of seeing and lack of sound which will mark the end of the poem. In the space left for her to imagine, she figures the inside of the church in her peculiar cold blue which clouds rather than clarifies the face of her fate. The only structure the "I" of this poem can enter is its own written words, a flow of desire Plath had called in "The Burnt Out Spa" the stream "that neither nourishes nor heals."

"The Moon and the Yew Tree" is a dark, satirical riposte to such affirmations of imaginative faith as Stevens' "Final Soliloquy of the Interior Paramour,"

> Within its vital boundary, in the mind.
> We say God and the imagination are one.
> How high that highest candle lights the dark.
>
> Out of this same light, out of the central mind,
> We make a dwelling in the evening air,
> In which being there together is enough.

In certain moods, Stevens could find all he needed within himself. Plath almost never could, for her mind is burdened with its charge. Her solitary poetic light neither beckons nor clarifies nor comforts. This is what sets her apart and what makes her a strange, disturbing, yet important poet who attains her own kind of poetic success.

Endnotes

[1]This count follows the selections of the editors of the *Collected Poems* (1982).

[2]I am indebted to Diann Blakely Shoaf for the insight "premature nostalgia," although her reading of "In Plaster" differs from mine in her essay "Thinking Back Through Our Mothers: Emily Dickinson and Contemporary Women's Poetry." Unpublished essay. 1987.

[3]Ted Hughes, "The Chronological Order of Sylvia Plath's Poems," *The Art of Sylvia Plath: A Symposium,* ed., Charles Newman (Bloomington: Indiana UP, 1970) 194.

[4]Denis Donoghue. Lecture. "T. S. Eliot." NYU. 19 December 1984.

[5]Robert Graves, "The Dedicated Poet" quoted in Judith Kroll, *Chapters in a Mythology* 221.

[6]Kroll quotes both Plath and Hughes, *Chapters in a Mythology* 43.

[7]Linda Wagner-Martin's biography offers evidence, especially in Chapter 13, "The Devon Life," SP 188–198. Anne Stevenson's, *Bitter Fame,* gives more evidence of Plath's pathological state and disturbing behavior during her last years, but this book also reveals Plath's efforts to make an enduring family in which she could be grounded. Plath's poetry alone gives only a glimpse of the actual woman who took pleasure in cooking, sewing, decorating, gardening, conversing and in the physical, affectionate presence of her husband and children. Her journals as well leave out much of her normal life experiences which she did have, in spite of her emotional extremes.

5

Dissolving to the Bone:
Poems of 1962–1963

Plath's first poem of 1961, "Parliament Hill Fields," resisted the impulse to be "too happy" in the face of loss, that is, too gaily self-inventing. Her speaker turned instead toward the "dregs and difficulties" of maternal and conjugal life. In the last line, the speaker enters a dwelling place, a "lit house" full of real things and a living child. The year 1962 began for Plath with the birth of her son Nicholas, and work on her verse play "Three Women" (CP 176–187) for the BBC. The drama consists of three monologues in counterpoint by women who experience pregnancy and childbirth. The First Voice gives birth to a wanted child and joyfully takes on her maternal role: motherhood totally absorbs her. The Second Voice asserts she wants a child, but miscarries, and not for the first time: she is filled with conflicting emotions. The Third Voice gives birth to an unwanted child whom she abandons. Empty by choice, she voices a strong will defying all claims on her.

The First Voice celebrates what Plath would call later, "the clearest thing I own," the love between mother and child: "What did my fingers do before they held him?/ What did my heart do with its love?/ I have never seen a thing so clear." She obeys the imperatives of both her body and the child's: "One cry. It is the hook I hang on./ I am a river of milk./ I am a warm hill." In such a relation, her energies will sustain the nurturing bond for as long as possible, though she knows the time will come when her body no longer can be the source of her child's well-being: "How long can I be/ Gentling the sun with the shade of my hand,/ Intercepting the blue bolts of a cold moon?" The First Voice is awed by the depth of her feeling which she believes must be clearly visible: "It is a terrible thing to be so open: it is as if my heart put on a face and walked into the world." Made capable by love which is a gift from the body, the First Voice wishes that the son be ordinary, that he "love me as I love him," and that she may enable him to love a woman so fully that he will leave her one day to "marry what he wants and where he will."

Weaving in and out of the First Voice's celebration of maternity is the Second Voice's lament for vacuity. She speculates that her emptiness is a sign of her deepest allegiances:

> ... Am I a pulse
> That wanes and wanes, facing the cold angel?
> Is this my lover then? This death, this death?
> As a child I loved a lichen-bitten name.
> Is this the one sin then, this old dead love of death?

She loves, not the flesh, but a lost ideal of perfection. The troubling and problematic Second Voice demands the reader's attention, for she has the closing lines of the play. Having confessed her limitations as best she can and feeling helpless but not hopeless in the face of them, she "wait[s] and ache[s]" in the last scene, at home with her husband: "And so we are at home together, after hours./ It is only time that weighs upon our hands./ It is only time, and that is not material." The dilemma of the Second Voice is that she knows she lacks an abundant life and she knows she cannot will it. An idea dominates her but a vital potential dies in her over and over.

The Third Voice in Plath's play refuses domination of any kind. She does not know what she wants, but she rejects what has been given to her, seeing only in the given "dangers: doves and words,/ Stars and showers of gold—conceptions, conceptions!" She is outraged by cause and effect: "every little word hooked to every little word, and act to act." The Third Voice resists her fate, blaming male doctors "for what I am," as she nears the end of her term: "I am not ready for anything to happen./ I should have murdered this, that murders me." She murders her past, for after giving birth and preparing to leave the hospital without her newborn daughter, she says: "There are the clothes of the fat woman I do not know." She departs: "I leave my health behind. I leave someone/ Who would adhere to me: I undo her fingers like bandages: I go." The will to be solitary and autonomous wins. After watching the landscape shimmer to white lights and clouds, she asks in her final line: "What is it I miss?" Hers is the voice of a will so strong that it represses the ordeal of separation from a human source of love into a blank of forgetfulness. Out of that vacancy, the reader suspects, will come something of the Third Voice's own powerful imaginings.

This refusal of the given contrasts with the First Voice's strongly felt acceptance of necessity: "I do not have to think, or even rehearse./ What happens in me will happen without attention.... Leaves and petals attend me. I am ready." She has no need to re-invent her fate. The Third Voice does and will. The Second Voice, then, is the most anguished of all three: "I have had my chances. I have tried and tried." She has tried to do everything right: "I have tried not to think too hard. I have tried to be natural." She lacks the unquestioning, obedient responses to life of the First Voice, but she also lacks the powerful will of the Third. The First Voice gives herself up to nature completely; the Third resists it just as completely. The Second Voice speaks as distressed self-consciousness: "I have tried to be blind in love, like other women,/ Blind in my bed, with my dear blind sweet one,/ Not looking, through the thick dark, for the face of another."

The Second Voice does, however, look for the face of perfection because that is what she really wants: "The face of the dead one that could only be perfect/ In its easy peace, could only keep holy so." This speaker becomes frightening here, more so than the Third Voice who gives up her child. The Third Voice knows she wants nothing to do with restraints of any kind, but the Second Voice cannot see her own negating imaginative power except by projecting it on others: "It is these men I mind:/ They are jealous of anything that is not flat! They are jealous gods/ that would have the whole world flat because they are." When the Second Voice imagines God saying: "Let us flatten and launder the grossness from these souls," she is giving form to her own obsessions which she has uneasily sensed as a gnostic distaste for the messiness of the flesh and an attraction to abstractions. The light of her mind is that same "blue, moony ray" of the speaker in "The Moon and the Yew Tree" complete with the O-gape and the sea: "I feel it enter me, cold, alien, like an instrument./ And that mad, hard face at the end of it, that O-mouth.... I am helpless as the sea at the end of her string...." Because she can neither fully engage life nor fully re-imagine it, the Second Voice vows to "be a heroine of the peripheral." She endures rather than defies time as she attends to things: sewing on buttons, mending socks, answering letters. No amount of attention to duties, to her own impeccable behavior and appearance will bring into being what she lacks: a living source of love which is not herself. She has a husband, but he seems less powerful than the absences that define her: a dead father or lover ("a lichen bitten name"); her dead children ("the little emptinesses I carry"). Her mind cannot console itself by creating, as Wallace Stevens' "mind of winter" could, a metaphor demonstrating that even the negating imagination can create one's fit with the world. In "a world of snow," says the Second Voice, "I am not at home." Plath's Second Voice waits for something other than her own fictions.

Sandra Gilbert has suggested that the Second Voice parallels Virginia Woolf's character Rhoda in *The Waves*, just as Plath's First Voice echoes Woolf's maternal Susan and Plath's Third Voice, Woolf's seductive Jinny.[1] Woolf's influence on Plath in this play and in the subsequent *Ariel* poems, which is indisputable, leads Plath, in Gilbert's view, to freeing herself, finally, in 1962 to explore the "'I am I' of female identity." Gilbert emphasizes, however, that poetic freedom for Plath is an exploration of "limited options" (218). Plath's three voices, like Woolf's, represent "the qualified power of maternity, the powerlessness of metaphysical consciousness, and the pseudo-power of seductive indifference" (218). Gilbert does not show just how Plath gave in *Three Women* her own version of Woolf, but Gilbert argues that, after this verse play, Plath became "the person she most feared and desired to be": the terrible queen bee of "Stings," the voracious self-resurrected woman in "Lady Lazarus," the glamorous murderess of "Purdah," the fierce virgin of "Fever 103°" (220). I would say that Plath became in these particular poems not a "person" but a creative surge in a form that she, as a person, had every reason to fear. Gilbert does not acknowledge that the speakers in these poems are visionaries with a "gnostic hatred of nature," yet aware that there is "no saving gnosis."[2] Gilbert and her colleague Susan Gubar favor the woman poet who recreates language "as a landscape, not of someone else's authority, but of her own desire."[3] This is the creed of ego-centered romanticism that asserts its essential rightness by breaking old forms and making new ones as acts of self-generated identity. In my readings that follow, I will question what this perspective calls the "triumph of identity" in Plath's late poetry, and will argue that we need to read Plath in yet another way. The Second Voice in *Three Women*, which echoes Woolf's Rhoda, can help form a fresh understanding of Plath's last poetry, the work of 1962–63. First, I will show how Plath revises Woolf's Rhoda.

In *The Waves*, Rhoda is a woman who keenly senses her unnaturalness. Unlike Susan who loves bodies maternally, and Jinny who loves bodies promiscuously (though not lasciviously), Rhoda loves what she cannot touch. Early in the novel, she seems to want another person: "I will give, I will enrich, I will return to the world this beauty.... Oh! to whom?" (57). Her subjectivity as desire cannot reach across the space between her and other people to make a satisfying relation that might reveal her to herself. When Rhoda cannot cross a puddle, she explains, "Identity failed me. We are nothing, I said and fell" (64). Rhoda is the supersensual who is wounded by desire but unable to be healed by human love. The following passages of Rhoda's monologue were underlined by Plath in her personal copy of *The Waves:* [4]

> The door opens and the tiger leaps ... I am afraid of the shock of sensation that leaps upon me, because I cannot deal with it as you do—I cannot make one moment merge in the next. To me they are all violent, all separate; and if I fall under the shock of the leap of the moment you will be on me, tearing me to pieces. I have no end in view. I do not know how to run minute to minute and hour to hour, solving them by some natural force until they make the whole world an indivisible mass you call life.... And I have no face.... (130) Yet there are moments when the walls of the mind grow thin; when nothing is unabsorbed, and I could fancy that we might take the blue of midday and the black of midnight and be cast off and escape from here and now.... [Plath not only underlines, she also stars this.] (224). The still mood, the disembodied mood is on us ... and we enjoy this momentary alleviation.... (228).

Rhoda had wanted to love a real person, but she is both intimidated by and unsatisfied with the actual. She wants a perfect relation, a vision she gets after the death of Percival, the central event for all the characters in the novel. Initially, his death is for Rhoda the shock of a "lightning flash" which leaves her "alone in a hostile world" to be terrorized and humiliated. Depressed by grief, Rhoda sees how "hideous" the human face can be: "faces and faces, served out like soup-plates by scullions; coarse, greedy, casual ... destroying everything..." (160). But upon hearing a woman singing in a music hall, Rhoda's vision is both cleaved and cleaned in a moment of poetic insight. She feels its given nature as a blow from an axe which

> ... split a tree to the core; the core is warm; sound quivers within the bark.... She has provided us with a cry. But only a cry. And what is a cry?... Now that lightning has gashed the tree and the flowering branch has fallen and Percival, by his death, has made me this gift, let me see the thing (163).

Rhoda sees a "perfect dwelling place" which she describes as "a square placed on an oblong" (163). This is an image of metaphor or, more specifically, of belief that meaning is generated by intuiting the similarities between two different things without abolishing their difference. The two geometric shapes relate in Rhoda's vision, but not so that their duality disappears and can be transcended. Rather, they allow Rhoda to perceive the split reference which is the creative core of metaphor.[5] The abstract forms place before Rhoda's eyes the meaning of metaphor: emotion transformed by seeing the similarities between dissimilars yields a place for the human mind to both think and feel its reality. This structuring of the mind is, in Rhoda's flash of insight, a "dwelling place," and that place is "our triumph" and "our consolation" (163). She affirms the human ability to create in the face of death relations which are beautiful and true and which death does not destroy. To this creative power she wants to give herself as a lover: "Now I will relinquish, now I will let loose. Now I will at last free the checked, the jerked back desire to be spent, to be consumed" (164). To be so smitten by an abstraction—an essence or mere theory—drives Rhoda to suicide. Rhoda cannot perceive the "dwelling place" in her lived relations to others as Susan and Jinny in their different ways can. Neither can Rhoda live with the "as if" of metaphoric fiction. If fictions urge us to desire new desires, Rhoda rejects such an endless pursuit because she has seen the end of desire: she has seen it perfectly abstracted and she cannot settle for less. Life's meaning remained for Rhoda only a vision, something seen, not touched, given her in rare moments of disembodied "alleviation" (228) from the anxiety of a quotidian life which became, finally, for this faceless, timid woman, intolerable. Woolf's Rhoda killed herself because she found no way to reconcile the hostile world, her own gnostic tendencies, and her visionary knowledge of a beautiful truth that was not a thing, but a relation, and not willed, but given.

Plath's Second Voice in *Three Women* evolves from Rhoda. Like her, the Second Voice wants more than her own inventions, and she is frustrated in her need. She fears some vacuous thing in her is more powerful than the life she tries to bear. This is her own "love of death," or perfection, a power which is the "vampire of us all." The Second Voice lives with the terrible suspicion that she is a killer and perhaps not against but in accordance with her solitary will. Leaving the hospital, she bitterly laments having "no attachments" and mocks her reflection in store windows:

> So neat she is transparent, like a spirit.
> How shyly she superimposes her neat self
> On the inferno of African oranges, the heel-hung pigs.
> She is deferring to reality.
> It is I. It is I—
> Tasting the bitterness between my teeth.
> The incalculable malice of the everyday.

The Second Voice cannot console herself with fictions, obsessed as she is with only one object of desire, an absolutely true one. Thus, the world grows intolerable along with the desiring self that wants what it cannot will and does not get. Plath, however, concludes her play allowing for a new possibility in the Second Voice that Woolf never conceded to Rhoda.

Rhoda's imaginings turn to "a thin dream ... a papery tree" (64). She cannot achieve the transparency of identity, "we are nothing, I said, and fell" (64), nor can she live with the given: "All palpable forms of life have failed me" (159). Neville, her friend, calls her a "fasting and anguished spirit" (197), one who "flies with her neck outstretched and blind fanatic eyes, past us" (198), "Rhoda, with her intense abstraction..." (200). Rhoda confesses her asceticism: "Life, how I have dreaded you... I have been stained by you and corrupted" (203). As she travels toward a rendezvous with the others, she imagines, blissfully, she is dying: "The lumps in the mattress soften beneath me... Everything falls in a tremendous shower, dissolving me" (206).

The final stanza of *Three Women* strongly echoes Rhoda's words in the dissolution of the world to papery images, in the fall after the failure to cross an expanse, and in the comfort of the mattress as a place to die. But Plath just as strongly re-imagines Rhoda, for the Second Voice recovers from the fall, resists the allure of dissolution and endures the pain of recovery.

> The streets may turn to paper suddenly, but I recover
> From the long fall, and find myself in bed,
> Safe on the mattress, hands braced, as for a fall.
> I find myself again. I am no shadow
> Though there is a shadow starting from my feet. I am a
> wife.
> The city waits and aches. The little grasses
> Crack through stone, and they are green with life.

Plath ends her play with a potentially life-denying ascetic in a conjugal relation; the fact of marriage and its possibility keep her facing the natural and the social world. Rhoda's mystic vision is for Plath's Second Voice a living couple: man and wife and the tenderness between them.

> I am at home in the lamplight. The evenings are lengthening.
> I am mending a silk slip: my husband is reading.
> How beautifully the light includes these things.
> There is a kind of smoke in the spring air,
> A smoke that takes the parks, the little statues
> With pinkness, as if a tenderness awoke,
> A tenderness that did not tire, something healing.

The "city" is, then, not the city of the will, as it was in Plath's poem "The Stones," but of the civilized mind that reads the world so that the structure of love, like the structure of metaphor, is perceived, felt as attunement, not as mere abstraction. Plath understood this redemptive power in humanist terms: "tenderness" was Krook's secular equivalent for the Holy Spirit. Plath concludes her play on the note of hope that such a spirit joins the man and the woman. Her effort is a brave one, but the Second Voice is still willing more than she is believing in that "dwelling place" in her own home and in the larger community. The play ends more with a spell, "Let this be," than with an affirmation, "This is."

Plath's Second Voice is as fragile as Woolf's Rhoda and just as repelled by fate. Both are kept from flying out of this world by the bonds of human relations, though Woolf's narrative lets the reader know that Rhoda eventually slipped free of them. Though Plath keeps the Second Voice firmly married, this wife's intensity is focused on what she does not have, children, not what she has, her husband. She is unable to live in the world with passionate, erotic belief, simply because she lacks too much; but neither can she overcome the world and her lack with passionate, gnostic defiance, simply because she does not want to invent. She wants (desires, lacks) the real, which is relation, and she does not believe she can actualize that with her solitary will to power. She must live patiently, obediently, trusting the human ties that keep her from dissolving the world into forms of her negating imagination, or dissolving herself into a shadow, falling, as Rhoda did in her dearest dream, "off the edge of the earth" (223). What kind of poetry can emerge from this stance? This is Plath's dilemma as a poet in 1962.

Plath knew she was marginal to the white heat of "doing" love in the Jamesian sense. Her Journals of that year attest to this: they have changed from intense introspection into a kind of spying on the world from which she is distanced. From that position, she can attack what is wrong, but she cannot create what is right, because she cannot repress strongly enough the fate she fears—the death of love in the fragility of human life. When the imagination confronts death and denies such fate's sufficiency, it can, if a powerful enough negation, revise that doom in sublime explorations of human potential. Plath praised the "hair-raising firmness" (J 165) of the last fifty pages of *The Waves* and underlined the closing lines of Bernard's long meditation as he recovers from depression and mourning: "<u>Death is the enemy. It is death against whom I ride with my spear couched and my hair flying back like a young man's.... I strike spurs into my horse. Against you I will fling myself, unvanquished and unyielding, O Death!</u>" (297).

In certain moods, Plath would try to do the same, but as the earlier chapters of this study have shown, she was afraid of her negating imagination, for it worked against her deepest need. That need was, I believe, not to defy death but to redeem her erotic sense. She did come to know that soundness of mind and body, at least for a time, in her marriage to Ted Hughes. Plath experienced as well the satisfying love of a mother for her young children whose well-being depended on her physical and emotional responsiveness to their needs. These relations affirmed the rightness and the richness of the given world which included her relation to others. This belief underlies the tradition of the symbolic imagination and casts the negating, gnostic imagination, at least for Plath, in a sinister role. I see a conflict of modes of imagination in Plath's poetry, not a "battle of the sexes" as Sandra Gilbert called Plath's internalized war (216). Plath's struggle reveals the two different ways of using language imaginatively.

One way Plath affirmed the symbolic imagination was to keep within her poems elements that resisted her will, or seemed to, such as the inscrutable alien crabs in "Mussel Hunter at Rock Harbor," the glow-in-the-dark child's picture in "Parliament Hill Fields," the nursing infant in "Morning Song," and the gift of red flowers in "Tulips." Such palpable, stubborn things will not allow the speaker to "have no face," a line from "Tulips" taken out of Rhoda's monologue in *The Waves*. Their opacity baffles gnostic desires to have everything on one's own terms as an expression of individual will. They will not dissolve, and thus they keep Plath facing them, not a transparent image for a sublime "self."

Many of Plath's poems of 1962 strive for opacity as a way of staying within the given. Only when human relations break down does she write her strongest and most furious poetry of the negating imagination. Those poems want to dissolve all limitations on their drive for poetic victory. Plath's gnostic mode is skewed, however, by a vengeance that results from her marginal stance as the "heroine of the peripheral." At the edge, not at the center, her unleashed desire sees its discontents too clearly to be able to repress them strongly enough for transumption. Plath transforms the given with corrosives only to make a stubborn skeleton visible. She etches on "intractable metal" the horrors of the solitary and arbitrary will, for, like other satirists, she wants to wound. Refusing to dissolve the pain of human existence, she insists on keeping present, that is metaphorically powerful, what is wrong with human will, thus making a satiric triumph out of her refusal of gnostic "identity."

The poems of 1962 chronicle the breakdown of Plath's marriage to Ted Hughes. To study Plath's most original works ignoring this biographical context would be unthinkable. Also, we must remember that Plath's muse is kin to Stevens' moony one but colder. Plath's is the metallic blue or stony Medusa-moon, the mother of "blackness and silence." Because Plath knows the dark side of the negating imagination, she can only use that power to say what it is not, and thus to affirm obliquely what is beyond her will to transform: human nature with its flawed and conflicting wills, and the human need of the body and of others in the search for what is true.

Why should Plath's imagination have found negation its most powerful expression? Plath asks the same question of herself, as she tried, as Woolf did in *The Waves*, "to uncover those hidden moments that dominate memory and shape development."[6] The poem which follows *Three Women* in Plath's *Collected Poems* is just such a probe. Written in April of 1962 when Plath sensed her husband's disaffection, "Little Fugue" is the first of several poems dealing with anxiety and death written in April and May of that year. The title suggests not only the interweaving of voices in a musical arrangement, but also the state of disturbed consciousness in which a person performs acts of which she appears to be conscious, but which she will not recollect when she recovers. The poem mimes disconnection. Things move in and out of proximity, but they do not relate and thus do not form any meaningful charge that helps a "self" become a reading soul. The speaker begins in proper romantic fashion, looking at nature, but the view is bleak:

> The yew's black fingers wag;
> Cold clouds go over.
> So the deaf and dumb
> Signal the blind and are ignored.

The yew tree is deaf and dumb; the clouds are blind. Because they do not touch, nothing proceeds from one to the other. A signaling system is at work, but without a receiver there is no shared meaning. What is the speaker to do with this state of affairs? She can exert her own power over blankness and declare she finds this satisfying:

> I like black statements.
> The featureless of that cloud, now!
> White as an eye all over!
> The eye of the blind pianist
>
> At my table on the ship.
> He felt for his food.
> His fingers had the noses of weasels.
> I couldn't stop looking.

The facetiousness in Plath's tone is unmistakable. The speaker is merely doing what tradition would have her do in the romantic lyric's drama of empirical loss and imaginative gain. This is Woolf's motive in *The Waves*. The moments of being Plath's speaker recollects in her dutiful turn toward memory are horrors, in a nightmare sequence in which fingers—long a Plathian metonymy for poetic making—become little predators:

> He could hear Beethoven:
> Black yew, white cloud,
> The horrific complications.
> Finger-traps—a tumult of keys.

There are at least two ways the artist can make a connection between separate voices that do not speak to each other but which both speak to her. She may intuit the similarities in their differences and make a metaphor which yields a satisfying image of her affective and intellectual relation to them; or she may refuse the metaphor in order to keep one voice or image from becoming "like" the other in the comparison. If so, she may be able to keep them in fugal tension, asserting their individual patterns to each other. The doubleness of the fugue will be a "trap" if the artist cannot hear and perform two melodic patterns simultaneously. If she can, she makes musical sense of incongruities. Plath's speaker admires such skill: "I envy the big noises/ The yew hedge of the Grosse Fugue." There is something to be heard and understood. Here the poem, if it were to be a romantic crisis lyric, would turn out again toward that desired compensatory gain of insight, but that does not happen. The speaker shifts her focus from blindness to deafness, and is pulled through an aperture into another memory which the reader can understand as the fugue of disturbed consciousness:

> Deafness is something else.
> Such a dark funnel, my father!
> I see your voice
> Black and leafy, as in my childhood,
>
> A yew hedge of orders,
> Gothic and barbarous, pure German.
> Dead men cry from it.
> I am guilty of nothing.

The speaker falls through the funnel of silence. Like Rhoda unable to cross the puddle, the speaker is unable to cross the abyss of loss which is "my father." The phrase seems more an appositive than an apostrophe. He is the gap that articulates a sequence of images from which she is distanced. Her denial of metaphoric connection with his authority as "yew hedge" is made to seem a betrayal in the next stanza:

> The yew my Christ, then.
> Is it not as tortured?
> And you, during the Great War
> In the California delicatessen
>
> Lopping off sausages!
> They color my sleep,
> Red, mottled, like cut necks.
> There was a silence!

The blind yew is silent before its accusers, like Christ. The father, imagined as a butcher, but not a Nazi or a killer, is just as silent before the speaker's address and her perhaps unfair recollection of him:

> Great silence of another order.
> I was seven, I knew nothing.
> The world occurred.
> You had one leg and a Prussian mind.
>
> Now similar clouds
> Are spreading their vacuous sheets.
> Do you say nothing?
> I am lame in the memory.

All Plath's speaker can manage in the way of connection with the lost, silent father are distinct figures of speech, a synecdoche and a metonymy, which, like disparate and fleeting fugal forms, she tries to present as a meaningful contrapuntal order of sound. How brief a performance!

> I remember a blue eye,
> A briefcase of tangerines.
> This was a man, then!
> Death opened, like a black tree, blackly.

The effort to play both patterns collapses into an even greater silence which ends the sequence of recollection. The last stanza should affirm the imaginative gain which traditionally results from facing and triumphing over loss. All Plath's speaker can say is that she is still alive:

> I survive the while,
> Arranging my morning.
> These are my fingers, this my baby.
> The clouds are a marriage dress, of that pallor.

The speaker does not remember her efforts to recollect the series of images of her father, or her failed effort to perform his parts into a unity. This seems so because the echo of "fingers" harkens back to the yew tree of the first stanza and the blind pianist's Grosse Fugue before the speaker's fall into "something else." Her use of "while" in the last stanza suggests, rather than time, a time out, a *quies* as rest or quiet, from which "while" is etymologically derived. Yet the speaker in her last stanza repeats the same efforts of her mental fugue to play a synecdoche and a metonymy as a way to perform herself, a poet and a mother: "These are my fingers, this my baby." Thus, she might say, repeating the earlier pattern, this is a woman, then! But she does not say that. Although she can make a metaphor in the last line, "The clouds are a marriage dress," its relation to the scene it cruises over is just as remote as the cold, blind sailing clouds of the first stanza. The white clouds are seen but they do not see; they do not register the distress of the speaker. The poem achieves no compensation for loss in satisfying metaphoric connections and brings painfully into focus just how little it can do to console, though it does strangely animate the speaker by keeping difference dominant.

A poem written a few days later, "Crossing the Water," rises to the power of consolation. In this little poem, Plath dissolved private fear and pain in a meditation on that which resists her will entirely. The early versions of the poem show its genesis in Plath's failing marriage. In one draft, the speaker "trails her hand in the cold water. At the close of the poem, with no explanation, the woman's hand is dead" (SP 204). The final version manages a frisson without such gothic effects and without inclusion of personal details. Plath achieves the emotion of art in this poem that moves from unease through fear to awe, as the speaker acknowledges that human love dies. In the first stanza, everything is black and moving through an immensity in which people have already turned unreal:

> Black lake, black boat, two black, cut paper people.
> Where do the black trees go that drink here?
> Their shadows must cover Canada.

The speaker is in that gliding boat, asking a childish question which no one answers in the first stanza. More mature in the second, she tries to read nature for herself:

> A little light is filtering from the water flowers.
> Their leaves do not wish us to hurry:
> They are round and flat and full of dark advice.

Do not rush this crossing, the leaves warn, and the third stanza shows why. The water will not be crossed in this poem because the journey is toward death by drowning:

> Cold worlds shake from the oar.
> The spirit of blackness is in us, it is in the fishes.
> A snag is lifting a valedictory, pale hand;

The only sign to be read now is the partially submerged branch that signals farewell. How can the speaker fare "well" if she knows she is doomed? She simply faces the truth in the last stanza. There, terror turns to awe before the unalterable facts:

> Stars open among the lilies.
> Are you not blinded by such expressionless sirens?
> This is the silence of astounded souls.

The watery blackness is an abyss Plath's speaker cannot cross. She finds in acknowledging this limitation a stunning beauty. Her blindness is not a repression of seeing the absolute knowledge which the sirens promise (they promise, as sirens do, death); her blindness is truly seeing, as a seer, and accepting in humility her fate—what is fixed, certain as the stars. Plath's stance is not one of resistance, but wonder at the human capacity to honor what is not in accordance with human will. Black is memory of fire that dominated the love poems Plath wrote to Hughes in 1956. "Crossing the Water" defers to difference, keeps sharp the edges of what is and what is not, and yet leaves the reader sensing relations that are true. We might paraphrase the poem's argument: If we cannot meet in passionate love, we can meet in some form of truth. Such mutuality creates

the clarification at the poem's end: the illuminating connection made between "astounded souls." The worst can be faced when truly shared.

The voice in "Elm," written in the same month, is urgent in its need
to share. Plath dedicated the poem to Ruth Fainlight, but it was already
finished when Plath read it to her poet friend in May (SP 203). The poem
had evolved through twenty-one worksheets (Heaney 20). Hughes in the
Collected Poems dated its final version April 19, 1962, just two weeks after
"Crossing the Water" was completed. "Elm" is the first poem of Plath's
final phase, when, as Seamus Heaney put it, her words come at the
"behest of some unforeseen but completely irresistible command" (20). The
imperative in "Elm" is to give voice to Plath's self-conscious and self-
critical negating spirit that is rooted in death.

> I know the bottom, she says. I know it with my great tap root:
> It is what you fear.
> I do not fear it: I have been there.
>
> Is it the sea you hear in me,
> Its dissatisfactions?
> Or the voice of nothing, that was your madness?
>
> Love is a shadow.
> How you lie and cry after it
> Listen: these are its hooves: it has gone off, like a horse.
>
> All night I shall gallop thus, impetuously,
> Till your head is a stone, your pillow a little turf,
> Echoing, echoing.
>
> Or shall I bring you the sound of poisons?
> This is the rain now, this big hush.
> And this is the fruit of it: tin-white, like arsenic.
>
> I have suffered the atrocity of sunsets.
> Scorched to the root
> My red filaments burn and stand, a hand of wires.
>
> Now I break up in pieces that fly around like clubs.
> A wind of such violence
> Will tolerate no bystanding: I must shriek.

The lyric cry comes in the midst of dispersal. The elm as speaker registers everything: the mind's discontent with its conditions, absence of meaning, loss of love, the deadly erosions of nature in rain, fire, wind, and the engagement with its force of articulation which is the O, the shape of grief as the deadly moon-muse who is "merciless and barren."

> I let her go. I let her go.
> Diminished and flat, as after radical surgery.
> How your bad dreams possess and endow me.

Who has bad dreams? The addressee, the one with whom the elm would share her knowledge. Part of the speaker's suffering results from the imaginings of another who wills her to be his/her/its own desire fulfilled. She, too, she confesses, has predatory desires with no sufficient objects:

> I am inhabited by a cry.
> Nightly it flaps out
> Looking, with its hooks, for something to love.
>
> I am terrified by this dark thing
> That sleeps in me.
> All day I feel its soft, feathery turnings, its malignity.
>
> Clouds pass and disperse.
> Are those the faces of love, those pale irretrievables?
> Is it for such I agitate my heart?

The elm has known the death of love and the continuing insistence of futile desire. This is a print out of Plath's gnostic mode: her own will seeing itself as all there is to see in the form of her muse as Medusa:

> I am incapable of more knowledge.
> What is this, this face
> So murderous in its strangle of branches?—

Its snaky acids kiss.
It petrifies the will. These are the isolate, slow faults
That kill, that kill, that kill.

Plath's negating imagination's refusal of death requires that it be itself deadly in its relation to nature. Thus, the poem as a lyric confesses the horror of its limits. This is what I do, says the spirit of the elm, and this is what you fear, yet you do the same. Do it, but know what it is, as I do. Do not kill everything. A. Alvarez has noted that Ted Hughes' "sense of menace and violence" comes straight out of some uncivilized center of himself, while Plath's similar expression "though often more powerful" is a "by-product of a compulsive need to understand" (204). The poem "Elm" springs out of such a compulsion, not only to understand but to teach.

In "Pheasant," also written in April, the speaker begs a hunter not to kill the bird that has appeared on his property. The poem exalts the pheasant's alien, natural existence, and asks the predator to "Let be, let be." In "The Rabbit Catcher," a speaker recalls what it was like to be desired as sexual prey: "It was a place of force.... There was only one place to get to ... the snares effaced themselves—/ Zeros, shutting on nothing." This reduction of eros to mechanism negates the triangulation which is love and turns the desired object into a thing to be possessed and destroyed. Plath knew she was capable of this reduction herself.

Love can die, Plath had acknowledged in "Crossing the Water," and the poetic will can defy limits, as it does in "Elm" but, Plath says in "The Rabbit Catcher," it is terrible willfully to destroy the fabric of life simply because it is possible. Yet, without desire, the "elements solidify" as the first line of Plath's May 21, poem "Event," declares. The world has turned solid and stony: moonlight is a "chalk cliff"; a child's face, "carved in pained, red wood"; stars are "ineradicable, hard"; and apple bloom "ices the night." Things are densely present, but nothing is clear. The space between lovers is a "black gap" where love "cannot come." The dark melts only in the last line when the man and wife touch each other "like cripples." By this time, Plath feared that her marriage had broken down completely, that there was no "dwelling place" for her in either passion, tenderness or trust. In her poem of almost unbearable opacity, "Words heard, by accident, over the phone," speech plops like mud on a phone table:

"...the spawn percolate in my heart. They are fertile./ Muck funnel, muck funnel—."

Earlier that July, Plath had written a long poem, "Berck-Plage," drawn from her memories of the French sea-side resort for wounded veterans, and the recent demise of her elderly neighbor Percy Keys. Keys' death from lung cancer, coinciding as it did with Hughes' infidelity, probably embodied for Plath the primal "betrayal" she had experienced in losing her father. Key's corpse was the first she had seen of someone she knew, and very likely his was the first funeral she ever attended. "Berck-Plage" concretizes loss with a vengeance in couplets that enact accretion without adding up to lucidity. The sea "creeps away, many-sided snake, with a long hiss of distress." A priest giving last rites is reduced to a "black high boot ... the hearse of a dead foot" who "plumbs the well of his book,/ The bent print bulging before him like scenery." A man dies exposing the pattern of his bed: "On a striped mattress in one room/ An old man is vanishing." Laid out, the dead man is "A wedding cake face in a paper frill.... This is what it is to be complete. It is horrible." The speaker, listening to the funeral liturgy, re-imagines the soul as a bride to a groom who is "red and forgetful, he is featureless." He is the grave: "... a naked mouth, red and awkward." Not even the air remains lucent for Plath but becomes a grotesque last minute expense as a gesture of resuscitation: "For a minute the sky pours into the hole like plasma./ There is no hope, it is given up."

"Berck-Plage" expresses revulsion at the barriers of oppressive, material density. Death as limitation is not repressed and re-imaged in a consolation, but shown as a brutal and unredeemed fact. Plath's images of disgust have the feel of Swift's satire or of Eliot in his most desperate days. That comparison can be instructive, for Swift (and Eliot, too, as a satirist) calls attention over and over to this: "The law of love is absolutely incompatible with things as they are" (Dyson 638). The other side of the intolerable, material universe of death is the inability to touch what might be a saving grace within it. In "Poppies in July," Plath uses images of Jinny in *The Waves:* "She was like a crinkled poppy, febrile, thirsty with the desire to drink dry dust ... little flames [that] zigzag over the cracks in the dry earth" (252).

Jinny was Woolf's indefatigable female lover. Plath had underlined and starred in her copy of *The Waves* Jinny's words: "Our hands touch, our bodies burst into fire. The chair, the cup, the table—nothing remains unlit. All quivers, all kindles, all burns clear" (140). The speaker in Plath's poem wants to get close to such fire, but more than proximity is required for energizing clarity:

> Little poppies, little hell flames,
> Do you do no harm?
>
> You flicker. I cannot touch you.
> I put my hands among the flames. Nothing burns.
>
> And it exhausts me to watch you
> Flickering like that, wrinkly and clear red, like the skin of
> a mouth.

A meeting of hands and poppies that would kindle a clear flame requires belief, such as Jinny had in the rightness of her imagination: "My imagination is the body's" (220). Plath's speaker, unlike Jinny, is a murderous and disembodied spirit who, if she cannot have the poppies, will destroy them in violent images: "A mouth just bloodied/ Little bloody skirts." The speaker wants release from the suffering of disconnection, but the poppies remain beyond her reach: "If I could bleed or sleep!—/ If my mouth could marry a hurt like that!" The necessity appears to be this: the speaker must make poetry (bleed) or die (sleep). Either her imagination works to relate her desire to the natural rhythms of the body and the actual world, or she perishes from its distillations, i.e., its abstractions. Plath may or may not have read Martin Buber, but her "Poppies in July" laments powerlessness in terms that echo one of Buber's passages about power in *I and Thou*:

> The *fiery stuff* of all my ability to will seethes tremendously, all that I might do circles around me, still without actuality in the world, flung together and seemingly inseparable, alluring glimpses of powers *flicker* from all the uttermost bounds: the universe is my temptation, and I achieve being in an instant, with both *hands plunged deep in the fire*, where the single deed is hidden, the deed which aims at me—now is the moment. Already the menace of the abyss is removed, the centerless Many no

longer plays in the iridescent sameness of its pretensions... [Italics mine] (52).

This passage tells how will is kindled by a sense of the holy, which was for
Buber, a relation with the "inborn Thou." In Buber's humanism, not unlike
Dorothea Krook's, submission to that power frees man from arbitrary
self-will and enables him both to accept necessity and to engage in moral
choices. Such energizing freedom occurs only when man "believes in
reality," which is a relation between persons that reveals the sacred. This
reality, for Buber, is man's destiny: "... what is to come will come only
when he decides on what he is able to will, which quits defined being for
destined being" (59). Plath had to find a way to be able to accept what had
happened to her in 1962, if she were to survive the loss of a relation without losing her belief in all relations.

Plath completed only one poem between July and September of 1962,
the spiteful "Burning the Letters." At the end of September, she began her
most productive period: forty poems in two months. There would be another lull during December when she moved from Devon back to London
with her two children, and then she would write twelve more poems the
first six weeks of the new year before she killed herself on February 11,
1963. Something is definitely different in Plath's first poem of this final period when she knew her marriage was in ruins. There is no attempt to
share or connect with a vital force that is not herself. Written on the last
day of September, 1962, "A Birthday Present" is addressed to no one but
Plath's own desire to know: what am I? what is my essence? The poem is a
gnostic quest for identity:

> What is this, behind this veil, is it ugly, is it beautiful?
> Is it shimmering, has it breasts, has it edges?
>
> I am sure it is unique, I am sure it is just what I want.

The tone is as facetious as in "Little Fugue." Of course "it" will be what she
wants, for "it" is, literally, her want, her own desire. As in the earlier
poem, a romantic convention is short-circuited and undone. The speaker

goes straight for the essence without the ritual of taking in a scene, reflecting on it, and projecting it outward again. Why bother with the natural world at all when she knows what she wants: her "want" or lack made visible in some satisfying way? Thus, she imagines "it":

> When I am quiet at my cooking I feel it looking, I feel it thinking
>
> Is this the one I am to appear for,
> Is this the elect one, the one with black eye-pits and a scar?
>
> Measuring the flour, cutting off the surplus,
> Adhering to rules, to rules, to rules.
>
> Is this the one for the annunciation?
> My god, what a laugh!

The veil for romantics, Rousseau, Blake, Wordsworth, Coleridge, Emerson, Shelley, is the undesired opacity of things. Because for them the veil hides a power which they desire, the obstruction must be removed. Plath's speaker never succeeds in lifting that veil to know her own essence, yet the speaker makes her relation only to that unseen "it" and to a "you" who is supposed to give "it" to her. The "it," she suspects, scorns her dull, ordinary self that obeys rules and honors limits. Moreover, "it" has designs on her: "I think it wants me." The birthday gift behind the opacity of existence is not a "given" in this poem, but a continuously expected thing which the speaker's speculations try to match and thus obtain. Her play of possibilities is a game of speculation, of making up. If only she guessed right, she would see and be satisfied. As she theorizes, she runs a gamut of emotions, from the meek "I would not mind if it was bones, or a pearl button," to the exigent: "Can you not give it to me?/ Do not be ashamed—I do not mind if it is small," to the exorbitant with echoes of Stevens:

> Do not be mean, I am ready for enormity.
> Let us sit down to it, one on either side, admiring the gleam,
> The glaze, the mirrory variety of it.
> Let us eat our last supper at it, like a hospital plate.

One echo seems to be Stevens' "Cuisine Bourgeoise" which meditates on lost feasts of holy communion, replaced by "human heads." "This bitter meat/ Sustains us," says Stevens of those who theorize out of themselves with no sense of the sacred: "Who, then, are they, seated here?/ Is the table a mirror in which they sit and look?/ Are they men eating reflections of themselves?" The other echo, less precise but surely vibrating here, is Stevens' "The American Sublime" which contemplates that mood as coming "down/ to the spirit itself/ The spirit and space/ The empty spirit/ In vacant space." No bread and wine there. In Plath's poem, the speaker's insistence grows as she continues to address vacuity. She promises no ridiculous displays: "No falling ribbons, no scream at the end," and her tone turns into outrageous affectation. "If you only knew how the veils were killing my days./ To you they are only transparencies, clear air." To the speaker, the natural is deadly: clouds are "carbon monoxide." She envies the "silver-suited" unnatural that is protected from materiality: "O adding machine." Its accretions will add up to nothing, because it is nothing: a zero. The speaker wants to be that, and so she turns vicious, feeling mutilated like purple-stamped meat rather than perfected by the power she addresses. Her plea grows desperate:

> Only let down the veil, the veil, the veil.
> If it were death
>
> I would admire the deep gravity of it, its timeless eyes.
> I would know you were serious.
> There would be a nobility then, there would be a birthday.
> And the knife not carve, but enter
>
> Pure and clean as the cry of a baby
> And the universe slide from my side.

The poem slides to its conclusion, not as desire satisfied but as desire momentarily exhausted. The "you" must be the poem itself, a structure of images. Clearly, the "want" as "it" is death, the absolute absence of relation. All Plath's images evoke death: bones, pearls (as pearls are drowned men's eyes), self-consumption, poison, and so on. The image of the knife turning from carving to cleanly piercing conveys intense need for release from the torture of natural existence. The speaker wants the poem to give her own desire as a pure essence. Those eyes will be hers looking back as she crosses that demonic threshold and sees her "I am I!," but this does not occur except in the speaker's imaginative projections, in her theories or speculations on that essence. She cannot see a "self"; she can muster images of "it"—her desire completed or perfected by its own fictions, and they are all forms of death.

For Plath, in the fall of 1962, there was one main fact to face: her undesired solitary existence, her severance from the conjugal relation in which she had believed and therefore from her own personhood. For Plath, the "self" as linguistic identity is elusive because it is easily dispersed among many possible scripts or theories as the proliferating speculations in "The Birthday Present" show. Moreover, all such theories in Plath's writing lead to death in reified forms. A theory is disposable; a belief is not. In a world or an imagination devoid of belief, there are only theories: fictional, provisional constructs to use as things, instruments, techniques. What to do? Shaken by the loss of her husband, Plath had to touch some sure thing, something in which she believed, which would help her survive not as a fictive "I" but as a person. This is the enterprise of Plath's next five poems, the so-called "bee sequence."

Plath wrote five poems about bee keeping during the first nine days of October, 1962. Susan Van Dyne's study of their various drafts concludes that this sequence was a "pivotal moment" in Plath's "search for an authentic and autonomous self."[7] Certainly Plath tried in her bee poems to give form to her articulating power as the queen bee who supplanted the old, distressing "disquieting muses." My reading differs from Van Dyne's, however, in my assessment of that new image of creativity. I think Plath is as critical of the killer queen bee as she was of the barren moon muses. In the bee poems, Plath follows her need to find a "dwelling place" which is not the grave. Such a place will be in the tradition of the symbolic imagination which affirms lived reality as relations within the given world.

Both Augustine and Martin Buber use the term "dwelling place" to designate human relations which are true, that is, which do not deny the personhood of another who is not the self. Augustine called that way of being in the world, *caritas*, and wrote that wherever man saw an act done in that spirit, man saw the Trinity. Woolf's Rhoda in *The Waves* saw the relation mystically as "a square supported by an oblong ... a perfect dwelling place." Buber called the "dwelling" the I-Thou relation which enables man to apprehend the world as the place where he belongs (14). With his questing spirit thus kindled, man is free, says Buber, to creatively shape his community, but "only so long as he possesses, in action and suffering in his own life, that act of the being—so long as he himself enters into relation" (54).

The bee sequence is an allegory devised by Plath to make clear a poetic stance which would affirm what Buber has called "relation," the primal I-Thou. Language in this tradition does not deconstruct or estrange meaning; it makes meaning, metaphorically and mythopoetically. For Plath, because of her particular history, such language was associated with the present and loving mother of her earliest years, not with the absent, willful father, or the deserted, "bony" moon-mother, both images for Plath that articulate the language of the negating, gnostic imagination. In her 1959 poem, "The Beekeeper's Daughter," Plath had acknowledged her gnostic spirit as she both married and "killed" her father in order to generate the power to create an autonomous self. In that poem the bees were metonymies for signification that was, itself, a metonymy for the displaced power of the dead "maestro" or god. The bees stand for language used as plays of desire in the face of the void. Plath had developed that poetic stance in the closing poems of *The Colossus* and continued it in the poems of 1960 and 1961. She had hoped, in "The Stones," that this mode would somehow "house the elusive rose," i.e., make the structure of love visible, but by the fall of 1962 when Plath wrote "The Birthday Present" she was giving up that hope. In that poem, she displays the drama of the "I" looking only for its own identity, but by wanting only a form for her solitary desire, her "I" will find, like Narcissus, death. Thus, the play of her desire must go on inventing forms that will delay an encounter which, though lethal, is desperately wanted. This is the spirit that wants to say, not "I-Thou," but "I am I" the hero's (and heroine's) boast of a tragically doomed spirit.

In the bee sequence, Plath tries to devise a new fiction of self that, paradoxically, will enable her to live by believing in something other than that fiction. The best mode for such a task is allegory used as satire, the mode she had used in her novel *The Bell Jar*, written in 1961. Lynda Bundtzen has observed the allegorical nature of *The Bell Jar*: the heroine points to lessons and morals to be read in her experiences (113). Esther Greenwood tries to learn from each dreadful situation in which she finds herself, but she does not, ever, establish what Buber would call "relation."

Her lessons are learned and her points are made in a world devoid of real meeting of persons. Esther does not interact with the world as a Thou, only as an "It." Although she wants something more, she can only keep trying to figure things out, which she usually does in some shrewd way, but her conclusions make the world look more terrible and herself more innocent. There is no genuine rebirth in this novel; Esther merely survives, her only triumph is her saying "I am, I am." The novel's brilliance lies in its steadiness of tone: a wry distance from an insufficient world, a brutal place which Esther learns how to negotiate a little better, for a little longer. Plath referred to *The Bell Jar* as a "pot boiler," and "an autobiographical apprentice work which I had to write in order to free myself from the past" (Harris 8). She would call, "Daddy," a later poem of satiric attack with the same purpose, an "allegory" and "light verse" (CP 293).

Allegory makes effective satire because it is the mode of metonymic estrangement and substitution, allowing the satirist to attack from the margins the problems that seem central. Her verbal slings and arrows are radii that keep her at a distance from a spoiled source. The danger in this kind of writing is finding the spoiled source is oneself, and so the satirist tries to stay peripheral. She wields her linguistic power arbitrarily because she knows in advance what she wants to rectify, though she may not know exactly how. She just knows her fictions serve her purpose. Plath's allegory in the bee sequence wants to destroy an old fiction of herself as the innocent devoid of relation and to replace it with something sustaining. The question is: can any mere theory of self be sustaining?

In the opening poem, "The Bee Meeting," the speaker undergoes an initiation into the craft of bee keeping by a group of *cognoscenti*. Allegorically, the speaker enters the life of writing. She does not know at the end of her ordeal whether her literate status will bring her life or death. The success of this poem resembles that of *The Bell Jar*: a sustained partial vision, a sort of perfectly pitched paranoia cataloguing its fears. When given a "black veil that molds to my face," the speaker thinks she is "being made one of them," but this assertion is immediately followed by uncertainty: "Is it the hawthorn that smells so sick?/ Etherizing its children...." The next stanza is all interrogative; nothing is sure except terror which the speaker, in her one aggressive act, projects upon the bees that are smoked out of the hive:

> The mind of the hive thinks this is the end of everything.
> Here they come, the outriders, on their hysterical elastics.
> If I stand very still they will think I am cow parsley....

Thus ordered by a comic device, the speaker speculates on the queen bee for which the keepers are searching: "Is she hiding, is she eating honey? She is very clever./ She is old, old, old, she must live another year and she knows it." The speaker imagines the queen displaced by other bees who will someday take the "bride flight.../ The uplift of the murderess into a heaven that loves her." Since no queen appears, there will be no "killing," that is, generating bee style, no powerful writing yet, in spite of being led through the motions. The speaker has learned little during the rite as a passive participant, though she has intimations of death waiting for her in the sacred grove:

> I am exhausted, I am exhausted—
> Pillar of white in a blackout of knives.
> I am the magician's girl who does not flinch.
> The villagers are untying their disguises, they are shaking
>   hands.
> Whose is that long white box in the grove, what have
>   they accomplished, why am I cold.

The poem remains in the realm of the magical. "Magic," as Martin Buber put it, "desires to obtain its effects without entering into a relation, and practices its tricks in the void" (83). Read as allegory, this initial bee poem tells the story of the entrance into the life of writing which will be mere magic if the novice remains innocent and without relation. Plath's stunning image for this phase of her development, the "magician's girl who does not flinch," recalls the terror and the brutality under the glittering surface of many of her Smith College poems. She performed, poetically and sexually, but without love.

In the second poem, "The Arrival of the Bee Box," the speaker timidly chooses to take responsibility for the power now in her hands: "I ordered this, this clean wood box...." She still sees the container as a coffin, but for things she will imagine, "a midget or a square baby," not for herself. The box houses a black inferno of angry energy she must deal with, though its sounds seems alien to her. She entertains the possibility of refusing to accept this mass of potential verbalization, thinking she might repress it, willfully, and make it die:

> I lay my ear to furious Latin.
> I am not Caesar.
> I have simply ordered a box of maniacs.
> They can be sent back.
> They can die, I need feed them nothing. I am the owner.

The speaker decides, however, to release the bees, her metonymic language of desire, only when convinced that she can protect herself from them, "in my moon suit and my funeral veil." The poem ends with an avowal, "Tomorrow I will be sweet God, I will set them free," and an ominous observation, "The box is only temporary." She must set them free if she is to avoid killing vitality. The bees are linguistic power as well as sexual power; the two, of course, are intimately related for the artist.

My reading of the entire bee sequence differ from Van Dyne's most in the next poem: Van Dyne reads "Stings" as Plath's triumph of identity. My question is: the identity of what? The speaker and a bee seller, "the man in white," order and arrange the hive, determined to see their enterprise as pure and under their control:

> He and I
>
> Have a thousand clean cells between us
> Eight combs of yellow cups,
> And the hive itself a teacup,
> White with pink flowers on it,
> With excessive love I enameled it
>
> Thinking 'Sweetness, sweetness '.

Their authority balks in the next lines, which focus on the ugly brood cells, "gray as the fossils of shells," and terrifying in their primal power. The old queen bee lies hidden there: "Poor and bare and unqueenly and even shameful." Yet the speaker wants to make that fecund queen her emblem, not the sexless honey bees:

> I stand in a column
>
> Of winged, unmiraculous women,
> Honey-drudgers.
> I am no drudge
> Though for years I eaten dust
> And dried plates with my dense hair.

The line of women suggests the matriarchy of Plath's family, her grand-mother and mother, who read and wrote but without genius or passion, without the divine right of the poet. Asserting this power means risking alienation. "Will they hate me…" the speaker wonders, but that is a moot point, for as the establishment of the hive ends, she does claim, "I am in control."

Is she? The queen bee is the proud and unaccommodated spirit that repeats over and over the drama of desire to keep the hive as a mechanism going. In the allegory, she is the phallic marker, the absence that keeps writing going. Once rightly established, the hive will "work without thinking … like an industrious virgin," mechanical but productive. The threat to such efficacy appears in the figure of another man, not the man in white:

> A third person is watching.
> He has nothing to do with the bee-seller or with me.

The bees attack him, drive him off the scene, "a great scapegoat." The figure is based on Hughes, who had in fact been stung during a bee meeting in June of 1962, wearing only a handkerchief on his head instead of more protective gear (LH 457):

Here is his slipper, here is another,
And here is the square of white linen
He wore instead of a hat.
He was sweet,

The sweat of his efforts a rain
Tugging the world to fruit.
The bees found him out,
Moulding onto his lips like lies,
Complicating his features.

Though a source of fertility and invention, the figure is sinister for he cannot humble himself to any rule but his own. Like Napoleon, whose "I" was his Cause and who said, "I am the clock, which exists, and does not know itself,"[8] the third man runs, following a destiny, but he cannot read the signs written on his own face. He is humbled and stung allegorically by language that, like the clock at Cinderella's ball, signs the end of the un-reality of his "I." Such language of satiric attack is, however, self-destroying: "They thought death was worth it...." It becomes clear that the speaker wants the hive to work following rules and rituals, but she also wants to be its animating, controlling spirit. Does she, like the stung man, overstep?

            ...but I
I have a self to recover, a queen.
Is she dead, is she sleeping?
Where has she been,
With her lion-red body, her wings of glass?

In spite of the grandeur of these lines, they contain hints of the ludicrous. An earlier image had the queen's long body "rubbed of its plush," and so of course that old form now needs, not discovering, but *re*-covering, i.e., new upholstery, a new fabric or fabrication as a new theory of self. If the self is such, it will have about it the self-consciousness of fiction, and that indeed occurs in the closing stanza. If the "Where has she been?" echoes a child's nursery rhyme, the closing lines echo a super-hero comic book:

Now she is flying
More terrible than she ever was, red
Scar in the sky, red comet
Over the engine that killed her—
The mausoleum, the wax house.

When the speaker appropriates the queen as her fiction of self, the hive suddenly becomes a death house, a place for effigies. The poem has stung its own images of community to death. Furthermore, in order to see the queen bee as a lion-red dragon, the reader must assent to the scale of fairyland. The magical still obtains. We are in the void of the unreal for no relation has yet been established in Plath's allegory of writing. The movement in the sequence has gone from sexual innocence to sexual experience, but the terrible queen is driven to repeat the old drama that ends in death over and over. In Plath's allegory, the queen bee becomes the emblem for the power to write this action. Is she, then, a triumphant identity, as many readers have interpreted her? Another way to put the question: *Is the writing self an adequate metaphor of self?* I do not think it was for Plath. That is why Plath uses the queen bee not as a metaphoric image but as a metonymic sign: she is a paper dragon, a self-conscious and arbitrary fiction, a theory only.

Theory quickly becomes a cause that turns everything into a function of itself. A cause must be interrogated. This is just what goes on in the next poem, "The Swarm." Here, the theory of the autonomous self as a basis for an ideology is ridiculed, not in the figure of the queen bee, but rather in the figure of a beekeeper as a little Napoleon whose imperious will defies limits and controls the energy of the bees. Van Dyne's reading makes sense of this poem's dense imagery by finding in its series of inversions a portrait of Hughes. He had recently captured a new "queen" but with the callousness of a chess player or military strategist. The speaker mocks him and those who have fallen into his "cocked hat." In my reading, the beekeeper as a "Napoleon" cannot enter into relation as a lover: he can only conquer and use. If Van Dyne is right, the poem is pure spite, and Hughes had every reason to exclude it from the English version of *Ariel*. My own sense is that Plath was questioning the very power she had claimed for herself in "Stings." If to create means to kill the other or turn the other into a "thing," there is no relation, no sense of attunement of difference between persons. The bee keeper bullies the bees into "a new mausoleum," protecting himself with gloves: "asbestos receptacles." There is no risk of being wounded and perhaps changed. As long as the beekeeper can use the bees as his tools, he is like "Napoleon," and "pleased with everything." In Plath's allegory of writing, the bees as signification articulated by this demonic will to power remain a "black intractable mind."

Plath's last poem in the bee sequence, "Wintering," strives for a new version of her creativity. Here, she tries to formulate a force that is not a Nietzschean super-woman, but a power that resists gnostic defiance of absence and instead suffers loss of relation without loss of belief that relation is possible. The bees in this conclusion to her allegory of her life in writing are put away in a dark, windowless room. As metonymies for her linguistic power as repressed desire, the bees are both her possessions and her possessors:

> It is they who own me.
> Neither cruel nor indifferent,
>
> Only ignorant.

The bees' honey has been usurped by the speaker, and so they must survive by eating a substitute:

> The refined snow.
> It is Tate and Lyle they live on, instead of flowers.
> They take it. The cold sets in.
>
> Now they ball in a mass,
> Black
> Mind against all that white.
> It spreads itself out, a mile long body of Meissen.

Divorced from the symbolic tradition which is grounded in the natural, temporal world and which ennobles erotic desire, the bees have been robbed of their culture which sustains life "without thinking." The speaker has their gold and will live off their capital, while they must feed during the winter on a blank, the "refined snow" of syrup. In this state, the bees "are all women,/ Maids and the long royal lady./ They have got rid of the men." Why do the bees in this allegory of writing eliminate the male component of the hive? Allegorically, the male stands for the will to power which is too aggressive to survive loss without pouring itself into the void. Plath did this herself, "like plasma," in such fearful poems as "Berck-Plage." The male drive, both sexual and creative, has little tolerance for lack, preferring to wound rather than be wounded, to invent rather than be invented or erased. Killing the male bees ("the boors") stands for Plath's own desire to control her drive to invent in the face of loss. Plath's new response is patience. She lays out dead black bees on an expanse of shining snow as signs of her own rejected will. Thus, she displays her desire to replace the world with a theoretical "self" and this confession leads the speaker to assert:

> Winter is for women—
> The woman, still at her knitting,
> At the cradle of Spanish walnut,
> Her body a bulb in the cold and too dumb to think.

The new stance is patience and endurance for the sake of relation; the emblem is that of mother and child. The enemy for the speaker is not men or a man, but her own mind, and what it can do to her when its powers are "wintering," that is, waiting out the season of death, the world's insufficiency that is the siren to the negating imagination. The greater the blank, the greater the desire to overcome it, but in this poem, Plath represses her too arbitrary will to power until it can respond to a given. Such waiting is an heroic effort to transform Plath's writing from allegories of gnostic practice into a symbol of her will to endure loss for the sake of relation:

> Will the hive survive, will the gladiolas
> Succeed in banking their fires
> To enter another year?
> What will they taste of, the Christmas roses?
> The bees are flying. They taste the spring.

The Christmas roses are children, love in the flesh as the Christ Child, the Christmas Rose, was Love Incarnate. Will the children taste only blankness, "refined snow," or will they taste of the real thing: the world made holy by relation in which they participate? In her last line, Plath affirms her belief in her poetic language to celebrate desire in its noblest form. The allegory finally points toward the symbolic. Her bees as poetic language are flying toward a source, "the spring," traditional season of generation of life, as well as the fountain of the muses, created by the hooves of Pegasus, born of the blood of the slain Medusa. Survival for mother and child, as well as for her poetry, depended for Plath in October 1962 on banked fires, conserved energy, patience and a sense of the holy found in relations within the actual world. This is the sense of herself Plath struggled to bring forth, not the terrible queen, who lies low in this last poem. Plath's language is still driven by desire, but it wants to meet, not to displace, another.

Plath must have thought she had succeeded in touching something life affirming in these five bee poems, for she placed them as the conclusion to her manuscript arrangement for her second volume of poems, *Ariel.* That entire collection, then, might have been meant to celebrate the desire to meet the other, beginning with the word "Love" in the opening poem, "Morning Song," and ending with the world "spring" in "Wintering." Plath's title has many possible allusions, the most obvious among them the freed spirit of *The Tempest*, but Plath knew the etymology of "Ariel" given in her copy of *Webster's New Collegiate Dictionary* (1949): a Hebrew name meaning "Lion of God." Pursuing this connection, Plath would have found "Ariel" as one of the Biblical names for Jerusalem, Augustine's "holy city" understood as the enlightened mind that knows love as a trinity. This is the mind that makes metaphors and makes visible the "dwelling place" that enables man to live in the real, not a magical, world.

Plath's plot for her second collection of poems was undone by Hughes' own choices and ordering, but perhaps his poetic judgment was better. As poems, the weakest "Wintering," is last; the strongest "The Bee Meeting," first. Although the sequence asserts more than it achieves, the bee poems show a complex of emotions: fear, rage, triumph, indignation, and hope. They are best understood as an allegory of Plath's relation to her writing which enabled her to write the poems that immediately follow this sequence.

In those poems, she was not concerned anymore with creating a gnostic identity, but with fighting the things she had come to see as wrong in the so-called "autonomous" self of the romantic sublime. She had found access to enough rage in the bee poems to become the allegorical satirist of later poems. Satire, though fueled by anger, is a form of pacifism: words are not guns or bombs. Words can wound the spirit and create a possibility for change without destruction of life. Plath resumed the passionate pacifism of her youth which she had expressed in "Bitter Strawberries," but which she could now display with the technique of satire. Thus, she could be powerful, not weak, "a person who, through love and indignation, has transcended her own violence, *not* one who is afraid to fight."[9]

After her bee sequence, done in the first nine days of October, Plath poured out a stream of poems that many critics have read as her most distinctive, as if in them she had finally shown her "true" self.[10] These biting and bitter works include "A Secret," "The Applicant," "Daddy," "Medusa," "The Jailor," "Lesbos," "Stopped Dead," "Fever 103º," "Amnesiac," "Lyonnesse," "Cut," "The Tour," "Purdah" and "Lady Lazarus." All can be read as allegories of writing divorced from the symbolic tradition of ennobled desire. They satirize desire that wants to see only itself as they dramatize gnostic enterprise as narcissism.

For example, in "The Applicant," the conjugal bond, the form of human love in which Plath had placed her faith, is reduced to a privileged purchase of an investment certificate, a paper doll that "in twenty-five years" will be silver, "In fifty, gold." This becomes the "last resort" for the applicant who has been interrogated by the speaker of the poem: "First, are you our sort of person?" The applicant has "nothing to show something's missing." Thus, he has no lack, that is no *bona fide* desire to meet and to relate to another. The poem's success is its swift and deadly accurate solution to this problem in a voice of an impatient adult talking to a spoiled brat: "Stop crying./ Open your hand./ Empty? Empty...." Continuing the staccato imperatives and interrogatives, "The Applicant" vacates the condition of mutuality and replaces it with instrumentality: "You have a hole, it's poultice./ You have an eye, it's an image./ My boy, it's your last resort./ Will you marry it, marry it, marry it." It: Not a person but a thing, not love but "will."

In "Daddy," the poem Plath called "an awful little allegory," the speaker negates a paternal bond by emptying out an image of father and of husband as a repeat of the father until that image is itself unfathered and thus finished: "Daddy, daddy, you bastard, I'm through." Broe, the first major critic to urge readers to look for comic and satiric protean displays in Plath, not a personal myth, reads "Daddy" as a "self-parody" in which a great mythological murder is reduced to a Hollywood B-movie spectacle, a performance that allows her to live with what is unchangeable (*Protean* 172–175). The speaker rejects father and husband, but they have already rejected her. In "Medusa," the maternal bond is even more fiercely denied but with less success. The jellyfish image of clinging death will not unstick. When the speaker closes with the command "Off, off eely tentacle!/ There is nothing between us," her efficacy is undercut by the word "nothing." With no relation there is no love, but that very reason may make the Medusa impossible to distance, for she is the imperious maternal will that is not a holy city but a "Ghastly Vatican," a vatic sham, "always there" controlling everything, even the outcome of this failed attempt to separate from her. Vacuity duplicates itself: the speaker's "I" who rejects relation and the Medusa-mother who insists on her own will, rather than love, collapse into identity *because* "there is nothing between us." They are the same and that is horrible.

Plath does the delusion and delirium of the drive for the *ignus fatuus* of "identity" brilliantly in "Fever 103°." My reading goes against interpretations of the poem as a positive enactment of the individual's realizing herself by rising from the "imprisonment of history" and "confronting the self at the most personal level of consciousness" (Sanazaro 92). In such readings, the speaker achieves transcendence by shedding all restraints— history, lover, her own body—and by becoming transparent, shimmering heat, an image for the liberation of that divine spark which empowers individual to realization of a "self." Plath shows instead that such a linguistic construct is insufficient as she performs satirically in the metonymic world of allegory, displacement and fiction, not the metaphoric world of analogy, relation and myth. Plath writes in this mode when she no longer believes in her imagination's promise to deliver what will suffice. Like the Second Voice in *Three Women*, she knows what she lacks but is too self-aware and skeptical to accept a theoretical consolation in the place of a real one. Plath gave her own explication of her poem on a BBC broadcast: we suffer either the fires of hell or the fires of heaven and in this poem, the "first suffers itself into the second" (CP 293). Plath's brief statement recalls Eliot's passage IV in *Little Gidding*. "Fever" can be read as a revision of Eliot which does not try to supplant his poem so much as to reaffirm it with new techniques. In ambiguous, unstable images, Eliot renders the constant flickering of possibility in human understanding. The "descending dove" may be received as the Holy Spirit or rejected as an enemy dive bomber about to torch and terrorize. Eros, for the ancient Greeks, was not a gentle god; and the God of Augustine was not either. In Eliot's tradition of the symbolic imagination, man must burn with desire in order to know the relation which is love. The spirit or creative spark that seeks to deny relation seeks death.

In Plath's poem, the second fire is the focus, but as a parody of Eliot's earlier lines from *Little Gidding:* "From wrong to wrong the exasperated spirit/ Proceeds, unless restored by that refining fire/ Where you must move in measure, like a dancer." Plath's "exasperated spirit" begins her poem with the question: "Pure, what does it mean?" If Plath was reading Buber, she might have been responding to his commentary on "absorption," which he calls the mistaken desire for gnostic unity of self: "Absorption wishes to preserve only the 'pure,' the real, the lasting, and to cast away everything else" (89). With Eliot as a matrix, she might have been thinking also of speech, and of Eliot's "compound ghost" speaking for Eliot in words taken from Mallarmé. Like that poet, Eliot had also wanted to "purify the dialect of the tribe." He simply had less confidence than many other poets in what language as a raid on the inarticulate could actually achieve, and he was not adverse to appropriating others' words for his personal rhythms. What, then, is pure speech or pure poetry? Can the absolute poetry of the symbolists, starting with Poe, reveal a pure or true self as "voice" or can it merely display a negating imagination struggling vainly to be free from restraints and limits of form?[11] Plath does in "Fever" what she does in her other satirical pieces: she mocks the symbolic seriousness of romantic expressionism by reducing it to a metonymy, a fable of failure. Her poem takes the reader through a series of increasingly heated situations, as specifically sexual desire refines itself to an hysterical pitch, ending in hilarity and then horror, not in sublime identity of "self." We have here what Frederick Buell calls a "willed dehumanization of the self" (149). The only problem with this excellent analysis is that Buell characterizes Plath only in the light of her late poems. Plath's most extreme work is best understood in relation to her entire poetic career in which both the symbolic and the negating imaginations are at work.

In "Fever," the speaker suffers the ache of desire for which Hell's "tongues" of fire are too "dull" a remedy. Deeming it better to extinguish a body which is merely a nasty, stubborn inferno, the speaker becomes a "snuffed candle"; however, the resulting rolls of smoke are as dangerous to the speaker as Isadora's scarves, for her unlit body pours out a density that might throttle her in the very means by which she hoped to deal with desire: the mechanism which is the poem. Denying the body is one wrong that proceeds to another, that of extinguishing the world, for "Such yellow sullen smokes/ Make their own element." Eliot's sinister yellow Prufrockian fog becomes Plath's more aggressive dead white "Devilish leopard!" A world wrapt in the denial of the human kills itself in radioactive ash, the afterward of human will in satanic form. So at the exact midpoint of this eighteen stanza poem, the speaker decides neither to pollute the world nor to endure it, but to burn fiercely, letting her own desire refine her out of the hell of human existence: "Three days, Three nights.... I am too pure for you or anyone" she tells her lover. "Your body/ Hurts me as the world hurts God." She will be her own god and redeem herself, as she becomes a pulsing radiance: "huge camellia, glowing and coming and going, flush on flush." There is hysteria in the self-assumption:

> I think I am going up
> I think I may rise—
> The beads of hot metal fly, and I, love, I
>
> Am a pure acetylene
> Virgin
> Attended by roses,
>
> By kisses, by cherubim,
> By whatever these pink things mean.
> Not you, nor him
>
> Not him, nor him
> (my selves dissolving, old whore petticoats)—
> To Paradise.

The acceleration of these last stanzas is that of an engine, "pure" sexual energy, ready to take off, melting all barriers, but it does not. The poem ends on a fragment that may complete with rhyme the earlier sentence, "I may rise," or it may be a command to a driver, "To Paradise," calling attention to the hazard in this situation. Those dissolving, impure selves may yet catch in her wheel of desire and throttle her. The speaker is not free from danger or suffering in the depravity of a world without relation. The refining fire of her own invention has not taken her beyond the theoretical or the fictive written "self." The speaker is just hotter than ever for release from forms without which there is no measure to dance to, only death. A collapsing of distinctions makes Heaven and Hell the same. Ted Hughes has commented that Plath's view of Paradise is a "burningly luminous vision" which is "eerily frightening, an unalterably spot-lit vision of death."[12]

When Plath said of her October poems, "They saved me" (SP 227), that was so because she was writing allegories of desire, arbitrary fictions of self over which she could say: "I am in control." With her energies put in the reductive form of a poetic satire, her drive toward death could be mocked. Such poems enact negation of relation as the reduction of spirit to theory, to thing or "it." At times, these reductions border on the pornographic,[13] but they are not. Her satirist's stance allowed Plath to continue affirming a fundamental belief in the transforming power of human love which requires relation as mutuality between persons who do not use each other as things. Though badly shaken, this belief still sustained Plath.

This is apparent because of three poems which punctuate the amazing October production of furious dramas. The first of these three is "Ariel," perhaps Plath's best known poem, but not at all a typical one.[14] "Ariel" can be misread as an expression of either mystic unification with the divine essence or identification with it. In the first, the "I" dissolves relation by emptying out and becoming dependent and without self-will. In the second, the "I" dissolves relation by asserting a tremendous will to power in order to overcome the duality of "I" and other, so that the "I" and its vision become all that there is. Both acts, one total passivity, the other total aggressivity, spring from the assumption that a divine spirit exists only within the individual, not in relation between one person and another, and thus both acts of "absorption" deny relation. "Ariel" read as an enactment of absorption is a poem either about the desire to die (unification) or the desire to be god (identification)—or both. Either way, the human subject dissolves. Because "Ariel" has none of the viciousness of other October allegories, the poem offers another experience: a unity of self that does not deny relation in either total submission or total domination.

"Ariel" can be experienced as a concentration of power within a person who rejoices in solitude without renouncing the desire to meet the other in lived relations. Buber calls this private act the "decisive moment" for an individual, without which he—or she—is "unfit for the work of the spirit." With it, he decides in his "innermost being, if this means a breathing space, or the sufficient end of his way" (86). The speaker in "Ariel" is joyous and fearless in a self-conscious and lonely unity, knowing she risks death if she does not turn back toward the world of relation. As an enlightened mind, the speaker understands her power to act and to choose: "Stasis in darkness/ Then the substanceless blue/ Pour of tor and distances./ God's lioness,/ How one we grow...." Plath now understands her desire in poetry as a place for sacrifice. Desire's object, the "tor" and desire's means for getting to it, "God's lioness," are both terms for a high place or altar,[15] a place for burnt offerings. The poet's desire as centered and burning all by itself, gives up drives to be divine in either transparency or identification. The desire of "Ariel" is the exhilaration of a thinking, feeling person who revels in her solitude while knowing the dangers of wanting to empty herself completely or of wanting her own power to be all there is. The speaker in "Ariel" risks the allure of those extremes in order to be free to choose to turn again with renewed force to the world of lived relations. The sign for her intelligence, which is the noble rider of desire, is the woman Godiva whose inner-focused intensity for the duration of her ride, which is the duration of the poem, distances her from even the most sacred of human bonds: "The child's cry/ Melts in the wall." Mutuality is not the focus of this poem, but rather the singular joy of the speaker's own power and destiny.

The moment cannot last, for as M. L. Rosenthal notes, near the end the poem's mood "suddenly becomes a desolate realization of the plunge into death that is going on:"[16] "And I/ Am the arrow,/ The dew that flies/ Suicidal...." The poem does not end in desolation. The sacrificial burning manages a turn that effects a change of direction so that life, and not death, is celebrated. The troubling word "suicidal" alerts the reader to ask: where can self-slaughter occur that is a true sacrifice in favor of ennobled life? The answer is in written language, of course, in language that confesses its limits by displaying a dead or fictive "I" as a witness to a living, real one. Thus, the poem ends in a turning toward the most impure coils of language in the brilliant concluding puns: "... at one with the drive/ Into the red/ Eye, the cauldron of morning." Only the "I" that is "read" is self-killed for love as it displays and confesses what such a sign is cut off from a lived relation. When writing is understood as a system of culturally overdetermined signs with no divine authority or origins to point to symbolically, but as mere agents to be manipulated in the service of any force, then writing is a "cauldron" of *mourning*—a place where absence is constantly articulating itself.[17] In Plath's satirical allegories of desire, the "I" has no reality because that "I" strives for pure subjectivity in transparency or identity. These states are fictive not real relations of a strictly linguistic "I" bearing witness to its limits. This sense of the insufficiency of language questions a strictly ego-positioned discourse and goads the reader to find a new relation with the printed words on the page.

"Ariel" is not, as Linda Wagner-Martin has suggested, a celebration of "aggression" which society had denied Plath (SP 220), but it is, as she has also said, the "portrait of the woman as artist." I differ from Wagner-Martin in our understanding of the imaginative force Plath celebrates, which is, in my reading, not the gnostic imagination that denies the world, but the symbolic imagination, that goes out to meet and receive the world. In "Ariel" a creative power kindles itself and then consumes its own extravagance, for it must choose to turn toward life lived among dregs and difficulties or die.

The same day Plath wrote "Ariel," she wrote "Poppies in October," a life affirming moment in a world that she refuses to extinguish, for all its horror and pollution, for in it she receives

> A gift, a love gift
> Utterly unasked for
> By a sky
>
> Palely and flamily
> Igniting its carbon monoxides, by eyes
> Dulled to a halt under bowlers.
>
> O my God, what am I
> That these late mouths should cry open
> In a forest of frost, in a dawn of cornflowers.

This encounter grounds the speaker in relation to what is not herself and leads her to a heightened sense of her reality. Two days later, Plath wrote "Nick and the Candlestick," in which she answers her own question by saying: "I am a miner. The light burns blue." Plath is saying, "I am a poet," to the reader who remembers the blue bolts and the blue light of the mind in the earlier poems. For seven stanzas, this poem takes the reader through intensifications of a cold interior: "Old cave of calcium/ Icicles, old echoer." Everything in this wintry echo chamber is frigid: "And the fish, the fish—Christ! they are panes of ice,/ A vice of knives,/ A piranha/ Religion, drinking/ Its first communion out of my live toes." The fish is a traditional sign for the Word made flesh, but in a world (or an imagination) devoid of relation, that sign would point to nothing, vacant as a "pane of ice," an image out of Plath's earlier poem, "Love Letter." There, she had tried to rise to gnostic identity, a state she fears now is deadly as a "vice of knives." That image also comes out of an earlier poem, "The Bee Meeting," in which the speaker was the "magician's girl who does not flinch," but who does not form a relation, either. At exactly midpoint, just as in "Fever 103º," the poem "Nick and the Candlestick" turns toward light and heat, but not to satirize the desire for release from the body. "Nick and the Candlestick" tries to celebrate desire's fulfillment in the body, for its energy is a flame that illuminates mother and child. If the poem succeeds, it does so because Plath's emphatic rhythms persuade the reader that a life is beating here, perhaps desperately against the odds:

> Love, love,
> I have hung our cave with roses,
> With soft rugs—
>
> The last of Victoriana.
> Let the stars
> Plummet to their dark address,
>
> Let the mercuric
> Atoms that cripple drip
> Into the terrible well,
>
> You are the one
> Solid the spaces lean on, envious.
> You are the baby in the barn.

A mother relates to her child, placing him at the center of her life; her echo chamber defers to his primacy as the opaque, pulsating presence she wants her words to house. For survival, his rhythms and hers require mutuality, attunement.

Plath's satirical allegories of desire, however, relate only to themselves, self-consciously cut off from full metaphoric reverberations by their dissatisfactions. Plath's most original poetry, such as "Purdah" and "Lady Lazarus," mock poetic "incarnation" as "self-destructive unity" (Buell 149), for the speaker becomes both victim and victimizer. These works confess the limits of the self that aspires to the sublime at the expense of relation. On a BBC broadcast, Plath said of the "professional suicide" (Pollitt 99) who is the heroine of Lady Lazarus: she has "the great and terrible gift of being reborn." Indeed it is terrible to be constantly revived in a myth that does not change its basic plot, or in language that is understood as an endless chain of metonymic displacements.

After the amazing October productions, Plath wrote a riddling poem, "The Couriers," in which she tells the reader, obliquely, what she is and is not doing. She is not writing as a traditional, romantic nature poet: "The word of a snail on the plate of a leaf? It is not mine, do not accept it." She is not writing as an aesthete: "Acetic acid in a sealed tin? Do not accept it. It is not genuine." She is not writing as a symbolist for a mythology: "A ring of gold with the sun in it? Lies. Lies and a grief." She is writing out of the fear she encountered in "Bluebeard" in 1955, when she suspected that an absolute absence, a cold and murderous indifference articulated her writing. Plath's cauldron in "The Couriers," as in "Ariel," is the space of writing as a place for sacrifice and for concentrating her power without succumbing to the craving for identity, which would be, for her, an anguished spirit writ large. Plath knew by November of 1962 the risks of such desires: they can deny the body, the world, all relation where love can be. She knew what she could do:

> Frost on a leaf, the immaculate
> Cauldron, talking and crackling
>
> All to itself on the top of each
> Of nine black Alps.

A disturbance in mirrors,
The sea shattering its gray one—
Love, love my season.

Rather than look to her poems for a reflection of her essence, Plath refuses identity by acknowledging her language as an unstable metonymic mechanism that enacts over and over loss of relation between the creator and her creations. When Plath's poems ask to be read as satire, they ask to be understood a marvelous things, but nevertheless as cunning devices which call attention to the results of turning a person into a thing, marvelous or otherwise. Her most original poetry confesses "love" as relation by displaying an "I" that functions without it and ends up reified, densely dead. Most of her October poems were satires of false relation. Succeeding poems of that kind written after her little manifesto "The Couriers" are "Getting There," "Death and Company," "Childless Woman," "Totem," "Paralytic," and "Gigolo."

Plath's variety of poetic performance increases and continues to diversify from November 1962 until her suicide in February 1963, because she was no longer asking "who" or "what am I?" In 1980, Mary Lynn Broe had urged readers to stop looking for unity in Plath's poetry by means of a personal myth of death and rebirth, especially death of a false self and birth of a pure, new one. Broe showed how Plath strives to celebrate her force in the face of great personal loss by flaunting a protean consciousness in rapid development, full of contradictions. Reading Plath's poems in the sequence in which she wrote them, available in the *Collected Poems* (1981), has enabled my study to follow Broe's lead. However, my study has both extended and contradicted Broe's by tracing in Plath's poetry a major dialectic in her developing awareness: that of a feared and resisted gnostic imagination and that of an ultimately failed relation in the symbolic tradition—failed unless we read Plath's most negating poems as confession, not as seduction or as subversion.

Plath's poetry is confessional, not because it is an out-pouring of intimate, painful and shameful detail, but because it bears witness in language to the death of the self when the self denies relation and thus finds no adequate metaphor to make it believable as a living soul. For Plath's gnostic, fictive self, the world remains unreadable. Plath's outrage at this state of her poetic affairs subsides in the last three months of her life. She becomes more meditative on her predicament but no less desperate. In spite of such poems as "Poppies in November" and "Nick and the Candlestick," her stance stiffens into that of the unconsoled whose poetic efforts turn into allegories of desire that despair of achieving their object. Plath's confessional poetry is a highly condensed drama of mourning, a display of the depressed mind which cannot create what is needed but which can reveal what is lacking.

"Winter Trees," dated November 26, 1962, is such a poem. The natural landscape in early morning is quickly taken over by the imagination in the first line: "The wet dawn inks are doing their blue dissolve." Dense parallelisms in sound coerce images out of blurring fog as a finely etched "botanical drawing," including invisible circular growth recording linear time: "Memories growing, ring on ring,/ A series of weddings." The metaphoric projections at first personify the trees, but the speaker quickly distances them from herself by means of contrast: "they seed so effortlessly!/ Tasting the winds, that are footless...." The poem seeks a metaphoric relation between the speaker and the scene without dissolving their differences: "Full of wings, otherworldliness./ In this they are Ledas." The trees have been figured in quick succession as diagrams, vegetable life, and mythological women chosen by a god to bear his fruit and make history. This string of images, more associational and contiguous than logical and similar, finally arrives at an image of the trees as mothers who cannot console themselves without a father. The speaker addresses one of them as if she were a muse: "O mother of leaves and sweetness/ Who are these pietàs?" The speaker then concludes by answering *as* one of them, but, characteristically, identity—which the poem tried but failed to avoid—brings Plath's speaker no comfort: "The shadows of ringdoves chanting, but easing nothing."

Plath's poem, "Winter Trees," emerging out of a need to find peace, becomes a pietà that offers none. Only a belief in a divinity who is a loving father could make the image of the grieving mother holding her dead son a symbol of love. Without that belief, Plath's trees become signs of unbearable loss; and the poem, a place for endless anguish. Plath wants here, as in other poems, to reject the gnostic mode engendered, not by a loving and present father, but by his absence. She could not, however, change her history, personal or cultural, though she perhaps could change her future.

The loss of the father for Plath's imagination meant acceptance of dissolution unless she exercised the will to overcome his void with her own creative spirit: she had to take the father's place and become a phallic power. This was the plot of *The Colossus*. Plath's apparent selection of poems for *Ariel* tried to make that defiant spirit holy by keeping it in the service of her desire for right relations, more than for self-justification or revenge, but in her last poems, she refuses to overcome loss by creating a "self." She is an exhausted magician who, having exposed the vacuousness of her efforts because of lack of belief in their efficacy, must now deal with the consequences. She must enact her refusal, in a word, *to be*. This seems a perverse use of her poetic gift unless the reader understands Plath's poems as confession, in an Augustinian sense: hers is the voice of a human spirit that cannot, that will not, save itself. Nevertheless, in her furious satires of the quest for identity as well as in her late evocations of desolation of spirit, Plath in the last two months of her life was writing the real thing, poetry that "carries by means of feeling truth alive into the heart" (Heaney 100). The truth that wounds the reader's heart is this: without the language of the father, Plath has no way to articulate her desire and thus distance herself from her source, the engulfing sea-mother. That relation remains benign, that is sustaining, only when there is no identity between speaker and her matrix. Maintaining the difference between self and source is possible when the imagination works within a symbolic tradition which allows for a sense of the holy between persons. Augustine's doctrine of the Trinity underlies that tradition in the West. Dorothea Krook's moral philosophy and Martin Buber's I-Thou paradigm are some of its humanist and ethical manifestations. Plath's humanist beliefs kept her aware of the dangers in negating the sacred intersubjective space, for then the self must either aggressively impose its own will or dissolve for lack of definition.

The speaker in "Sheep in Fog" is on the brink of dissolution.[18] In this poem, the first completed in 1963, there are no tricks in the void, no magic, but rather the estrangement of the speaker in the poem from any personal, sustaining relation. Here is the published version:

> The hills step off into whiteness.
> People or stars
> Regard me sadly, I disappoint them.

The train leaves a line of breath.
O slow
Horse the color of rust,

Hooves, dolorous bells—
All morning the
Morning has been blackening,

A flower left out.
My bones hold a stillness, the far
Fields melt my heart.

They threaten
To let me through to a heaven
Starless and fatherless, a dark water.

Like "Winter Trees," this "mourning" poem darkens the will rather than refines it into the capable spirit of "Ariel." The solitude of "Sheep in Fog" is not a place for sacrifice of burning energy that gathers itself to turn again toward the life of lived relations, but a place for melting the heart as dissolution of the will to relate to others. Instead of providing a breathing space, "Sheep in Fog" reveals the end of Plath's way. The horse, the color of oxidation not flame, is desire at such a low ebb that it will destroy its mechanism for producing energy. Plath had earlier drawn "pietàs" out of fog, but here the damp blank menaces the speaker. The oddest thing about "Sheep in Fog" is this: in the final version, there are no sheep in the poem. The poem's speaker indeed disappoints. The reader follows the lines of sound which flow, going places like trains, one thing after another, but with no defining action. A horse's hooves are named and so are bells, but they do not do anything. The speaker can acknowledge the one flower that decorates the landscape only by saying that she leaves it out. Sheep occupied the unpublished December version of this poem in which they are seen as "Patriarchs" deliberately moving away from the speaker. Thomas Bredsdorff's comparison of the two versions leads him to conclude that Plath's "universe, as recorded in her last poems, changed from one dominated by parental figures to one of utter solitude" (190). Certainly the father is gone, but "the dark water" remains as either the fatherless abyss or the maternal sea which becomes a sinister source when the speaker refuses to exercise her will to power in any form—joyful, lamenting, or satiric—

and allows the fog to portend a region without markers of any kind.[19] Faced with the blank, Plath's poetic voice is doomed if she refuses articulation in the language of her gnostic imagination. This is the source of Plath's outrage: she wanted desire bestowed by a real person who engenders love, the symbolic I-Thou, but her power came from an inner absence that engenders desire as will, the gnostic "I am I." "The Stones" of 1959 marked the beginning of Plath's attempts to accept the dominant mode of her creativity. "Sheep in Fog" in 1963 marks an end, a letting go of the hope that such poems could, after all, "house the elusive rose." Even when the fury of her satires abated, her quieter poems of January and February are still saying: the law of love is incompatible with things as they are, and I cannot change things as they are.

The "dwelling place" where an authentic metaphoric self can be, which Plath sought most of her short life, is not within the structure of her most original poems. Her distinctive achievements remain cauldrons of mourning, crackling all to themselves, which must be read as signs not symbols, as labels for an inaccessible essence, not a real or a true "self." As fictions they remind the reader that the real thing, if it exists, is elsewhere. Plath's readers must bring to her allegories, her fictive selves, the specific moral and historical correlatives that enable a more complete understanding of her poetry. Thus, we must read and interpret Plath's life in a full critical assessment of her art.

Plath can be understood as a woman who believed that the world was readable and habitable when there were other people in it, but who, as a poet, found her power came from a form of the imagination that tended to deny everything but itself. Her response to the drive to create an identity in her poetry, perhaps many identities, was full of anxiety and doubt, for she felt more benevolently defined in lived relations with others than in her art. To take up the gnostic stance that fathered her poetics was to deny the given world of nature, other people, and her own fecund body in favor of a cold cave of echo, yet her strongest poetry is just that and she was writing it almost to the last day of her life.

Plath continued to seek a way out of her gnostic quest. By the fall of 1962 she had come to see it as shabby magic which in "Totem" she would image as "no terminus, only suitcases/ Out of which the same self unfolds like a suit/ Bald and shiny, with pockets of wishes...." Allegory offers a way out of failure to achieve or to believe in an adequate metaphoric image of self, for allegory opposes the symbolic in its separation of the imagination from the forms that the imagination manipulates. In her October 30, 1962, BBC interview with Peter Orr, Plath had been frank about her distaste for the "shut box" and "mirrors" of "narcissistic" poetry and emphatic about her newly felt strength to "manipulate" with an "informed and intelligent mind" the previously taboo "sensuous" and "emotional experiences" of her life. She used the word "manipulate" twice as she affirmed her intent to make her poetry "relevant to the larger things ... to Hiroshima and Dachau." She was aware she was doing something new. We can see now that she was getting rid of gnostic magic: the debased cult of autonomous will which tended to deny human relations that respect difference and thus to deny human reality. Her tactic developed as satirical reduction of poetic making to densely physical acts, a power that continued to intensify, as in the stunning poem "Words," written on 1 February 1963. Plath's inscribed signs for speech cut like "Axes..." to the same core of emotion that gave the grieving Rhoda in *The Waves* an image for the creation of meaning. The metaphoric power of Plath's words gallops away, full of thunder but "dry and riderless." She has generated art, but she will not pretend that its power can save her: "From the bottom of a pool/ fixed stars govern a life."

On February 5, Plath completed her last poems, "Balloons" and "Edge." In "Balloons" she made a final effort to warm her images, as she had done in earlier work, by placing a beloved person in the poem, but even the child in "Balloons" turns into a sign for absence. When the little boy breaks one of the "oval soul-animals" that have floated about their apartment since Christmas, his surprise and delight are reduced to Plath's allegory of loss. The final image, "the red shred in his little fist," is a reminder that a son's acts repeat the father's.

In "Edge," a far superior poem, Plath makes no effort to realize personal relations of any kind. The split reference that generates her metaphoric images drives a mechanism for producing self-conscious fictions. Plath's last line, "Her blacks crackle and drag," mocks what the poem has claimed to achieve: the perfected woman. As letters or signs for sound (as the bees were signs), the "blacks" are the lackeys of the feminine sign for absence, the bloodless, electric Medusa-moon "staring from her hood of bone." The language Plath articulates in her gnostic mode, no matter how brilliant the technique, offers no release from a theory of poetry into romantic belief. If the reader believes this image of perfection identifies its creator, the reader has been seduced by a fiction. Plath is not there except as a negation of her personal existence as she creates signs of her absence instead of an adequate, unifying metaphoric image of self. The reader is simply commanded, and she feels the satiric force of Plath's fiat: *let this not be!*

Allegory quickly becomes satire when the poet knows what is wrong. Plath came to feel it wrong to desire either pure subjectivity or pure objectivity, for both stances deny mutuality as well as distinctions between subjectivities, between persons. That she continued to hope for the balance and health which come from being in the world of others and from relating to them seems evident from Plath's staying in touch with a number of people even while she was being treated medically for severe depression during her last month. Plath had kept up several correspondences, including one begun in October with a young American priest studying at Oxford who had written Plath asking for a critique of his poetry. Besides commenting on his poems, she alludes to her harassed domestic life as a setting for her writing, thanks him for his prayers for her, and tells him that they have helped her find a flat in Yeats' house in London. After moving there, she writes that she hopes the priest might visit her and her children, adding that they frequent the zoo. She asserts her difference from the priest as she calls her atheism "irredeemable" and compares herself with the Troll King in *Peer Gynt* who believes only in himself; however, she considers this belief a "blessing" for which she says, "Thank God." After learning that "Fr." means "Father" not "frère or friar" as she supposed, she chose to write out the title "Father," adding "I like it better written out, why not, it is a fine word." Her last letter to the priest, written on February 4, 1963, is brief but cheerful and ends with a question that furthered their discussion of poetry. Her signature is firm. Though he sensed her need for a dialogue with him, the priest did not suspect how ill she was becoming or how urgently she needed psychiatric and medical help.[20] After February 5, her poetry stopped; less than a week later, she committed suicide. Recent biographies have disclosed something of Plath's frantic and fatal descent that winter into despair, but much remains a mystery, even to those who were closest to her. Although no one can know for certain the state of Plath's mind on February 11, 1963, when she took her life, the parallel between her dead body and the character of her confessional poetry cannot be dismissed. Plath's final act was appalling, but like her most shocking and memorable poetic acts, it can be read allegorically: a sign for her longing to be in a relation that, in her melancholy, she simply could not—or would not—imagine.

Endnotes

[1]Sandra M. Gilbert, "In Yeats' House: The Death and Resurrection of Sylvia Plath," Wagner-Martin 204–222.

[2]Frederick Buell, "Sylvia Plath's Traditionalism," Wagner-Martin 144.

[3]Sandra Gilbert and Susan Gubar, *No Man's Land: The Place of the Woman Writer in the Twentieth Century*, Vol. I (New Haven: Yale UP, 1988) 270.

[4]Plath's personal, annotated copy of *The Waves* is in The Sylvia Plath Collection at Smith College. Citations to the text are from *The Waves* (New York: Harcourt Brace Jovanovich, 1978).

[5]Paul Ricoeur, "The Metaphorical Process as Cognition, Imagination, and Feeling," *Critical Inquiry* (Autumn 1978): 143–159. Ricoeur uses Roman Jakobson's definition of poetry as language characterized by ambiguity ("it is and it is not"), but Ricoeur extends this concept of "split reference" in his general theory of metaphor.

[6]Lyndall Gordon, *Virginia Woolf: A Writer's Life*, (New York: W.W. Norton, 1984), 208.

[7]Susan Van Dyne, "More Terrible than She Ever Was: The Manuscripts of Sylvia Plath's Bee Poems," Wagner-Martin 154–170. Mary Lynn Broe's analysis ("The Bee Sequence," Bloom, *Plath* 95–108) finds the queen bee an ambivalent image of "self" affirming not only power but also passivity and a "scaled down life" (108). Broe's essay, based on a chapter in *Protean Poetic: The Poetry of Sylvia Plath* (1980) places "The Beekeeper's Daughter" (1958) first in the sequence and "The Swarm" last, an arrangement which explains much of the difference between our two readings.

[8]Buber, 68. Interestingly, Buber calls the self as "Cause" the "third" variation on the stance that denies relation. Also, in an October 30, 1962, interview with Peter Orr of the BBC, Plath stressed her interest that fall in Napoleon. *Plath*. Credo Records. 1975.

[9]Teresa Bernardez, M.D., "Women and Anger—Cultural Prohibitions and the Feminine Ideal," *Realia* (Wellesley College) 78, 5 December 1988: 10.

[10]The notion of Plath's true and false selves, with a true self finally exposed in an authentic poetic voice, has dominated much of Plath criticism since Judith Kroll's *Chapters in a Mythology* (1976) and Ted Hughes' Introduction to *The Journals of Sylvia Plath* (1982).

[11]See Mutlu Blasing, "Sylvia Plath's Black Car of Lethe," *American Poetry: The Rhetoric of its Forms* (New Haven: Yale UP, 1987) 50–63, for a discussion of the symbolist tradition from Poe through Eliot to Plath that reads her as an allegorist of the limits of form. See also Edward Butscher, "Sylvia Plath's Metaphors of Madness," *Bluefish* III (Spring/Summer 1987): 45–64, for a discussion of how Plath dealt with the limits of the Freudian "schema" with "a Blakean praxes" in her efforts to "escape the inherent entropy" of ego-centered fictiveness. Butscher recognizes Plath's drive for "moral legitimacy" (61). In his 1976 biography of Plath, Butscher had noted Plath's need for a "positive system of spiritual meaning" (MM 317).

[12]M. L. Rosenthal quotes Hughes in Newman 73.

[13]Richard Howard compared Plath's voice to that of the French pornographic novel *The Story of O*, "Sylvia Plath: 'And I have wanted to efface myself,'" *American Poetry: 1946–1965*, ed. Harold Bloom (New York: Chelsea House, 1987) 349–357. Missing Plath's peculiarly pitched satire, Howard took Plath at her word and understood her as an "oracle at the world's funneling center" who asks for death proudly, as "O, naked and chained in her owl mask … asks Sir Stephen for death" (357). He does not account for the two forms of the imagination that I have tried to emphasize in Plath's poetic.

[14]Lynda Bundtzen in *Plath's Incarnations: Woman and the Creative Process* (Ann Arbor: U of Michigan P, 1983) traces Plath's efforts to achieve autonomy as a woman with control over her own body as a process analogous to becoming a strong woman poet. For Bundtzen, "Ariel" is Plath's greatest poetic achievement, for that poem is not "directed toward vengeance or turning the tables on a male victimizer, nor does it depict a woman's body to be dragged toward rebirth. She does not simply repossess her body from an old usurpation, but in 'Ariel' she is possessed by and in possession of that instant when the Word is incarnated, when the word

becomes a vision of energy unfettered by mortal substance, and in Plath's development as a poet, freed from the carnal sting. She is, in this moment, the presiding genius of her own body" (256). Bundtzen's approach to Plath's work, though brilliant, misses Plath's need for an erotic sense redeemed through relating in love to another body not her own.

[15]Kroll, 181. Also, according to *New Catholic Encyclopedia*, "ariel" can mean etymologically either "lion of God" or "hearth of God." Ezekiel uses the term to designate the hearth of the altar in the Temple of Jerusalem (Ez 43: 15–16) while Isaiah uses the term as a poetic synonym for the city of Jerusalem (Is 29. 1–2, 7). The notion that Ariel was the name of an angel comes from "rabbinical speculation" that misunderstood the phrase "messengers of Salem" as "messengers of peace."

[16]Rosenthal in Newman, 73.

[17]Walter Benjamin's account of the German baroque *trauerspiel* (mourning drama) suggest fruitful ways of thinking about modern allegory which is cut off from access to the spirituality of the Middle Ages. *The Origin of German Tragic Drama*. Trans. John Osborne (London: NLB, 1977). Benjamin privileges allegory over symbol in order to read signs of absence as they show themselves in the secular world and in the depressed mind: "The only pleasure the melancholic permits himself, and it is a powerful one, is allegory" (185). Allegorical signs are "monograms of the essence, never the essence in a mask"(214).

[18]M. L. Rosenthal and Sally M. Gall find the twelve 1963 poems, beginning with "Sheep in Fog" and ending with "Edge," a "sequence in formation" which deals with the problem of death as perfection. See "The Confessional Mode: Lowell and Others," *The Modern Poetic Sequence: The Genius of Modern Poetry* (New York: Oxford UP, 1983) 428–443. The authors read "Edge" as "autobiographical confession" of utter solitude (435–437). My use of "confession" extends, rather than limits this critical term in relation to Plath: she is confessing the limits of her negating imagination as they are revealed in writing.

[19]Julia Kristeva describes the "call of the mother" when the woman has given up "desperate attempts to identify with the symbolic paternal order." The matrix is a silent irruption that unmoors "the word, the ego, the superego," which then founder and sink: "Life itself can't hang on: death quietly moves in." Kristeva places Plath among other women who choose "not to be" when "disillusioned with meanings and words." "About

Chinese Women," in *The Kristeva Reader*, ed. Toril Moi (New York: Columbia UP, 1986) 156–159.

[20]Plath's letters are privately held by the man who received them. Although he and Plath never met, he was sure that "she was searching for belief. I was ready to lend a hand—not to change her into anything but to help her think. I was going to see her in London that very Sunday...." (Letter to author. 7 April, 1989).

Appendix

The following letters were written by Sylvia Plath to an American Roman Catholic priest then studying at Oxford. He had written to Plath asking for a critique of his poetry. She typed her responses. Her signatures as well as her hand-written postscripts and additions appear in this appendix in italics. Her correspondent's name has been deleted at his request.

Court Green
North Tawton
Devonshire

October 23, 1962

Dear _____,

Please do forgive me for not answering your letter sooner, but I have been laid low by influenza on my small farm with two very small children, so my correspondence has suffered as a result.

I should be very happy to have a look at your poems. The one thing I can't promise is to tell you whether or not to go on writing! If you enjoy it, do it, and fine! "Success" or publishing should be no guide as to whether you should write or not, your own feelings must tell you that. I shall certainly tell you frankly what I think is good and less good in your work. But do go on drinking with the gods and goddesses at Pieria in any case!

And if you ever care for lesser fare, in the form of a cup of tea, while in England, do feel welcome at the above address (half an hour from Exeter by train) until December at least, after which date I shall be trying to finish a novel in the wilds of Western Ireland.

Yours sincerely,

Sylvia Plath

I send the book under separate cover.

Court Green
North Tawton
Devonshire

Wednesday: November 21

Dear Fr. _____,

Do forgive me for being so long in writing, but I have been juggling two infants, 70 apple trees, syrup-eating bees and all sorts of negotiations which may get me a flat in London for the winter—hopefully the house of W. B. Yeats, plaque and all. Now for being frank. First let me say I love your pseudonym, _____ of the Six Dreams. How many languages do you know? Your epigraphs come from several.

I see two poets in you. The first is what I would call lyrical-traditional, a bit too much given to whimsy and the fey. The second, the much more interesting one, to my mind, is the one who produces meticulously-observed phrases like "wrapped in a mouse-colored twilight", "geraniums drenched in blood", "corrugated sands", "relax their boas' hold", "petroleum frenzy", "black macadam altars" and passages in The Shetlands like

Day and night the ocean speaks
And rage is in his breath.
Eternal: the wedlock of wave to seacrag.

These are phrases and lines of the 20th century—they have a power and
vitality you must develop. How much poetry do you read, and by read I
mean study. Read Thomas Wyatt for lyrics, but tense and special ones.
Read, of course, Gerard Manley Hopkins. I think you have learned much
from Anglo-Saxons, that your May Mourning poem has lots of exciting
things in it & shows a real development. Beware, for Heaven's sake, the
fey, the pretty, the "cute"—you know what I mean—the "butterscotch
curls & marshmellow [sic] ears". This is fun, but only fun. It is "verse", en-
tertainment. I think you should let the world blow in more roughly. Read
Eliot, Pound (you do dedicate a poem to him), study the assonances & con-
sonances in Emily Dickinson (beloved of me) for a subtlety far beyond exact
rhyme. And sweep out the archaicisms "Tis," "Opes", "Alway". Modern
poetry has blown these out. Do read Hopkins. Have you read his note-
books? I believe Penguin has a paper edition. Rhymes, exact rhymes, and
especially feminine rhymes tend to "jingle" too much. Try more free things
like Fragment XXXVIII which I love. Speak straight out. You should give
yourself exercises in roughness, not lyrical neatness. Say blue, instead of
sapphire, red instead of crimson. Forget witches and elves for a bit.

I am myself, ironically, an atheist. And like a certain sort of atheist,
my poems are God-obsessed, priest-obssessed. Full of Marys, Christs and
nuns. Theology & philosophy fascinate me, and my next book will have a
long bit about a priest in a cassock. Did you ever live in Boston? That is my
birth city. I think I will send you a poem of my own, very rough, but about
the Christ-ness in all martyrs, and written by a mother of a son.

Warmest good wishes,

Sylvia Plath

P. S. What does Fr. stand for?
Frère? Friar? Do say God bless.
I need it, God knows!

Court Green
North Tawton
Devonshire

November 29, 1962

Dear Fr. _____,

The blessing was lovely & I do feel better for it. I know why you had the 'horrible sinking feeling' that you called me Edith—Edith is the name of my mother-in-law. How odd of you.

I didn't mean <u>dissect</u> by study, which is the process you describe as study. I meant learn by <u>heart</u>. The same thing happened to me with Milton; I hate him too, although by myself I did not. It was a horrid dull studious teacher did it!

I would answer the autobiographical questions if I knew what you meant by <u>what</u>. Dear Father _____, I meant above. I like it better written out, why not, it is a fine word.

Sincerely,

Sylvia

Please could you bless Yeats' house as well! I think it is coming through, & Lord knows I need it!

23 Fitzroy Road
London N. W. 1

Sunday: December 16

Dear Father _____ ,

The various blessing have triumphed & the babies & I installed over the Yeats plaque. We moved in by candlelight, as the Electricity Board hadn't bothered to connect it, in spite of my smog-muffled arrangements the previous week, so it was very Dickensian. We will be camping out more or less until I get several acres of ancient floorboards painted by hand, rather a trial as I would, in the evenings, much rather write poems. Do drop by for the cup of tea I couldn't give you in North Tawton anytime you happen to be up around Primrose Hill. It's my very favorite district in London, for when I was reading English on a Fulbright at Cambridge I was first installed in the middle of Regents' Park to be 'initiated'. And we spend a great deal of time at the Zoo!

My answer to the 'what' question is the Troll King's answer out of Peer Gynt—'Myself'. Very much so, thank God. Now you will surely think I am unredeemable, but do go on blessing me nonetheless!

And best Christmas wishes,

Sylvia Plath

23 Fitzroy Road
London N. W. 1

February 4, 1963

Dear Father _____,

Please don't worry about critiques or harshness, I enjoy both. I've been silenced by everybody's having flu & fevers & am just now creeping enough out of my post-flu coma to start to cope with sewing curtains & writing dawn poems, and minding babies.

I don't think any good poet <u>wishes</u> to be obscure. I certainly don't; I write, at the present, in blood, or at least with it. Any difficulty arises from compression or the jaggedness of images thrusting up from one psychic ground root.

How about Yeats for the lyrical?

All best wishes,

Sylvia

Sources

The works listed below were especially helpful for this study. An abbreviation in brackets after a title indicates the form of the title that is used in the parentheical notes within the chapters.

Works by Sylvia Plath:

Ariel. New York: Harper and Row, 1966.

The Bell Jar. New York: Harper and Row, 1971.

The Collected Poems: Sylvia Plath [CP]. Ed. with Introduction and Notes by Ted Hughes. New York: Harper and Row, 1981.

The Colossus and Other Poems. 1960. New York: Alfred Knopf,

Letters Home: Correspondence, 1950–1963 [LH]. Ed. with Introduction and Commentary by Aurelia Schober Plath. New York: Harper and Row, 1975.

Johnny Panic and the Bible of Dreams: Short Stories, Prose, and Diary Excerpts [JP]. Introduction by Ted Hughes. New York: Harper and Row, 1980.

The Journals of Sylvia Plath [J]. Ed. Frances McCullough and Ted Hughes. Foreword by Ted Hughes. New York: Ballentine, 1982.

Unpublished material:

Diaries and calendars, 1948–1957; High school, Smith College and Newnham College essays; Uncollected juvenilia; Smith College teaching notes. The Sylvia Plath Collection. The Lilly Library. Indiana U. Bloomington, Ind.

Letters to Priest. October 1962 to February 1963. Privately held.

Journal entries; Underlinings and annotations in books from Plath's personal library. The Neilson Library, Rare Book Room, Smith College. Northampton, Mass.

The Magic Mirror: A Study of the Double in Two Novels by Dostoevsky. Senior Thesis. 1955. Smith College. Northampton, Mass.

Biography:

Butscher, Edward. *Sylvia Plath: Method and Madness.* [MM] New York: Washington Square P, 1976.

Steiner, Nancy Hunter. *A Closer Look at Ariel: A Memory of Sylvia Plath.* Introduction by George Stade. New York: Harper's Magazine, 1974.

Stevenson, Anne. *Bitter Fame: A Life of Sylvia Plath.* [BF] Boston: Houghton Mifflin, 1989.

Wagner-Martin, Linda. *Sylvia Plath: A Biography.* [SP] New York: Simon and Schuster, 1987.

Bibliography:

Tabor, Stephen. *Sylvia Plath: An Analytical Bibliography.* London: Mansell, 1987; Westport, Conn.: Meckler, 1987.

Collections of Critical Essays:

Alexander, Paul, ed. *Ariel Ascending: Writings about Sylvia Plath.* New York: Harper and Row, 1985.

Bloom, Harold, ed. *Sylvia Plath.* Modern Critical Views. New York: Chelsea House, 1989.

Butscher, Edward, ed. *Sylvia Plath: The Woman and the Work.* New York: Dodd, Mead, 1977.

Lane, Gary, ed. *Sylvia Plath: New Views on the Poetry.* Baltimore: The Johns Hopkins UP, 1979.

Newman, Charles, ed. *The Art of Sylvia Plath: A Symposium.* Bloomington: Indiana UP, 1970.

Wagner, Linda, ed. *Critical Essays on Sylvia Plath.* [CE] Boston: Hall, 1984.

_____, ed. *Sylvia Plath: The Critical Heritage.* [CH] London: Routledge,1988.

Individual Books and Essays about Sylvia Plath:

Alvarez, A. "Sylvia Plath: A Memoir." Alexander 185–213.

Axelrod, Steven Gould. *Sylvia Plath: The Wound and the Cure of Words.* Baltimore: The Johns Hopkins UP, 1990.

Bayley, John. "Death and Company." rev. of *The Collected Poems. New Statesman.* 2 October 1981, 19–20.

Bennett, Paula. *My Life a Loaded Gun: Female Creativity and Feminist Poetics.* Boston: Beacon P, 1986.

Buell, Frederick. "Sylvia Plath's Traditionalism." Wagner [CE]140–154.

Blasing, Mutlu Konuk. "Sylvia Plath's Black Car of Lethe." *American Poetry: The Rhetoric of its Forms.* New Haven: Yale UP, 1987, 50–63.

Bredsdorff, Thomas. "The Biographical Pursuit: Biography as a Tool of Literary Criticism, Sylvia Plath—a Test Case." *Orbis Litterarum* 44 (1989): 181–190.

Broe, Mary Lynn. *Protean Poetic: The Poetry of Sylvia Plath.* Columbia: U of Missouri P, 1980.

Bundtzen, Lynda. *Plath's Incarnations: Woman and the Creative Process.* Ann Arbor: U of Michigan P, 1983.

Butscher, Edward. "Sylvia Plath's Metaphors of Madness." *Bluefish* III (Spring/Summer 1987): 45–64.

Crockett, Wilbury. Personal interview.1 August 1987. Wellesley, Mass.

Davison, Peter. *Half Remembered: A Personal History.* New York: Harper and Row, 1973.

Gilbert, Sandra. "In Yeats' House: The Death and Resurrection of Sylvia Plath." Wagner [CE] 204–222.

Heaney, Seamus. "The Indefatigable Hoof-taps: Sylvia Plath." *The Government of the Tongue.* New York: Farrar, Straus, and Giroux, 1989. 148–170.

Howard, Richard. "Sylvia Plath: 'And I have no face, I have wanted to efface myself.'" *American Poetry: 1946–1965*. Ed. Harold Bloom. New York: Chelsea House, 1987. 349–357.

Holbrook, David. *Sylvia Plath: Poetry and Existence*. London: Athlone P, 1976.

Hughes, Ted. "The Chronological Order of Sylvia Plath's Poems." Newman 187–195.

————. "Sylvia Plath and her Journals." Alexander 152–164.

————. "Introduction," *Johnny Panic*. 1–9.

Kopp, Jane Baltzell. "'Gone, Very Gone Youth': Sylvia Plath at Cambridge, 1955–1957." Butscher 61–80.

Kroll, Judith. *Chapters in a Mythology: The Poetry of Sylvia Plath*. New York: Harper and Row, 1976.

Krook, Dorothea. "Recollections of Sylvia Plath." Butscher 49–60.

————. Letters to author. 12 February 1988; 4 September 1988.

Oberg, Arthur. *Modern American Lyric: Lowell, Berryman, Creeley and Plath*. New Brunswick: Rutgers UP, 1978.

Ostriker, Alicia. "The Americanization of Sylvia Plath." Wagner [CE] 97–109.

Perloff, Marjorie. "The Confessional Mode: Romanticism and Realism." *The Poetic Art of Robert Lowell*. Ithaca: Cornell UP, 1975. 80–99.

Phillips, Robert. "The Dark Funnel: A Reading of Sylvia Plath." Butscher 186–205.

Plath, Aurelia S. "Letter Written in Early Spring." Alexander 214–217.

————. Letters to author, 13, 14, 15 March 1987; 4 October 1987.

————. Letter to Ted and Carol Hughes. Plath MSII. The Lilly Library.

Pollitt, Katha. "A Note of Triumph." Alexander 94–99.

Quinn, Sister Bernetta. "Medusan Imagery in Sylvia Plath." Lane 97–115.

Rosenblatt, Jon. *Sylvia Plath: The Poetry of Initiation*. Chapel Hill: U of North Carolina P, 1979.

Rosenthal, M. L. *The New Poets*. New York: Oxford UP, 1967.

————. "Sylvia Plath and Confessional Poetry." Newman 69–76.

———— and Sally M. Gall. "The Confessional Mode: Lowell and Others." *The Modern Poetic Sequence: The Genius of Modern Poetry*. New York: Oxford UP, 1983.

Sanazaro, Leonard. "The Transfiguring Self: Sylvia Plath, a Reconsideration." Wagner [CE] 87–97.

Shoaf, Diann Blakely. "Thinking Back Through Our Mothers: Emily Dickinson and Contemporary Women's Poetry." Unpublished essay. 1987.

Van Dyne, Susan. "More Terrible Than She Ever Was: The Manuscripts of Sylvia Plath's Bee Poems." Wagner [CE] 154–170.

Vendler, Helen. "Sylvia Plath." *Part of Nature, Part of Us.* Cambridge: Harvard UP, 1980. 271–276.

Other Sources, a Selected Bibliography:

"Ariel (Jerusalem)." *New Catholic Encyclopedia.* 1967 ed.

Saint Augustine. *Confessions.* Trans. R. S. Pine Coffin. London: Penguin, 1961.

Benjamin, Jessica. *The Bonds of Love: Psychoanalysis, Feminisim, and the Problem of Domination.* New York: Pantheon Books, 1988.

Benjamin, Walter. *The Origin of German Tragic Drama.* Trans. John Osborne. London: NLB, 1977.

Bloom, Harold. *A Map of Misreading.* New York: Oxford UP, 1975.

_____. *The Breaking of the Vessels.* Chicago: U of Chicago, 1982.

_____, ed. *Elizabeth Bishop.* Modern Critical Views. New York: Chelsea House, 1985.

Bowie, Malcolm. *Freud, Proust and Lacan: Theory as Fiction.* New York: Cambridge UP, 1987.

Burke, Kenneth. *The Philosophy of Literary Form: Studies in Symbolic Action.* Baton Rouge: Louisiana State UP, 1967.

Buber, Martin. *I and Thou.* Second Edition. Trans. Ronald Gregor Smith. New York: Charles Scribner's Sons, 1958.

Burnaby, John, ed. *Augustine: The Later Works.* Philadelphia: The Westminster P, 1955.

Caramagno, Thomas. "Manic-Depressive Psychosis and Critical Approaches to Virginia Woolf's Life and Work." *PMLA* 103 (January 1988): 10–23.

Diel, Paul. *Symbolism In Greek Mythology: Human Desire and its Transformations.* Trans. Vincent Stuart et al. London: Shambhala, 1980.

Donoghue, Denis. "The American Style of Failure." *The Sovereign Ghost: Studies in the Imagination.* Berkeley: U of California P, 1976. 103-127.

212

Dyson, A. E. "Swift: The Metamorphosis of Irony." *The Writings of Jonathan Swift*. New York: W. W. Norton, 1973. 672–684.

Eagelton, Terry. *Literary Theory: An Introduction*. Minneapolis: U of Minnesota P, 1983.

Gilbert, Sandra and Susan Gubar. *No Man's Land: The Place of the Woman Writer in the Twentieth Century. Vol. I*. New Haven: Yale UP, 1980.

Gordon, Lyndall. *Virginia Woolf: A Writer's Life*. New York: W.W. Norton, 1984.

Gusdorf, Georges. "Conditions and Limits of Autobiography." Olney 28–48.

_____. "Scripture of the Self: 'Prologue in Heaven,'" *The Southern Review* 22 (April 1986): 280–295.

Gordon, Lyndall. *Viginia Woolf: A Writer's Life*. New York: W. W. Norton, 1984.

Jakobson, Roman. "The Metaphoric and Metonymic Poles." *Modern Criticism and Theory: A Reader*. Ed. David Lodge. New York: Longman, 1988, 57–61.

James, Henry. "The Golden Bowl." *Henry James: French Writers, Other European Writers, The Prefaces to the New York Edition*. Ed. Leon Edel. New York: The Library of America, 1984. 1322–1341.

Keefer, Michael. "Deconstruction and the Gnostics," *University of Toronto Quarterly* 55 (Fall 1985): 74–93.

Kristeva, Julia. "About Chinese Women." *The Julia Kristeva Reader*. Ed. Toril Moi. New York: Columbia UP, 1986. 138–159.

Krook, Dorothea. *The Ordeal of Consciousness in Henry James* Cambridge: Cambridge UP, 1962.

_____. *Three Traditions in Moral Thought*. [TTMT] Cambridge: Cambridge UP,1959.

Lacan, Jacques. "The Insistence of the Letter in the Unconscious." *Modern Criticism and Theory: A Reader*. Ed. David Lodge. New York: Longman, 1988. 79–106.

Lang, Andrew. *The Yellow Fairy Book*. New York: Dover, 1966.

Miller, J. Hillis. *The Ethics of Reading*. New York: Columbia UP, 1987.

Olney, Jame. *Metaphors of Self: The Meaning of Autobiography*. Princeton: Princeton UP, 1972.

_____, ed. *Autobiography: Essays Critical and Theoretical*. Princeton: Princeton UP, 1980.

Radin, Paul. *African Folktales and Sculpture.* Bollingen Series XXXII. New York: Pantheon Books, 1952, 250–253.

Ricoeur, Paul. "The Metaphorical Process as Cognition, Imagination, and Feeling." *Critical Inquiry* (Autumn 1978): 143–159.

Rousseau, Jean-Jaques. *The Confessions of Jean-Jaques Rousseau.* Trans. W. Conyngham Mallory. New York: Tudor, 1928.

Santayana, George. *The Sense of Beauty.* New York: Collier Books, 1961.

Starobinski, Jean. *Jean-Jaques Rousseau: Transparency and Obstruction.* Trans. Arthur Goldhammer. Chicago: U of Chicago, 1988.

————. "The Style of Autobiography." Olney 73–83.

Tate, Allen. "The Angelic Imagination," and "The Symbolic Imagination." *Essays of Four Decades.* Chicago: The Swallow P, 401–423; 424–446.

Wellek, René and Austin Warren. *Theory of Literature.* Third Edition. New York: Harcourt Brace Jovanovitch, 1977.

Writing About Women
Feminist Literary Studies

This is a literary series devoted to feminist studies on past and contemporary women authors, exploring social, psychological, political, economic, and historical insights directed toward an interdisciplinary approach.

The series is dedicated to the memory of Simone de Beauvoir, an early pioneer in feminist literary theory.